William Robert Bernard Brownlow

Lectures on Slavery and Serfdom in Europe

William Robert Bernard Brownlow

Lectures on Slavery and Serfdom in Europe

ISBN/EAN: 9783744760256

Printed in Europe, USA, Canada, Australia, Japan

Cover: Foto ©ninafisch / pixelio.de

More available books at **www.hansebooks.com**

LECTURES

ON

SLAVERY AND SERFDOM IN EUROPE.

BY

W. R. BROWNLOW, M.A.,
Trinity College, Cambridge,
CANON OF PLYMOUTH.

BURNS AND OATES LIMITED.

London . .
28, Orchard Street, W.

New York:
Catholic Publication
Society Co.

1892.

TO

WILLIAM PENGELLY, ESQ.

F.R.S. F.G.S. ETC. ETC.,

THE FOUNDER OF THE

Torquay Natural History Society

AND OF

The Devonshire Association,

IN GRATEFUL RECOLLECTION OF MANY PLEASANT

HOURS SPENT IN CONNECTION WITH THESE TWO INSTITUTIONS,

THESE LECTURES

ARE,

BY HIS PERMISSION,

RESPECTFULLY DEDICATED.

TABLE OF CONTENTS.

	page
INTRODUCTION. General Design of the Work	xv
The Abolition of Slavery a proof that Christianity is Divine	xv
Difficulty put by Cardinal Newman as to Roman Slavery	xvii
St. Chrysostom on, *If thou canst be free, use it rather*	xviii
Answer to the difficulty	xix
Branches of the subject omitted: Orders for Redemption of slaves	xx
Slavery in British India. Sources of information	xxiii
Slavery in the New World, Mexico, and Peru	xxiv
Action of the Church thwarted by the conquerors	xxv
LETTER OF POPE LEO XIII. TO THE BISHOPS OF BRAZIL IN 1888	xxviii

LECTURE I.

SLAVERY IN THE ROMAN EMPIRE	1
The effects of Slavery on the Romans—on the labouring classes	4
All work done by slaves, free labour unable to find work	6
Slavery crushed the motive for invention, and division of labour	8
Enormous number of slaves. St. Clement of Alexandria	10
Entertainment given by a wealthy patrician. His slaves	11
Effect of Slavery on the masters from their boyhood	13
Evidence from Terence and Plautus	14
Legal condition of slaves according to Gothofred	17
Laws of Constantine mitigating the sufferings of slaves	17
Roman ladies and their slaves, according to Juvenal and Ovid	18
Effect on the slaves—reduced to the level of cattle	20

viii *Contents.*

	page
No legal marriage among slaves. No rights over their children	22
Female slaves, their helpless condition	25
Wholesale execution of the slaves of Pedanius Secundus	26
Christianity restored the dignity of labour	27
Justinian abolished slavery as a penalty for crime	29
The means used by the Church to abolish Slavery	29
She taught both slaves and masters their duties towards each other	30
The Christian slave had limits to obedience. St. Potamiæna	31
The Church admitted slaves to equal spiritual rights	32
St. Chrysostom on this matter	33
Slaves might become priests, bishops, and even Popes	34
No instance of the term *servus* on a Christian epitaph	35
Validity and sacredness of the marriage of Christian slaves	36
Emancipation of slaves facilitated and promoted by Christianity	37
Deed of manumission preserved by Ennodius	38
Justinian declared freedom given by ordination or the monastic tonsure	39
Pagans, Jews, and heretics forbidden to possess Christian slaves	40

LECTURE II.

ROMAN SLAVERY AND MEDIÆVAL SERFDOM	42
Authorities on the subject, copious in French, rare in English	43
What Christianity had effected in the fourth century	45
Legislation of the Christian Emperors	46
The rehabilitation of the dignity of labour	47
A Roman *villa rustica* according to Vitruvius and Columella	48
The *coloni*, originally conquered natives, bound to the soil	49
This binding to the soil made more stringent by Christian laws	50
Example of the *Scyri* in the fifth century	51
Letters of St. Gregory the Great on manumission of slaves	52
Slavery in the Byzantine Empire, from M. Biot	54
The barbaric invasions, scene described by Salvian	55
First effects of invasions calamitous for slaves	56
Serfs and slaves confused under the Goths	57

Contents.

	page
Action of the Church, through the Councils, on slaves	58
Churches opened as sanctuaries for ill-treated slaves	60
Example of tyrannical conduct towards slaves. St. Gregory of Tours	62
Councils insisted upon Sunday being a day of freedom for slaves	64
Slaves of bishops and monasteries, their emancipation	65
Charlemagne revived the privileges of the serfs	69
Rise of the feudal system. Its effect on slavery	71
How freemen sometimes fell into serfdom. Example	72
Why freemen often wished to become serfs of Abbeys	73
Story of a serf of the Abbey of Fleury.	74
The *Polypticon* of Irmino, Abbot of St. Germain des Prés	75
Its evidence on the condition of serfs and free labourers	76
The *villani* free in France, serfs in England	78
Life of a serf in the ninth century	79
The serf protected by "customs" which had the force of law	80
Serfdom in Germany. The Sclaves	81
Slavery in Italy in mediæval times. Examples	82
Decrees of Popes Pius II. and Paul III. against slavery	83
Slavery and serfdom in Spain affected by Moorish conquest	84

LECTURE III.

SLAVERY AND SERFDOM IN THE BRITISH ISLES. I. *England*	87
Sir Thomas Smith's *Commonwealth of England*	87
Various classes of freemen described	88
Villeins in grosse and *villeins regardants*, both extinct	89
How this extinction came about	90
Mr. Seebohm on the manor of Winslow under Edward III.	91
The value of the labour dues of a *villanus* in 1279	94
The labour dues of a *cotarius* at the same period; the difference	95
The manors of England from the eleventh to the thirteenth century	96
Maps showing the proportion of various classes in *Domesday*	97
The *villani*	97

Contents.

	page
The *bordarii* and *cotarii*	98
The *sochmanni* or *liberi homines*	99
The *servi*, most numerous in the south	100
The male population of Devonshire from *Domesday*	102
Manors of Osbern, Bishop of Exeter, and the serfs on them	103
The grievances of a *servus* or "theow" in Saxon times	104
How Saxon manors were formed in the time of Alfred	105
Emancipation of slaves in England	106
Archbishop Brihtwald redeems a slave from Abbot Beorwald	107
St. Wilfrid emancipates two hundred and fifty slaves in Sussex	108
And three hundred families in the Isle of Wight	109
Emancipations registered in the Bodmin Gospels	110
Slaves captured by the Danes, and sold	111
Slave trade forbidden in 1102 by St. Anselm. St. Wolstan at Bristol	112
Manumission encouraged by William the Conqueror	113
2. *Ireland*. The Brehon laws	114
The *Senchus Mór*. Its correction by St. Patrick	116
Story in *Senchus Mór* showing the extent of slavery in Ireland	117
No serfdom in Ireland. Tanistry	121
The *saer-tenant* and the *daer-tenant*	122
The plebeian families and noble tribes	123
The *Book of Rights*. Slaves regarded as chattels	124
St. Patrick complains that the Welsh had enslaved his converts	126
Adamnan redeems slaves made by Egfrid of Northumbria	127
St. Laurence O'Toole abolishes slavery in Ireland	128
3. *In Wales*. Ancient Welsh canons on slaves	129
Laws of Howel the Good, their compilation	130
Privileges of the free Cymri	131
The *taeogs* or serfs, distinguished from *cacths* or slaves	132
The *taeog* had to pay food rents and honey and wax	134
Welsh measures of land and co-tillage	136
4. *Scotland*. Difference between the Highlanders and Lowlanders	138
Example of an English lord claiming his *villani*, in 1312	141

LECTURE IV.

	page
ABOLITION OF SERFDOM IN ENGLAND	145
All *villani, cotarii, bordarii* in *Domesday* were serfs	146
Their servile condition described by Blackstone	147
Henry de Bracton on serfdom in 1270	148
His distinction of the various kinds of villenage	150
The condition of serfs lighter in Norman than in Saxon times	153
No trace of the German "mark system" in England	154
Mr. Thorold Rogers on the condition of labourers in England	155
English serf lost the land, which French serf retained	156
Effects of the "Black Death" on serfdom	157
The "Statute of Labourers"	158
Socialism spread among the serfs by Wycliffe's preachers	160
Mr. R. Lane Poole on Wycliffe's socialistic theories	160
Wat Tyler's rebellion. Bishop Stubbs' account of it	163
Preaching of John Ball. The wrongs of the serfs	165
The mob enter London and demand the surrender of Archbishop Sudbury	167
They invade the Tower, seize and murder the Archbishop	169
Demands of the peasants granted, and then revoked	170
Designs of the rebels according to Jack Straw	171
Confession of John Balle in *Fasciculi Zizaniorum*	172
Evidence of Wycliffe's complicity. Nicolas Hereford and John Bedeman	173
Rapid emancipation of the serfs	174
No mention of serfs in the "Paston Letters"	175
Emancipations in fifteenth and sixteenth centuries	176
Emancipation of serfs by Queen Elizabeth, in 1574	176
The last trace of villenage in 1602. Legal abolition	177
Effects of abolition of serfdom. Unemployed *villeins*	178
Cruel laws of Henry VIII. against vagrants. Of Edward VI.	179
Treatment of vagabonds under Elizabeth	181
Dissolution of monasteries brought misery on the cottagers	183
England at its lowest degradation. The "Poor Laws" of Elizabeth	184

LECTURE V.

	page
SLAVERY IN BRITISH COLONIES. Slavery revived in 1442	186
Portuguese and Spaniards commenced negro slavery	186
Sir John Hawkins, the first English slave-dealer	187
Progress, continuance, and abolition of the slave trade	188
Sale of Spaniards in England. Slaves in Barbadoes in 1647	189
Sale of a slave related by Ligon	190
Ligon's account of Sambo who wished to be a Christian	191
Story of Yarico, sold into slavery by him whose life she saved	192
Sale of English and Irish into slavery by Cromwell	193
Thousands of Irish boys and women sold as slaves in West Indies	194
Twenty-five thousand Irish slaves in St. Kitts	195
Father Morison on sale of Irish young ladies	197
Slavery of political convicts made perpetual by Cromwell	197
Irish girls kidnapped and transported into Jamaica	198
The same practice continued under Charles II.	199
English, Scotch, and Irish slaves in Barbadoes under James II.	200
Rebels in Monmouth's rebellion sent as slaves by Judge Jeffreys	201
Henry Pitman's account of his own sufferings there	202

LECTURE VI.

THE ABOLITION OF SLAVERY IN EUROPE. 1. *France*	204
The chartulary of the Abbey of St. Bertin	205
The four chains of slavery which bound the serf	206
Emancipations from twelfth to fifteenth century. Their motives	207
Emancipations not always accepted	208
Village communes for mutual protection	209
Effect of Crusades on emancipation. Communities of serfs	210
Family communities in Croatia and Servia	214
Serfdom existed in some parts of France until 1789	215
2. *Germany.* *Hörigen*, or serfs, and *leibeigener*, or slaves	215
Emancipation slower in Germany than in France	218
The Peasants' War in the sixteenth century	219

Contents.

	page
Robertson on the influence Luther had in the rebellion	220
Demands of the peasants not unreasonable	222
The emancipation of serfs thrown back by the Reformation	222
Serfdom in the eighteenth century	223
Dates of abolition of serfdom in German States	224
Traces still in Mecklenburg. Serfdom in Hungary	225
Has emancipation benefited Hungarian peasants?	227
In Denmark, serfdom re-appeared in the twelfth century	228
3. *Russia.* How the Russian peasants became serfs	230
Catherine II. deprived serfs of legal protection	232
Free labour ceased to exist in Russia under Peter the Great	234
Discontent of serfs. Their miseries under Catherine II.	235
Paul I. interfered to protect the serfs	236
Power of nobles over their serfs. Their numbers	237
Mr. Wallace on the condition of serfs under a kind master	238
The emancipation of the serfs in 1856—1861	239
Whether the serfs are the better for emancipation	241
Justification of the action of the Church towards serfdom	243
Note. Specimen of a manumission by Bishop Grandisson	244
General Index	245

ERRATA ET CORRIGENDA.

Page 6, *line* 3 from bottom, for "bossum" read "possum."
,, 42, ,, 4, for "Emperor" read "Bishops."
,, 43, ,, 12, omit "though never abolished by law."
,, 62, ,, 2, for "twelfth" read "eighth."
,, 62, ,, 3, for "Fourth" read "First."
,, 133, ,, 16, for "in" read "of."
,, 133, ,, 17, for "estates" read "system."
,, 136, ,, 14, for "twelve trevs macnols" read "twelve macnols."

INTRODUCTION.

THE following Lectures were given at various times in the Museum at Torquay, before the "TORQUAY NATURAL HISTORY SOCIETY," but have since been re-written, and a great deal of additional matter has been incorporated with them.

The first Lecture is almost entirely an epitome of the work of M. Paul Allard, *Les Esclaves Chrétiens*, published in 1876. It was the reading of that book that first impressed me with the sense of how great a debt the world owes to Christianity in the abolition of slavery. It seemed to me that, at a time when people are asking, What benefits has the Christian religion conferred upon the human race? the abolition of slavery is at once a ready and a solid answer. It gives the strongest grounds for hope that the same power that solved the grave Social Problem in the past may be confidently trusted to lead the way in the solution of the Social Problem of the present, and of the future. It seemed to me that it only requires the facts to be made known, for the most sceptical mind to draw the conclusion for itself, that only a Divine religion could have succeeded in accomplishing what no other religion has ever attempted. Another volume of M. Allard, *Esclaves, Serfs, et Mainmortables*, carries the same thought still further, although the brevity of the work makes the reader wish for fuller details. It begins with the most remote antiquity, summarizes his previous work, and then proceeds to trace the action of Christianity in the softening of Slavery into Serfdom, and finally sketches the abolition of Serfdom in the different countries of Europe. Whatever there may be of value in my Lectures they owe to M. Allard. But, while gratefully acknowledging my obligations to him, I have consulted every other work that seemed to promise help in elucidating the subject. M. Allard naturally devotes the chief part of his work to Serfdom in France. My readers wish, of course, to be informed most fully as to Slavery and Serfdom in the British Isles. Hence I had to seek such information in other works. Fortunately for me, Mr. Seebohm's *English Village Community*, although treating on quite a different subject, supplied me with almost all that was required. Mr. Wallace's *Russia* enabled me to complete the account of the emancipation of the Serfs in Europe. In all cases I have verified my references where possible.

It may be said that the first Lecture draws too

dark a picture of Roman Slavery. Mr. Allies, in *The Formation of Christendom* in his Lecture on *The Consummation of the Old World*, gives an equally frightful account of the evils of Slavery. I could not perhaps put the objection more strongly than by quoting a criticism of my Lecture, which the late Cardinal Newman was kind enough to send me in 1878. He says:

My only difficulty is, whether what Seneca, Ovid, or Juvenal may say of the slaves of the upper society of Rome applies generally to Roman Slavery. Satirists and moralists are apt to take extreme instances. How could St. Paul write so strongly on their duties of obeying their masters, if obeying them was, from the very nature of the institution, a state of mortal sin? How is it that such martyrdoms as St. Potamiaena's did not occur every day? How is it that St. Chrysostom, who, if any one, was a denouncer of sin in high places, does not inveigh against slavery on far more simple and solemn grounds than those which, as far as I know him, he puts forward? I really think, unless my memory fails, he interprets "Use it rather," Use slavery rather,—continue a slave. But anyhow, in that passage, 1 Cor. vii., St. Paul makes very light of slavery, whereas Allies and you make it a first class evil.

It will help to illustrate the subject if I give the passage of St. Chrysostom alluded to by the Cardinal, from the Oxford Translation:

Hast thou been called, being a slave? Care not for it. Continue to be a slave. . . . We are not ignorant that some say the words, *Use it rather*, are spoken with regard to liberty: interpreting it, "If thou canst be made free, become free." But the expression would be very contrary to Paul's meaning. . . . But meaning to point out that a man gets nothing by being made free, he says, "Though thou hast it in thy power to be made free, remain rather in slavery."

Then, giving the example of Joseph, while a slave, being in reality more free than his mistress, who was a slave to her passions, he continues:

For it is possible for one who is a slave not to be a slave; and for one who is a free man to be a slave. And how can one be a slave and not a slave? When he does all things for God: when he feigns nothing, and does nothing out of eye-service towards men: That is how one that is a slave to men can yet be free. Or, again, how does one that is free become a slave? When he serves men in any evil service, either for gluttony, or desire of wealth, or for office' sake. . . . In fact, there are limits set to slaves by God Himself; and up to what point one ought to keep them, this is also exacted, and to transgress them is wrong. When your master commands nothing which is displeasing to God, it is right to follow and obey, but no further. For thus the slave becomes free. But if you go further, even though you are free, you become a slave."[1]

Mr. Allies, in the very lecture in which he speaks so strongly of the evil of slavery, gives a summary of the revolution which was to be brought about by the mission of St. Peter in the Roman Empire, and says:

He is come to found a society by means of which all that he sees around him, from the emperor to the slave,

[1] *Hom*. xix. on 1 Cor. vii.

shall be changed. He will first teach that slave, now the secret enemy in every household, to "be subject to his master with all fear, not only to the good and gentle, but also to the froward;" and reciprocally he will teach the master "to give to his slave that which is just and equal, because he has himself a Master in Heaven." But more, under the effect of his teaching, that great work of injustice and oppression, which had grown up, flourished and increased in all nations, will be dissolved as it were of itself, and the master accept the slave to an equality of civil rights.[1]

From the time when the Christian Emperor Justinian declared that slavery was founded on the law of nations contrary to the law of nature,[2] there has been no reserve in the language of Christian authorities on the inherent wrong of slavery. Pope Leo XIII. has traced in his letter to the Bishops of Brazil, in his own clear and forcible way, the action of the Church in grappling with this gigantic evil, "for the system is one which is wholly opposed to that which was originally ordained by God and by nature." There would have been danger of a social revolution if St. Chrysostom had used such language to the crowds of slaves who hung upon his words in Antioch and Constantinople. The picture given of slavery in the first lecture was not intended to depict the condition of every household in heathen

---

[1] *Formation of Christendom*, i. p. 102.
[2] *Inst. Justin.* i. tit. iii. 2. See p. 46.

Rome, but to show what was always possible, and too often actually took place. I cannot see much difference between the accounts given by Ovid and Juvenal, and those to be found in Plautus and Terence, and the latter are generally considered to give a fairly truthful picture of Roman society.

My aim has been to show, as the Pope expresses it, "how tenderly and with what prudence the Church has cut out and destroyed this dreadful curse of slavery." I have therefore endeavoured to call attention especially to the *indirect* action of the Church, rather than to her direct efforts for the emancipation of the slave. And yet it would be ungrateful to omit all mention of the heroic and persevering struggle against slavery made in the middle ages by those religious orders which devoted themselves to the great work of the Redemption of Captives. Two Orders, the *Trinitarians*, and the *Order of Mercy* had for their special object the redemption of Christians held in slavery by the Moors. Both arose about the same time, the end of the twelfth century, and they had houses in most of the countries of Europe. The Irish Franciscan, Father Baron, whose latinized name has sometimes caused his Annals to be confused with those of the more famous Oratorian Baronius, has recorded the history of the Trinitarians.

The monks of this Order, in 1199, with money given by Pope Innocent III., ransomed in Morocco 186 Christians, whom they brought to Marseilles. In the course of the following century successive bands of captives were led by these devoted men back to their homes. Thus:

In 1202, St. John Matha ransomed in Valentia, then Moorish...............	207	slaves.
„ 1203, two Fathers, with money collected in Catalonia...................	208	„
„ 1204, St. John Matha brought to Rome from Tunis......................	104	„
„ 1205, two other Fathers brought back to Barcelona...................	190	„
„ 1206, two others ransomed in Algiers	340	„
„ 1207, two Brothers of the Order ransomed and brought home............	109	„
„ 1208, another Brother redeemed......	94	„
„ 1209, Father Bernadine Zabata ransomed in Murcia......................	209	„
„ 1210, St. John Matha, on a second visit to Tunis, redeemed............	220	„
„ 1210, two Brothers of the Order ransomed in Grenada...............	140	„
„ 1211, two Brothers led to Rome from Tunis	114	„

&c. &c.

It will be seen that each year added to the glorious records, and from 1198 to 1787, no fewer than 900,000 Christian slaves had been redeemed by this Order alone.

The *Order of Mercy* was no less zealous. Their

Chronicles have been written from the year 1218 to 1632, and within that period they had ransomed 490,736 captives. These achievements had been effected not only by incessant labour in begging for alms, but also by the sufferings of torture and death which many met with at the hands of the Mahomedans. To the usual three vows of Religious they added a fourth, "To take the place of a captive if there were no other means of effecting his ransom." Numbers passed long years in captivity in fulfilment of this vow, and many suffered martyrdom. One heroic Spanish Bishop detained in slavery, twice expended in the ransom of others the money that had been sent by his diocese for his own redemption, and finally resolved to remain in slavery for the rest of his days, that he might console and support those who were in danger of losing faith and hope under the grinding tyranny of their inhuman masters. Among the martyrs of these Orders were several English and Irish monks; one was Blessed Arthur O'Neil, son of Prince O'Neil, Irish Provincial, who was burned alive on September 1st, 1282. Mr. Kenelm Digby gives a most interesting account of the labours and sufferings of these two Orders, in the eighth chapter of the third book of *Compitum*, "The Road of Captives." The heroic labours of Blessed Peter Claver, S.J., who spent thirty-nine years in alleviating the miseries of the negro slaves in Carthagena, where in seven years he baptized 30,000 of them, are well known; but this is another branch of the subject into which I have not entered.

In the following pages I have confined myself almost entirely to slavery and serfdom in Europe, and have only touched very lightly upon slavery in British Colonies in order to embrace the sale of white slaves that went on during the sixteenth and seventeenth centuries. I have said nothing about the slavery and serfdom that existed up to very recent times in British India. In 1826 the House of Commons ordered to be printed

Copies or Abstracts of all Correspondence between the Court of Directory of the East India Company and the Company's Governments in India, touching the state of Slavery in the Territories under the Company's Rule, or respecting any Slave Trade therein, &c.

These papers fill a thick folio volume of nearly a thousand pages and extend from 1772 to 1827, and contain an immense amount of interesting information on the subject. The case of Mr. Murdock Brown, who carried on a traffic in slaves for his pepper plantation in Malabar occupies two hundred and thirty pages. The condition of slaves appears to have varied greatly in different parts of the peninsula. In some places there were none but agrestic slaves; or those attached to the soil, in other places they were at the absolute disposal of their masters. Mr. Campbell, after twenty-two years' experience in Madras, in answer to questions circulated by the commissioners for the affairs of India in 1834, states:

> There is no enactment of the British Government, under the Madras presidency, either to hinder or promote the manumission of slaves. . . . Their female domestic slaves are seldom made free; but if they have children by their master, such progeny is free: and the children of a male domestic Mussulman slave, married to a free woman, would I think be exempted from bondage. With regard to agrestic slaves, I never heard of any instance of manumission (Appendix, p. 35).

Those who wish to pursue the subject further should read the volume referred to.

Another chapter in the history of slavery has been omitted from these lectures, viz. the Slavery into which the natives of Mexico and Peru were reduced by their Spanish conquerors, in defiance of the remonstrances of Las Casas and other devoted men who laboured hard for the liberty as well as for the conversion of the unfortunate inhabitants. The Queen Isabella issued a Decree prohibiting their reduction to Slavery, and the exertions of Las Casas induced Charles V. to repeat a Decree to the same effect. But the greed of the conquerors rendered this Decree ineffective. Even the condemnation of slavery by the Pope was disregarded, and it has only been in our own days that the natives of Mexico, Peru, and Brazil have been admitted to equal rights with their Spanish and Portuguese conquerors.[1]

As I have endeavoured in these lectures to trace the action of the Church and the Holy See during the last eighteen centuries with regard to slavery, I cannot do better than insert, at the conclusion of this Introduction, the Letter of our Holy Father, Pope Leo XIII., to the Bishops of Brazil, in which he sets forth the line taken by the Popes and the principles that have guided their acts on the subject of Slavery. I trust that my lectures may serve in some measure to illustrate that noble Letter, and show how consistently it follows the traditions of his predecessors in the Apostolic See.

W. R. B.

Plymouth, December 8th, 1891.

---

[1] Isabella's indignation at the enslavement of the Indians is related by Prescott, *Ferdinand and Isabella*, vol. ii. pp. 126, 127, 140, 141. For her condemnation of the Repartimientos, see *Conquest of Mexico*, i. 121, and for a note on Las Casas, see pp. 206—212. The arguments of Las Casas for the suppression of slavery are given in *Conquest of Peru*, ii. pp. 161, 162. Their result in the Decree of Charles V. in 1542, and the tumult they raised in Peru, are described in pp. 165—170. The wise and philanthropic reforms made by the clerical Governor, Pedro de la Gasca, show what efforts true Catholics made against the revival of slavery, see vol. ii. p. 297.

LETTER

OF OUR MOST HOLY LORD

LEO XIII.

BY DIVINE PROVIDENCE

POPE

TO HIS VENERABLE BRETHREN
THE BISHOPS OF BRAZIL.

VENERABLE BRETHREN,
Health and the Apostolic Benediction.

(In plurimis).

AMID the many and great demonstrations of affection which from almost all the peoples of the earth have come to Us, and are still coming to Us, in congratulation upon the happy attainment of the fiftieth anniversary of Our priesthood, there is one which moves Us in a quite special way. We mean one which comes from Brazil, where, upon the occasion of this happy event, large numbers of those who in that vast empire groan beneath the yoke of slavery, have been legally set free. And this work, so full of the spirit of Christian mercy, has been offered up in co-operation with the clergy, by charitable members of the laity of both sexes to God, the Author and Giver of all good things, in testimony of their gratitude for the favour of the health and the years which have been granted to Us. But this was specially acceptable and sweet to Us because it lent confirmation to the belief, which is so welcome to Us, that the great majority of the people of Brazil desire to see the cruelty of slavery ended, and wholly rooted out from the land. This popular feeling has been strongly seconded by the Emperor and his august daughter, and also by the Ministers, by means of various laws which, with this end in view, have been introduced and sanctioned. We told the Brazilian Ambassador last January what a consolation these things were to Us, and We also assured him that We would address letters to the Bishops of Brazil on behalf of these unhappy slaves.

We, indeed, to all men are the Vicar of Christ, the Son of God, Who so loved the human race, that not only did He not refuse, taking our nature to Himself, to live among men, but He delighted in the name of the Son of Man; openly proclaiming that He had come upon earth "to preach deliverance to the captives"[1] in order that, rescuing mankind from the worst slavery, which is the slavery of sin, "He might re-establish all things that are in Heaven and on earth,"[2] and so bring back all the children of Adam from the depths of the ruin of the common fall to their original dignity. The words of St. Gregory the Great are very applicable here: "Since our Redeemer, the Author of all life, deigned to take human flesh, that by the power of His Godhead, the chains by which we were held in bondage being broken, He might restore us to our first state of liberty, it is most fitting that men by the concession of manumission should restore to the freedom in which they were born those whom nature sent free into the world, but who have been condemned to the yoke of slavery by the Law of Nations."[3] It is right, therefore, and

---

[1] Isaias lxi. 1; St. Luke iv. 19.　　[2] Ephes. i. 10.
[3] *Epist.* lib. vi. 12.

obviously in keeping with Our Apostolic Office, that We should favour and advance by every means in Our power whatever helps to secure for men, whether as individuals or as communities, safeguards against the many miseries which, like the fruits of an evil tree, have sprung from the sin of our first parent; and such safeguards, of whatever kind they may be, not only help to promote civilization and the amenities of life, but lead on to that universal restitution of all things which Our Redeemer Jesus Christ contemplated and desired.

In the presence of so much suffering, the condition of slavery, in which a considerable part of the great human family has been sunk in squalor and affliction now for many centuries, is deeply to be deplored: for the system is one which is wholly opposed to that which was originally ordained by God and by nature. The Supreme Author of all things decreed that man should exercise a sort of royal dominion over beasts and cattle and fish and fowl, but never that men should exercise a like dominion over their fellow-men. As St. Augustine puts it: "Having created man a reasonable being, and after His own likeness, God willed that he should rule only over the brute creation; that he should be the master, not of men, but of beasts."[1] From this it follows that "the state of slavery is rightly regarded as a penalty upon the sinner, thus the word slave does not occur in the Scriptures until the just man Noe branded with it the sin of his son. It was sin, therefore, which deserved this name; it was not natural."[2] From the first sin came all evils, and specially this perversity, that there were men who, forgetful of the original brotherhood of the race, instead of seeking, as they should naturally have done, to promote mutual kindness and mutual respect, following their evil desires began to think of

---

[1] *De Civ. Dei*, lib. xix. c. 15. [2] *Ibid.*

other men as their inferiors, and to hold them as cattle born for the yoke. In this way, through an absolute forgetfulness of our common nature and of human dignity, and the likeness of God stamped upon us all, it came to pass that in the contentions and wars which then broke out, those who were the stronger reduced the conquered into slavery; so that mankind, though of the same race, became divided into two sections the conquered slaves and their victorious masters. The history of the ancient world presents us with this miserable spectacle down to the time of the coming of our Lord, when the calamity of slavery had fallen heavily upon all the peoples, and the number of freemen had become so reduced that the poet was able to put this atrocious phrase into the mouth of Cæsar: "The human race exists for the sake of a few."[1]

The system flourished even among the most civilized peoples, among the Greeks and among the Romans, with whom the few imposed their will upon the many. And this power was exercised so unjustly and with such haughtiness, that a crowd of slaves was regarded merely as so many chattels, not as persons but as things. These were held to be outside the sphere of law, and without even the claim to retain and enjoy life. "Slaves are in the power of their masters, and this power is derived from the Law of Nations; for we find that among all nations masters have the power of life and death over their slaves, and whatever a slave earns belongs to his master."[2] Owing to this state of moral confusion it became lawful for men to sell their slaves, to give them in exchange, to dispose of them by will, to beat them, to kill them, to abuse them by forcing them to serve for the gratification of evil passions and cruel

---

[1] "Humanum paucis vivit genus." (Lucan, *Pharsal.* v. 343.)
[2] Justinian, *Instit.* i. tit. viii. n. 1.

superstitions; these things could be done, legally, with impunity, and in the light of Heaven. Even those who were wisest in the pagan world, illustrious philosophers and learned jurisconsults, outraging the common feeling of mankind, succeeded in persuading themselves and others that slavery was simply a necessary condition of nature. And they did not hesitate to assert that the slave class was very inferior to the free-men both in intelligence and perfection of bodily development; and, therefore, that slaves, as beings wanting in reason and sense, ought in all things to be the instruments of the will, however rash and unworthy, of their masters. Such inhuman and wicked doctrines are to be specially detested; for, when once they are accepted, there is no form of oppression so wicked but that it will defend itself beneath some colour of legality and justice. History is full of examples showing what a seed-bed of crime, what a pest and calamity, this system has been for states; hatreds are excited in the breasts of the slaves, and the masters are kept in a state of suspicion and perpetual dread; the slaves prepare to avenge themselves with the torches of the incendiary, and the masters continue the task of oppression with greater cruelty. States are disturbed alternately by the number of the slaves and by the violence of the masters, and so are easily overthrown; hence, in a word, come riots and seditions, pillage and fire, wars and slaughter.

The greater part of humanity were toiling in this abyss of misery, and were the more to be pitied because they were sunk in the darkness of superstition, when in the fulness of time and by the design of God, light shone down upon the world, and the merits of Christ the Redeemer were poured out upon mankind. By that means they were lifted out of the slough and the distress of slavery, and recalled and brought back from the terrible bondage of sin to their high dignity as the sons of God. Thus the Apostles, in the early days of the Church, among other precepts for a devout life taught and laid down the doctrine which more than once occurs in the Epistles of St. Paul addressed to those newly baptized: "For you are all the children of God by faith, in Jesus Christ. For as many of you as have been baptized in Christ, have put on Christ. There is neither Jew, nor Greek; there is neither bond, nor free; there is neither male nor female. For you are all one in Christ Jesus."[1] "Where there is neither Gentile nor Jew, circumcision nor uncircumcision, Barbarian nor Scythian, bond nor free. But Christ is all and in all."[2] "For in one Spirit were we all baptized into one body, whether Jews or Gentiles, whether bond or free, and in one Spirit we have all been made to drink."[3]

Golden words indeed, noble and wholesome lessons, whereby its old dignity is given back and with increase to the human race, and men of whatever land or tongue or class are bound together and joined in the strong bonds of brotherly kinship! Those things, St. Paul, with that Christian charity with which he was filled, learned from the very Heart of Him Who, with such surpassing goodness, gave Himself to be the brother of us all, and in His own Person, without omitting or excepting any one, so ennobled men that they might become participators in the Divine nature. Through this Christian charity the various races of men were drawn together under the Divine guidance in such a wonderful way that they blossomed into a new state of hope and public happiness; as with the progress of time and events and the constant labour of the Church the various nations were able to gather together, Christian and free, organized anew after the manner of a family.

[1] Galat. iii. 26—28. [2] Coloss. iii. 11. [3] 1 Cor. xii. 13.

From the beginning, the Church has spared no pains to make the Christian peoples, in a matter of such high importance, accept and firmly hold the true teaching of Christ and the Apostles. And now, through the new Adam, who is Christ, there is established a brotherly union between man and man, and people and people. Just as in the order of nature they all have a common origin, so in the order which is above nature they all have one and the same origin in salvation and faith. All alike are called to be the adopted sons of God and the Father, Who has paid the self-same ransom for us all. We are all members of the same Body, all are allowed to partake of the same Divine banquet, and offered to us all are the blessings of Divine grace and of eternal life.

Having established these principles as beginnings and foundations, the Church, like a tender mother, went on to try to find some alleviation for the sorrows and the disgrace of the life of the slave. With this end in view, she clearly defined and strongly enforced the rights and mutual duties of masters and slaves, as they are laid down in the letters of the Apostles. It was in these words that the Princes of the Apostles admonished the slaves they had admitted to the fold of Christ. "Servants, be subject to your masters with all fear, not only to the good and gentle, but also to the froward."[1] "Servants, be obedient to them that are your lords according to the flesh, with fear and trembling, in the simplicity of your heart, as to Christ. Not serving to the eye, but as the servants of Christ, doing the will of God from the heart. With a good will serving as to the Lord and not to men. Knowing that whatsoever good thing any man shall do, the same shall he receive from the Lord, whether he be bond or free."[2] St. Paul says the same

---

[1] 1 St. Peter ii. 18.   [2] Ephes. vi. 5—8.

to Timothy: "Whosoever are servants under the yoke, let them count their masters worthy of all honour; lest the name of the Lord and His doctrine be blasphemed. But they that have believing masters, let them not despise them because they are brethren, but serve them the rather, because they are faithful and beloved, who are partakers of the benefit. These things teach and exhort."[1] In like manner he commanded Titus to teach servants "to be obedient to their masters in all things pleasing, not gain saying. Not defrauding, but in all things showing good fidelity, that they may adorn the doctrine of God our Saviour in all things."[2]

Those first disciples of the Christian faith very well understood that this brotherly equality of all men in Christ ought in no way to diminish or detract from the respect, honour, faithfulness, and other duties due to those placed above them. From this many good results followed; so that duties became at once more certain of being performed, and lighter and pleasanter to do, and at the same time more fruitful in obtaining the glory of Heaven. Thus they treated their masters with reverence and honour as men clothed in the authority from Whom comes all power. Amongst these disciples the motive of action was not the fear of punishment, or any enlightened prudence, or the promptings of utility, but a consciousness of duty and the force of charity.

On the other hand masters were wisely counselled by the Apostle to treat their slaves with consideration in return for their services. "And you, masters, do the same things unto them, forbearing threatenings; knowing that the Lord both of them and you is in Heaven, and there is no respect of persons with Him."[3] They were also told to remember that the slave had no reason to regret his lot, seeing that he is "the freeman of the

[1] I Timothy vi. 1, 2.   [2] Titus ii. 9, 10.   [3] Ephes. vi. 9.

Lord;" nor the freeman, seeing that he is "the bondman of Christ,"[1] to feel proud, and to give his commands with haughtiness. It was impressed upon masters that they ought to recognize in their slaves their fellow-men, and respect them accordingly; recognizing that by nature they were not different from themselves, that by religion and in relation to the majesty of their common Lord all were equal. These precepts, so well calculated to introduce harmony among the various parts of domestic society, were practised by the Apostles themselves. Specially remarkable is the case of St. Paul when he exerted himself in behalf of Onesimus, the fugitive slave of Philemon, with whom, when he returned him to his master, he sent this loving recommendation: "And do thou receive him as my own bowels, not now as a servant, but instead of a servant a most dear brother. . . . And if he have wronged thee in anything, or is in thy debt, put that to my account."[2]

Whoever compares the Pagan and the Christian attitude towards slavery will easily come to the conclusion that the one was marked by great cruelty and wickedness, and the other by great gentleness and humanity, nor will it be possible to deprive the Church of the credit due to her as the instrument of this happy change. And this becomes still more apparent when we consider, carefully, how tenderly and with what prudence the Church has cut out and destroyed this dreadful curse of slavery. She has deprecated any precipitate action in securing the manumission and liberation of the slaves, because that would have entailed tumults and wrought injury, as well to the slaves themselves as to the commonwealth, but with singular wisdom she has seen that the minds of the slaves should be instructed through her discipline in the Christian faith,

[1] 1 Cor. vii. 22.   [2] Philemon 12—18.

and with baptism should acquire habits suitable to the Christian life. Therefore, when, amid the slave multitude whom she has numbered among her children, some, led astray by some hope of liberty, have had recourse to violence and sedition, the Church has always condemned these unlawful efforts and opposed them, and through her ministers has applied the remedy of patience. She taught the slaves to feel that, by virtue of the light of holy faith, and the character they received from Christ, they enjoyed a dignity which placed them above their heathen lords; but that they were bound the more strictly by the Author and Founder of their faith Himself never to set themselves against these, or even to be wanting in the reverence and obedience due to them. Knowing themselves as the chosen ones of the Kingdom of God, endowed with the freedom of His children, and called to the good things that are not of this life, they were able to work on without being cast down by the sorrows and troubles of this passing world, but with eyes and hearts turned to Heaven were consoled and strengthened in their holy resolutions. St. Peter was addressing himself specially to slaves when he wrote: "For this is thanks-worthy, if for conscience towards God a man endure sorrows, suffering wrongfully. For unto this you are called; because Christ also suffered for us, leaving you an example that you should follow His steps."[1]

The credit for this solicitude joined with moderation, which in such a wonderful way displayed the Divine powers of the Church, is increased by the marvellous and unconquerable courage with which she was able to inspire and sustain so many poor slaves. It was a wonderful sight to behold those who, in their obedience and the patience with which they submitted to every

---

[1] 1 St. Peter ii. 19—21.

task, were such an example to their masters, refusing to let themselves be persuaded to prefer the wicked commands of those above them to the holy law of God, and even giving up their lives in the most cruel tortures with unconquered hearts and unclouded brows. The pages of Eusebius keep alive for us the memory of the unshaken constancy of the virgin Potamiaena, who, rather than consent to gratify the lusts of her master, fearlessly accepted death, and sealed her faithfulness to Jesus Christ with her blood. Many other admirable examples abound of slaves who, for their souls' sake and to keep their faith with God, have resisted their masters to the death. History has no case to show of Christian slaves for any other cause setting themselves in opposition to their masters, or joining in conspiracies against the State.

Thence, peace and quiet times having been restored to the Church, the holy Fathers made a wise and admirable exposition of the Apostolic precepts concerning the fraternal unanimity which should exist between Christians, and with a like charity extended it to the advantage of slaves; striving to point out that the rights of masters extended lawfully indeed over the works of their slaves, but that their power did not extend to using horrible cruelties against their persons. St. Chrysostom stands pre-eminent among the Greeks. He often treats of this subject, and affirms with exulting mind and tongue that slavery, in the old meaning of the word, had at that time disappeared through the beneficence of the Christian faith; so that it both seemed, and was, a word without any meaning among the disciples of the Lord. For Christ indeed (so he sums up his argument), when in His great mercy to us He wiped away the sin contracted by our birth, at the same time healed the manifold corruptions of human society; and that, as death itself by His means has laid aside its terrors and become a peaceful passing away to a happy life, so also has slavery been banished. Do not then call any Christian man a slave, unless, indeed, he is in bondage again to sin; they are altogether brethren who are born again and received in Christ Jesus; our advantages flow from that new birth and adoption into the household of God, not from the eminence of our race; our dignity arises from the praise of our truth, not of our blood; but, in order that that kind of evangelical brotherhood may have more fruit, it is necessary that in the actions of our ordinary life there should appear a willing interchange of kindness and good offices, so that slaves should be esteemed of nearly equal account with the rest of our household and friends, and that the master of the house should supply them, not only with what is necessary for their life and food, but also with all necessary safeguards of religious training. Finally, from the marked address of Paul to Philemon, bidding "grace and peace *to the Church which is in thy house*,"[1] the precept should be held in respect equally by Christian masters and servants; that they, who have an intercommunion of faith should also have an intercommunion of charity. Of the Latin authors we worthily and justly call to mind St. Ambrose, who so earnestly inquired into all that was necessary in this matter, and so clearly ascribes what is due to each kind of man according to the laws of Christianity, that no one has ever achieved it better. His sentiments, it is unnecessary to say, fully and perfectly coincide with those of St. Chrysostom.

These things were, as is evident, most justly and usefully laid down. But more, the chief point is that they have been observed wholly and religiously, from

[1] Philemon 2.

the earliest times, wherever the profession of the Christian faith has flourished. Unless this had been the case, that excellent defender of religion, Lactantius, could not have maintained it so confidently, as though a witness of it. "*Should any one say: Are there not among you some poor, some rich, some slaves, some who are masters; is there no difference between different persons? I answer, There is none, nor is there any other cause why we call each other by the name of brother, than that we consider ourselves to be equals; for when we measure all human things, not by the body but by the spirit, although their corporal condition may be different from ours, yet in spirit they are not slaves to us, but we esteem and call them brethren, fellow-workers in religion.*"[1]

The care of the Church extended to the protection of slaves, and without interruption tended carefully to one object, that they should finally be restored to freedom, which would greatly conduce to their eternal welfare. That the event happily responded to these efforts, the annals of sacred antiquity afford abundant proof. Noble matrons, rendered illustrious by the praises of St. Jerome, themselves afforded great aid in carrying this matter into effect; so that, as Salvianus relates, in Christian families, even though not very rich, it often happened that the slaves were freed by a generous manumission. But also St. Clement long before praised that excellent work of charity by which some Christians became slaves, by an exchange of persons, because they could in no other way liberate those who were in bondage. Wherefore, in addition to the fact that the act of manumission began to take place in churches as an act of piety, the Church ordered it to be proposed to the faithful when about to make their wills, as a work very pleasing to God and of great merit and value with Him.

[1] *Div. Inst.* i. v. 16.

Hence those precepts of manumission to the heir were introduced with the words "*for the love of God, for the welfare or benefit of my soul.*" Neither was anything grudged as the price of captives; gifts dedicated to God were sold, sacred vessels of gold and silver melted down, the ornaments and gifts of the basilicas alienated, as, indeed, was done more than once by Ambrose, Augustine, Hilary, Eligius, Patrick, and many other holy men. Moreover, the Roman Pontiffs, who have always acted, as history truly relates, as the protectors of the weak and helpers of the oppressed, have done their best for slaves. St. Gregory himself set at liberty as many as possible, and, in the Roman Council of the year 597, desired those to receive their freedom who were anxious to enter the monastic state. Hadrian I. maintained that slaves could freely enter into matrimony even without their master's consent. It was clearly stated by Alexander III., in the year 1167, to the Moorish King of Valencia, that he should not make a slave of any Christian, because no one was a slave by the law of nature, all men having been made free by God. Innocent III., in the year 1190, at the prayer of its founders, John de Matha and Felix of Valois, approved and established the *Order of the Most Holy Trinity for Redeeming Christians* who had fallen into the power of the Turks. At a later date, Honorius III., and afterwards Gregory IX., duly approved the *Order of St. Mary of Help*, founded for a similar purpose, which Peter Nolasco had established, and which included the severe rule that its Religious should give themselves up as slaves in the place of Christians taken captive by tyrants, if it should be necessary in order to redeem them.

The same Pope Gregory passed a Decree, which was a far greater support of liberty, that it was unlawful to sell slaves to the Church; and he further added an exhortation to the faithful that, as a punishment for their faults, they should give their slaves to God and His saints as an act of expiation. There are also many other good deeds of the Church in the same behalf. For she, indeed, was accustomed by severe penalties to defend slaves from the savage anger and cruel injuries of their masters; and to those upon whom the hand of violence had rested she was accustomed to open her sacred temples as places of refuge, to receive the freed men into her good faith, and to restrain those by censure who dared by evil inducements to lead a free man back again into slavery. In the same way, she was still more favourable to the freedom of the slaves whom, by any means, she held as her own, according to times and places; when she laid down, either that those should be released by the Bishops from every bond of slavery who had shown themselves during a certain time of trial of praiseworthy honesty of life, or when she easily permitted the Bishops of their own will to declare those belonging to them free. It must also be ascribed to the compassion and virtue of the Church, that somewhat of the pressure of civil law upon slaves was remitted; and, as far as it was brought about, that the milder alleviations of Gregory the Great, having been incorporated in the written law of nations, became of force. That, however, was done principally by the agency of Charlemagne, who included them in his *Capitularia*, as Gratian afterwards did in his *Decretum*. Finally, monuments, laws, institutions, through a continuous series of ages, teach and splendidly demonstrate the great love of the Church towards slaves, whose miserable condition she never left destitute of protection, and always to the best of her power alleviated. Therefore sufficient praise or thanks can never be returned to the Catholic Church, the banisher of slavery, and the author of true liberty, fraternity, and equality among men, for, through the fulness of the beneficence of Christ our Redeemer, she has merited it by the prosperity of nations.

Towards the end of the fifteenth century, at which time, the base stain of slavery having been nearly blotted out from among Christian nations, States were anxious to stand firmly in evangelical liberty, and also to increase their empire, this Apostolic See took the greatest care that the evil germs of such depravity should nowhere revive. She therefore directed her provident vigilance to the newly discovered regions of Africa, Asia, and America; for a report had reached her that the leaders of those expeditions, Christians though they were, were wickedly making use of their arms and ingenuity for establishing and imposing slavery on those innocent nations. Indeed, since the crude nature of the soil which they had to overcome, and also the wealth of metals which had to be extracted by digging, required very hard work, unjust and inhuman plans were entered into. For a certain traffic was begun, slaves being transported for that purpose from Ethiopia, which at that time, under the name of *La tratta dei Negri*, too much occupied those colonies. An oppression of the indigenous inhabitants (who are universally called Indians), much the same as slavery, followed with a like maltreatment. When Pius II. had become assured of these matters, without delay, on October 7th, in the year 1462, he addressed a letter to the Bishop of the place, in which he reproved and condemned such wickedness. Some time afterwards Leo X. lent, as far as he could, his good offices and authority to the kings of both Portugal and Spain, who took care to radically extirpate that licence, opposed alike to religion, humanity, and justice. Nevertheless, that evil having grown strong remained there, its impure cause, the unquenchable desire of gain, remaining. Then Paul III., anxious with a fatherly love as to the condition of the Indians and of the Moorish slaves, came to this last determination, to declare in open day, and, as it were, in the sight of all nations, that they all had a just and natural right of a threefold character, namely, that each one of them was master of his own person, that they could live together under their own laws, that they could acquire and hold property for themselves. More than this, having sent letters to the Cardinal Archbishop of Toledo, he pronounced an interdict and deprival of Sacred Rites against those who acted contrary to the aforesaid Decree, reserving to the Roman Pontiff the faculty of absolving them.[1]

With the same forethought and constancy, other Pontiffs, at a later period, as Urban VIII., Benedict XIV., and Pius VII., showed themselves strong asserters of liberty for the Indians and Moors, and even those who were as yet not instructed in the Christian faith. The last Pope, moreover, at the Council of the confederated Princes of Europe held at Vienna, called their attention in common to this point, that that traffic in negroes of which We have spoken before, and which had now ceased in many places, should be thoroughly rooted out. Gregory XVI. also severely censured those who neglected the duties of humanity and the laws, and restored the decrees and statutory penalties of the Apostolic See, and he left no means untried, that foreign nations also, following the kindliness of the Europeans,

---

[1] *Veritas ipsa*, 29 May, 1537. See the Letter of Gregory XVI., given at full length in Note 15 to Balmez' *European Civilization*. The whole Note is most valuable, and occupies pp. 420—437 of the English Edition.

should cease from and abhor the disgrace and brutality of slavery.[1] But it has turned out most fortunately for Us that We have received the congratulations of the chief princes and rulers of public affairs for having obtained, thanks to Our constant pleadings, some satisfaction for the long continued and most just complaints of nature and religion.

We have, however, in Our mind, in a matter of the same kind, another care which gives Us no light anxiety and presses upon Our solicitude. This shameful trading in men has, indeed, ceased to take place by sea, but on land it is carried on to too great an extent and too barbarously, and that especially in some parts of Africa. For, it having been perversely laid down by the Mahommedans that Ethiopians and men of similar nations are very little superior to brute beasts, it is easy to see and shudder at the perfidy and cruelty of man. Suddenly, like plunderers making an attack, they invade the tribes of Ethiopians fearing no such thing, they rush into their villages, houses, and huts; they lay waste, destroy, and seize everything; they lead away from thence the men, women, and children, easily captured and bound, so that they may drag them away by force for their shameful traffic. These hateful expeditions are made into Egypt, Zanzibar, and partly also into the Soudan, as though so many stations; men bound with chains are forced to take long journeys, ill supplied with food, under the frequent use of the lash; those who are too weak to undergo this are killed; those who are strong enough go like a flock with a crowd of others to be sold, and to be passed over to a brutal and shameless purchaser. But whoever is thus sold and given up is

---

[1] *In supremo Apostolatus fastigio*, 3 Dec. 1839. "We absolutely prohibit and interdict all ecclesiastics and laymen from venturing to maintain that this traffic in negroes is permitted, under any pretext or colour whatsoever."

exposed to a miserable rending asunder of wives, children, and parents, and is driven by him into whose power he falls into a hard and indescribable slavery; nor can he refuse to conform to the religious rites of Mahomet. These things We have received not long since, with the greatest bitterness of feeling, from some who have been eye-witnesses, though tearful ones, of that kind of infamy and misery. With these accounts what has been related lately by the explorers of equatorial Africa entirely coincides. It is indeed manifest, by their testimony and word, that each year about four hundred thousand Africans are thus sold like cattle. And of these one half, wearied out by the roughness of the tracks, fall down and perish there; so that, sad to relate, those travelling through such places see the pathway strewn with the remains of bones. Who would not be moved by the thought of such miseries? We, indeed, who bear the person of Christ, the loving liberator and Redeemer of all mankind, and who so rejoice in the many and glorious good deeds of the Church to all who are afflicted, can scarcely express how great is Our commiseration for those unhappy nations, with what fulness of charity We open Our arms to them, how ardently We desire to be able to afford them every alleviation and support, with the hope that, having cast off the slavery of superstition as well as the slavery of man, they may at length serve the one true God under the gentle yoke of Christ, partakers with us of the Divine inheritance. Would that all who hold high positions in empires or states, or who desire the rights of nations and of humanity to be held sacred, or who earnestly devote themselves to the interests of the Catholic religion, would all, everywhere, acting on Our exhortations and wishes, strive together to repress, forbid, and put an end to that kind of traffic, than which nothing is more base and wicked. In the meantime, while by a more strenuous application of ingenuity and labour new roads are being made, and new commercial enterprises undertaken in the lands of Africa, let apostolic men endeavour to find out how they can best secure the safety and liberty of slaves. They will obtain success in this matter in no other way than if, strengthened by Divine grace, they give themselves up to spreading Our most holy faith and daily caring for it, whose distinguishing fruit is that it wonderfully favours and developes the liberty *with which Christ made us free*. We therefore advise them to look, as if into a mirror of apostolic virtue, at the life and works of St. Peter Claver, to whom We have lately added a crown of glory; let them look at him who, for full forty years gave himself up to minister with the greatest constancy in his labours, to a most miserable assembly of Moorish slaves, truly he ought to be called the apostle of those whose constant servant he professed himself and gave himself up to be. If they endeavour to take to themselves and reflect the charity and patience of such a man, they will shine indeed as worthy ministers of salvation, authors of consolation, messengers of peace, who, by God's help, may turn solitude, desolation, and fierceness into the most joyful fertility of religion and civilization.

And now, venerable brethren, Our thoughts and letters desire to turn to you that We may again announce to you and again share with you the exceeding joy which We feel on account of the determinations which have been publicly entered into in that empire with regard to slavery. If, indeed, it seemed to Us a good, happy, and propitious event, that it was provided and insisted upon by law that whoever were still in the condition of slaves ought to be admitted to the status and rights of free men, so also it confirms and increases our hope of future acts which will be the cause of joy, both in civil and religious matters. Thus the name of the Empire of Brazil will be justly held in honour and praise among the most civilized nations, and the name of its august Emperor will likewise be esteemed; for his excellent speech is on record, that he desired nothing more ardently than that every vestige of slavery should be speedily obliterated from his territories. But on the other hand, until those precepts of the laws are carried into effect, earnestly endeavour, We beseech you, by all means, and press on as much as possible the accomplishment of this affair, which no light difficulties hinder. Through your means let it be brought to pass that masters and slaves may mutually agree with the highest good-will and best good faith. Do not let there be any transgression of clemency or justice, but, whatever things have to be carried out, let all be done lawfully, temperately, and in a Christian manner. It is, however, chiefly to be wished that this may be prosperously accomplished, which all desire, that slavery may be banished and blotted out without any injury to Divine or human rights, with no agitation of the State, and so with the solid benefit of the slaves themselves, for whose sake it is undertaken. To each one of these, whether they have already been made free or are about to become so, We address with a pastoral intention and fatherly mind a few salutary cautions culled from the words of the great Apostle of the Gentiles. Let them then endeavour piously and constantly to retain a grateful memory and feeling towards those by whose counsel and exertion they were set at liberty. Let them never show themselves unworthy of so great a gift nor ever confound liberty with licence; but let them use it as becomes well ordered citizens for the industry of an active life, for the benefit and advantage both of their family and of the State. To respect and increase the dignity of their princes, to obey the magistrates, to be obedient to the laws, these and similar duties let them diligently fulfil under the influence, not so much of fear as of religion; let them also restrain and keep in subjection envy of another's wealth or position, which unfortunately daily distresses so many of those in inferior positions, and presents so many incitements of rebellion against security of order and peace. Content with their state and lot, let them think nothing dearer, let them desire nothing more ardently, than the good things of the heavenly Kingdom, for the sake of which they have been brought to the light and redeemed by Christ; let them feel piously towards God, Who is their Lord and Liberator; let them love Him with all their power; let them keep His Commandments with all their might; let them rejoice in being sons of His spouse, the Holy Church; let them labour to be as good as possible, and, as much as they can, let them carefully return His love.

Do you also, Venerable Brethren, be constant in showing and urging on the freed men these same doctrines; that that which is Our chief prayer, and at the same time ought to be yours and that of all good people, religion, amongst the first, may ever feel that she has gained the most ample fruits of that liberty which has been obtained wherever that empire extends.

But, that that may happily take place, We beg and implore the full grace of God and the motherly aid of the Immaculate Virgin. As a foretaste of heavenly gifts and witness of Our fatherly good-will towards you, Venerable Brethren, your clergy, and all your people, We lovingly impart the Apostolic Benediction.

Given at St. Peter's at Rome, May 5th, in the year MDCCCLXXXVIII., the eleventh of Our Pontificate.

LEO PP. XIII.

LECTURE I.

SLAVERY IN THE ROMAN EMPIRE.

SLAVERY, in a more or less aggravated form, is still a sadly practical question in every country where Christianity is not dominant, and is likely to be so for many generations yet to come. It is a phenomenon in the natural history of man extending through all periods of which we have any records; and therefore, human nature continuing the same, the lessons of the past have an important influence on the mind and action of the present.

As a nation we have happily been, for nearly a generation, delivered from the reproach of slavery ourselves. Our American cousins have not yet recovered from the violent shock which the Republic felt in the contest that resulted in the abolition of slavery in the Southern States. Even these last few years have seen our African Colonial Governments sorely exercised with the difficulties of the slave question in tribes subject to British rule, while it is hard to speak confidently about the success of our attempts to repress the slave-trade on the East Coast of Africa.

It is therefore a practical, as well as an interesting study, to inquire into the history of slavery in any case where it has existed and has been successfully abolished, and trace how that abolition has been effected.

We may, with M. Paul Allard,[1] divide the history of slavery during the last eighteen hundred years into three epochs:

1. Under the Roman Empire, in which it was carried to an excess never known elsewhere, before or since. Christianity found it permeating and corrupting every domain of human life, and in six centuries of conflict succeeded in reducing it to nothing.

2. The second epoch may be taken to embrace the barbarous nations who overran and finally overthrew the Roman Empire, and who re-established slavery in Europe, until they too submitted to the influence of Christianity, and by the twelfth century slavery had again been proscribed and expelled from Europe.

3. The third epoch is that melancholy history of the revival of this hateful bane of humanity among nations professing Christianity, but acting in defiance of its spirit and its laws. The Portuguese have the unhappy distinction of having reintroduced slavery on the coast of Africa in the fifteenth century. The Spaniards were not slow to catch the infection; and, in defiance of the clear prohibitions of religion, slavery was established in the New World. The Puritans attempted to make out that the Christian religion sanctioned and

---

[1] *Les Esclaves Chrétiens.* Par Paul Allard, pp. 492, seq. Paris: Didier et Cie.

enforced it, and modern Christian slavery reached its most revolting climax when Oliver Cromwell shipped off thousands of Irish boys and girls and sold them in the slave-market of Barbadoes. "Sir William Petty states that six thousand were sent out as slaves to the West Indies. The Bristol sugar-merchants traded in these human lives. . . . Even girls of noble birth were subjected to this cruel fate. Morison mentions an instance of this kind which came to his own knowledge. He was present when Daniel Connery, a gentleman of Clare, was sentenced to banishment by Colonel Ingoldsby for harbouring a priest. Mrs. Connery died of destitution, and three of his daughters, young and beautiful girls, were transported as slaves to Barbadoes."[1] We are only just emerging from this third and last epoch of slavery in civilized Europe.

The first epoch is the most easy to treat impartially, and the contending forces are more distinct and less complicated than during the other two epochs, and hence the results of the conflict are more easy to estimate. We shall in this lecture confine ourselves to slavery under the Roman Empire, and sketch briefly—

I. The effects of slavery in the Roman Empire.

II. Its diminution and all but extinction during the fourth and fifth centuries.

III. The cause of this extinction, and the manner in which it was effected.

---

[1] Miss Cusack's *History of Ireland*, p. 465.

I. *The effects of slavery on the Romans.* Let us begin at the bottom of the social scale, with that wide base upon which the pyramid of society ultimately rests—the poor labouring classes—and see how it affected them. The population of the Roman Empire in the first century consisted of three classes—masters, slaves, and poor freemen. The master bought his slaves and fed them, but paid them nothing—they were his machines. He needed no hired labourer, for his slaves did all that was wanted. The free labourers found themselves reduced to idleness, and congregated together in the large cities, where the State silenced their discontented clamours with bread and games. Not to have more than one slave was thought extreme poverty. When Horace sat at his frugal table, three slaves waited on him,[1] and he had nine in his little Sabine farm. On an average, a capital of £80 implied one slave. Under Augustus, a simple freedman, C. Cæcilius Isodorus, is described by Pliny as "having lost a considerable part of his fortune during the civil wars, yet at his death he left four thousand one hundred and sixteen slaves."[2] Another freedman, Demetrius Pompeianus, is stated by Seneca to have had repeated to him the number of his slaves every morning, like a general who examines the muster-roll of his troops.[3] In fact it was necessary, for Petronius—we may suppose without exaggeration—makes one of his characters, a freedman, Trimalcion, to ask one morning how

---

[1] "Cœna ministratur pueris tribus." (*Sat.* i. vi. 116.)
[2] *Hist. Nat.* xxxiii. 47. [3] *De Tranquil. Anim.* 9.

many infant slaves had been born on his estates the preceding day, and was informed that there had been an increase to his property of thirty boys and forty girls.[1] Now we cannot suppose that such vast numbers of slaves would be allowed to be idle. A comparatively few personally ministered to the pleasures of their master, but the vast majority were incessantly employed in work of various kinds. In a moderate Roman establishment there was a mill to grind the corn, and bakers to make it into bread: the flax was spun and the wool, and in the same farm there were looms where the cloth was woven; and dyers, tailors, and embroiderers, all under the superintendence of the *lanipens*, had each their allotted task. There were shoemakers, huntsmen, fishermen, carpenters, masons, carvers, mosaic workers, glaziers, joiners, architects, surgeons, and physicians —all slaves. In great houses the various classes of slaves were divided into *decuriæ*, or bands of ten, with a slave officer over each.[2] Roman patricians took a pride in having everything that they could require manufactured by their own slaves. So Petronius makes Trimalcion boast: "Thanks to the gods, there is nothing in my house that you admire which has been bought."[3]

With us a large establishment encourages labour and stimulates trade in its neighbourhood; but

---

[1] *Satyricon*, 53.
[2] In the *columbarium* of Livia are found enumerated: "Decurio cubicular, Mensor decurio, Strator decurio, Decurio medicus, Lector decurio, Ostiarius decurio, Pedisequus decurio, Decurio a tabulis, Decurio femina, Vernarum decurio." (Orelli, *Inscr.* 2973.)
[3] *Satyric.* 47.

these Roman establishments had precisely the opposite effect. There was nothing for the labourer to do, no want for the tradesmen to supply. Nay, there was a superfluity of manufactured goods; and the wants of less extensive establishments were supplied from the warehouses, which every great slave-holder found himself obliged to open. No small farmer, no small tradesman, could compete with these vast manufactories. Lucullus had in his warehouse five thousand purple cloaks.[1] When extraordinarily grand public entertainments had to be given, and a prætor wished to put on the stage a few hundred actors, he did not apply to a costumier or a clothier, but borrowed the dresses from Lucullus. The poet Martial writes to a rich man: "Your wardrobes are over-full of brilliant robes, your presses are crammed with festive garments without number, you have enough white wool to clothe a whole tribe."[2] When slaves were thus productive, it became a necessity for every tradesman to invest his capital in slaves, and thus every shop was filled with them. A slave workman ordinarily cost about £18 or £20, and a female slave £6 or £8, and their food did not cost above £5 or £6 a year. Slaves never grumbled about wages; they had no rights. When they attempted to escape, they were condemned by the

[1] Chlamydes Lucullus, ut aiunt,
Si posset centum scenæ præbere rogatus,
Qui dossum tot? ait : tamen et quæram, et quot habebo,
Mittam. Postpaulo scribit, sibi millia quinque
Esse domi chlamydum ; partem, vel tolleret omnes.
(Hor. Epist. i. vi.)

[2] Epigramm. ii. 46.

law for stealing themselves from their masters, and terrible punishments and the red-hot iron brand cautioned them against a repetition of the offence. Letting out slaves on hire for every conceivable purpose became in Rome as common as letting out horses in England.[1] A man of small means who wanted to give an entertainment would hire a slave cook to prepare his dinner, slave waiters to attend upon his guests, and a slave dancing girl or musician to amuse them. These hired slaves were called *operarii*, and Plutarch tells us that Crassus had five hundred slave builders and architects, by means of whom he amassed an enormous fortune; for whenever a fire took place, Crassus was ready to rebuild the ruined houses for the citizens with his army of slave masons, who were more profitable to him than his silver mines and all his vast domains.[2]

The only employments that thus remained open to poor freemen of humble means were the lower offices about the temples or the courts of justice, and even here they sometimes met with formidable rivals in slaves. These offices were gained by favour, and thus the mass of the population became pauperized parasites, who lived by flattering the great. Here and there an independent spirit, like the poet Plautus, would insist upon the rights of labour, and hire himself out for eightpence a day to work among the slaves. The poor generally

---

[1] "Mercedes servorum vel jumentorum . . . possunt locari." (Ulpian, *In Dig.* xlii. v. 8.)
[2] Plutarc. *Marc Crassus*, 2.

became pensioners of the State. Under Pompey 320,000 Romans received regular supplies of bread. Septimius Severus reduced the number to 155,000. In 270, under Aurelian, every pensioner received two pounds of bread a day. From the time of Cicero one-fifth of the whole *vectigalia* or revenue from indirect taxation was absorbed by the distributions made in the single city of Rome. This relief does not include the largesses of from £5 to £50 a head for each of the idle rabble which the Emperors showered from time to time on the restless clamorous crowd of beggars.[1] Excuses for sumptuous feasts were never wanting. And so the populace forgot its degradation in the gratification of every passion and every caprice at the public expense. Thus slavery, by destroying free labour, corrupted and undermined the very basis of society.

2. Necessity is the mother of invention. Our brains are taxed to discover new machines for lightening labour, and enable one man to do what requires the strength of a multitude. Our machines are our slaves. But the Roman slave-holder had no such stimulus to his invention. He cared not to lighten a burden which a few blows could extract from those whom Varro called speaking machines—*instrumenti genus vocale*.[2] The slave workman had no interest in improving his tools. Such improvement would not benefit him in the least, for his master would merely insist upon an

---

[1] See M. Allard's *Les Esclaves Chrétiens*, pp. 35—37.
[2] *De Re Rustica*, i. 17.

extra amount of work. Thus art and skill alike languished. Lucian in his *Dream* makes Science speak, "If you make yourself a sculptor, you will be only an artisan. Even if you were a Phidias or a Polycletes, it is only your workmanship that all will praise. Among those who see them there will not be a single man of common sense who will desire to resemble you; for, however skilful you may be, you will always pass for an artisan, a vile workman, a man who lives by the labour of his hands." It would be a mistake to suppose that there was not a highly cultivated and most fastidious taste among the Roman patricians; what was wanting was that due appreciation of the skill and genius of the artist which is essential if freshness and originality are to be brought out. There was none of that delicate economy of a skilled workman's brain and strength which marks our fine-art manufactures. The waste of human force under the crushing weight of slavery was immense. The division of labour depended on the caprice of the master, who, for some imaginary offence, would degrade a highly accomplished artist or musician to labour in the mines, perhaps for life. Then the pride of rich men and women led them to waste the lives of multitudes of their fellow-creatures on the petty requirements of their own vanity and idleness. The very minute division of labour was a degradation.[1] Imagine a man

---

[1] St. Clement of Alexandria describes them: "Men, avoiding working with their own hands and serving themselves, have recourse to slaves, purchasing a great crowd of fine cooks, and of people to set out the table, and of others to divide the meat skilfully into

whose sole occupation in life was to carve fowls![1] Even the slaves themselves had a multitude of slaves of their own—*vicarii*.

In a *columbarium* near the Gate of St. Sebastian there is found an inscription which is now in the Lateran Museum, describing the retinue of a rich slave employed in the customs in Gaul, who died in Rome. He had brought with him sixteen *vicarii*, one who had to look after his commercial affairs, *negotiator;* another who regulated the household expenses, *sumptuarius;* three slave secretaries, *a manu;* one slave doctor, *medicus;* two slaves to look after the silver, *ab argento;* one to take care of the wardrobe, *a veste;* two valets de chambre, *cubicularius;* two footmen, *pedissequus;* two slave cooks, *cocus;* and a woman named Secunda, whose occupation is not specified. If such was the travelling suite of a slave, what must have been the household of his master?

Let us picture a wealthy patrician going to spend the evening with his friends. His equipage starts. His arrival is announced by *cursores*, who run before his litter. He is surrounded

pieces. And the staff of slaves is separated into many divisions: some labour for their gluttony, carvers and seasoners, and the compounders and makers of sweetmeats, and honey cakes, and custards; others are occupied with their too numerous clothes; others guard the gold like griffins; others keep the silver, and wipe the cups, and make ready what is needed to furnish the festive table; others rub down the horses; and a crowd of cup-bearers exert themselves in their service, and herds of beautiful boys, like cattle, from whom they milk away their beauty. And male and female assistants at the toilet are employed about the ladies—some for the mirrors, some for the head-dresses, others for the combs." (*Pædagog.* iii. c. 4.)

[1] Seneca, Epist. 47.

by a crowd of pages and footmen, who accompany him everywhere like an army. There are the *lanternarii*, with their torches in their hands. The house of his friend is alive with a crowd of slaves carrying bronze or terra-cotta lamps, the *lampadarii*. The *janitor*, represented by Ovid as dragging a long chain behind him, must open the door; the *velarii* slaves hold back the curtains which close the *atrium*, where the *atriarii* are ranged to pay their respects to the distinguished guest. The *nomenclator* announces the visitor, who is politely invited to recruit himself with a bath. The *fornicator* has heated the chamber, the *balneator* has prepared everything, elegant slaves attend the stranger at the bath, after which the *alipilus* gently draws out any hairs that may mar the smoothness of his skin, and the *unctor* applies his perfumes. Then he is conducted to the gymnasium, where slave acrobats display their powers. He amuses himself with the contests of slave boxers or wrestlers. While thus occupied a troop of slave cooks are busy in the kitchen, crowds of beautifully attired waiters dress and serve the table. Supper is ready, and a young page at the door warns the guest to enter the *triclinium* with the right foot first, for good luck. While the repast is going on, troops of slaves enter one after another—dwarfs, clowns, mountebanks, male and female singers, musicians, and dancers, transform the *triclinium* into a theatre, while private gladiators turn it into an arena. The troop of beautiful youths, arranged according to their height or nation, who attend the guests, themselves require the services of a crowd of slaves, *pædagogi* to train them, *ornatores glabrorum* to dress them and cover them with jewels. Seneca tells us that to such a pitch of languid torpor had luxury reduced many noble Romans that they required a slave to tell them whether they were sitting or standing.[1] He describes one of them at table: "Around him stand caterers who know exactly all the wants of their master's palate, who understand what dishes will tickle his taste, what will please his eyes, what novelty will excite his nauseated appetite, what he disliked yesterday and what he fancies to-day."[2] He lies on a bed of roses, and waits for his repast. A fresh pleasure is prepared for each of his senses. "Harmonious songs sound in his ears, voluptuous spectacles present themselves to his eyes, and most delicate morsels attract his taste, his whole body is enveloped in the softest and smoothest clothing, and that pleasure may not be excluded from any of his senses, the fragrance of varied perfumes reach his nostrils."[3] Lest he should die of very languor, select slaves revive his fainting body. He stretches out his lazy fingers, and a slave who is obliged to keep his hands day and night in gloves to preserve the delicacy of their touch, takes off these gloves and strokes dexterously the enervated limbs of his

---

[1] "Audio quemdam ex delicatis . . . cum ex balneo elatus, et in sella positus esset, dixisse interrogando: *Jam sedeo?*" (*De Brev. Vit.* xii.)
[2] Epist. 47.
[3] *De Vita Beata*. xi.

fainting master, in order to re-awaken some sensation in that half-dead carcase.[1] Well may Seneca add: "Such men care more for the ruffling of their hair than for the ruin of their country; the curling of their head touches them more than the salvation of the State."[2]

3. It will be seen from such sketches as these that slavery not only ousted free labour, degraded industry and art, but produced the most deleterious effect on the *masters themselves*. Slavery corrupted life at its very outset. Tacitus traces the debasement of morals to the all but universal custom of mothers giving their children to be suckled by slaves.[3] Cato allowed his own wife to give suck to the infants of his slaves, but he refused to entrust his son to the care of a slave tutor or *pædagogus*, though he might be a very honest man and a good grammarian.[4] The *pædagogus*, from being the slave appointed to conduct his young master to school, often became his tutor himself, and a highly educated slave tutor, or *literator*, is said by Suetonius to have been bought for £2,000 of our money;[5] but the mere fact of his being a slave was sufficient to destroy all respect for him in the mind of his pupil, and it was only too natural that the unhappy tutor should seek to gain the affections of his charge frequently by flattering his worst vices. Thus pædagogues would

---

[1] Percurrit agili corpus arte tractatrix,
Manumque doctam spargit omnibus membris:
Martial, Epigr. iii. 82.)
[2] *De Brev. Vit.* xii.
[3] *De Oratoribus,* 28. [4] Plutarc. *Cato Maj.* 20.
[5] *De Illustr.-Gramm.* 4, 5.

become the notorious corrupters of youth. A young man often signalized the attainment of his majority by giving freedom to his *pædagogus*, and thus the tutor was dependent on his pupil, and afraid of incurring his dislike lest he should fail in obtaining his liberty. Terence, in his *Phormio*, introduces two pædagogues, Geta and Davus, who converse thus:

Geta. The two old people on leaving for Lemnos entrusted their sons to me, and constituted me their preceptor.

Davus. A trying charge, Geta.

Geta. Yes, I know it by experience. I began by opposing their passions. But how shall I tell you? For my fidelity to our master, my poor back had to suffer (*scapulas perdidi*).

Davus. That is easy to understand: It is hard to kick against the goad.

Geta. And so I set myself to do and to let them do all that they pleased.

Davus. You are a wise man, Geta. *Scisti uti foro.*[1]

Plautus, who, as we have seen, mixed freely with the slaves and knew what he was saying, tells us:

The child is hardly seven years old when it is quite impossible for the *pædagogus* to touch him with the tip of his finger, unless he wants to have his head broken with the writing-tablets. And if at length he goes to complain to the father, the parent says: "Well, my son, you are my son indeed, you know how to resist injustice! And you, you worthless old wretch, don't you attempt to whip my good child." The teacher goes away with his

---

[1] *Phorm.* Act. i. Scene 2

face burning like a lamp. And this is how justice is done. What authority will you assign to a teacher whose pupil is the first to beat him?[1]

The same Plautus, in his *Bacchides*, gives us a significant dialogue between a pædagogue and a youth whom he is trying to rescue from the toils of an abandoned woman:

Lydus. You destroy yourself, you destroy me, you destroy the good lessons which I have so often given you.

Pistoclerus. Eh—well—I have lost my labour and you yours. The education you have given me has profited neither you nor me.

Lydus. Oh, what an enslaved heart!

Pistoclerus. Come, come, you are tiresome. Hold your tongue, Lydus, and come along with me.

Lydus. He calls me no longer, "my teacher," he calls me now, "Lydus." ... You are going to have a mistress?

Pistoclerus. Well. When you see her, then you'll know.

Lydus. You shall not have one. I shall not allow it. I am going home to your father.

Pistoclerus. Do nothing of the sort, Lydus, or else look out for yourself.

Lydus. What! "Look out for yourself!"

Pistoclerus. Yes. I am old enough to be no longer under your tutelage.

Lydus. Ah! What an abyss you are in now! Oh, how gladly would I help you! I see to-day more than I ever wished to see. I had rather have died first. A disciple threaten his master! I have indeed much too

[1] *Bacchides,* iii. 36.

fiery pupils; they will kill me, poor weak man that I am.

Pistoclerus. Yes, I think I shall become Hercules, and you Linus.

Lydus. Alas! I fear I shall be more like Phœnix. However, I shall go and tell your father that he has no longer a son.

Pistoclerus. Come, enough of this idle talk.

Lydus. Ah! He has cast off all shame! You made a sad bargain when you purchased to yourself this shamelessness. He is a lost man! Do you then forget that you have a father?

Pistoclerus. And you, do you forget that you are my slave?[1]

Here is the root of the whole matter, the secret of that corruption from which Cato wished to save his sons. It would not be fitting to follow the young Roman in his career of self-indulgence and vice. Never before or since had men of wealth such power of gratifying their passions: the flower of the human race were at the disposal of the conquerors of the world, and every indulgence was not merely permitted but protected by the laws. Resistance on the part of a slave was unheard of, and regarded as impossible. Absolute power and unrestrained self-indulgence produced their necessary results in the destruction of that grandeur of character for which the Romans under the Republic had been famous.

By the most ancient Roman law, says Gothofred,[2]

---

[1] "Tibi ego, ut tu mihi servus es?" (*Bacchides*, i. ii. 24, &c.)
[2] *Cod. Theodos.* lib. ix. tit. 12; *Commentar*, Gothofred, tom. iii. p. 88.

the master had absolute power of life and death over his slaves, without any fear of being called to account for any consequences. The *Lex Petronia* forbade masters to expose their slaves to contests with wild beasts. Hadrian prohibited masters from putting their slaves to death, and ordered that they should be condemned by the judges if guilty of capital offences. Marcus Aurelius appointed several judges to receive the complaints of slaves treated with excessive cruelty, and these judges were empowered to compel the sale of slaves so ill-treated, on the ground that it was for the public good that no one should be allowed to misuse his own property.

We may form some idea of the hard condition of the slaves when we read the law of Constantine the Great, which was regarded as a miracle of humanity toward the slave. The first Christian Emperor enacted A.D. 319: "If any master shall chastise his slaves with rods or thongs, or for safe keeping put him in chains, he shall not incur any danger of a criminal charge if his slave die, whether that death take place after few or many days. But let him not use his right beyond moderation, for he is guilty of homicide if he slay him wilfully either with the blow of a club or with stones, and certainly if he use a weapon and inflict a deadly wound: or if he order him to be hanged by a halter, or by a foul mandate have him cast down a precipice. If he have him poisoned, or his body flayed by public tortures, such as tearing open his sides with iron claws, or burning his limbs with red-hot plates; or when his fainting limbs are naked and streaming with gore and blood, add to his very torments by leaving life in him,—almost the cruelties of pitiless barbarians."[1]

Roman ladies were no less cruel to their unfortunate handmaids. Surrounded by a multitude of slaves, each of whom had charge of some fantastic implement of vanity, the patrician lady went through the important business of the toilet with a small stiletto always at hand to punish, with spiteful stabs, any want of success in her tire-woman, and sometimes an executioner, paid by the year, to flog the poor slaves who had offended her.

Juvenal describes the scene: "The executioner strikes. While it is going on she applies the paint, talks to her friends, or she has unfolded before her robes of embroidered gold; they go on striking all the time until the arms of the executioners drop with fatigue. 'Get out,' she cries, in a voice of thunder, when the punishment is over."[2] Again: "The unhappy Psecas, with her hair in disorder, her shoulders and her bosom bare, dresses the hair of her mistress. Why is that ringlet so rebellious! The scourge punishes the crime of those hairs that will not curl. In what, then, is Psecas to blame?

---

[1] Gothofred, tom. iii. p. 86.

[2] Hic frangit ferulas, rubet ille flagellis,
Hic scutica: sunt, quæ tortoribus annua præstent.
Verberat, atque obiter faciem linit; audit amicas,
Aut latum pictæ vestis considerat aurum,
Et cædit; longi relegit transversa diurni,
Et cædit, donec lassis cædentibus EXI
Intonet horrendum, jam cognitione peracta.
(*Sat.* vi. 480.)

Is it her fault, if your looks don't please you?"[1] Ovid's Corinna presents a more pleasing picture. He tells us: "Her hair is subtle, and allows itself to be curled round and round a hundred times, without making her suffer the slightest pain. Neither pin nor comb tear it. And so her *ornatrix* has a whole skin. Many a time has she had her hair dressed before me, and never once has she torn with her stiletto the arms of her slave."[2] Ovid evidently considered this a rare exception, for he warns ladies in general: "Don't be peevish at the time of your toilette; let your tire-women have a respite from your blows. I hate those women who scratch with their nails the face of that poor wretch, and plunge their stiletto into her arms. The slave then curses her as she touches the head of her mistress, and cries bleeding over that detested hair of hers."[3] We can hardly wonder at the atrocities committed so calmly by such women as Agrippina, when we remember that a Roman palace was a very school of cruel caprice.

[1] Disponit crinem laceratis ipsa capillis
Nuda humero Psecas infelix nudisque mamillis,
Altior hic quare cincirus? taurea punit
Continuo flexi crimen facinusque capilli:
Quid Psecas admisit? quænam est hic culpa puellæ,
Si tibi displicuit nasus tuus?
(*Sat.* vi. 490.)

[2] Adde quod et dociles, et centum flexibus apti,
Et tibi nullius causa doloris erant,
Non acus abrupit, non vallus pectinis illos;
Ornatrix tuto corpore semper erat.
Ante meos sæpe est oculos ornata; nec unquam
Brachia derepta saucia fecit acu.
(*Amor.* i. 14.)

[3] Tuta sit ornatrix. Odi, quæ sauciat ora
Unguibus, et rapta brachia figit acu
Devovet, et dominæ tangit caput illa: simulque
Plorat ad invisas sanguinolenta crines.

4. From the masters and mistresses let us pass to the slaves themselves and see the effect of slavery upon them. In Roman law a slave had no rights: *Servile caput nullum jus habet.* Seneca says they were used just as animals are. A slave was not a person, *persona*. The slave had no name of his own. "The *prænomen*, the *nomen*, the *cognomen*, belong to free men," says Quinctilian, "he who is not free cannot pretend to them."[1] The slave had a sort of *agnomen*, just as we give a name to a horse or a dog, but he could not transmit it to his children.

Sometimes these names showed to whom the slave belonged—*Marcipor*, *Lucipor*, the slave of Marcus or Lucius. When slaves came more numerous their masters used to call them by names of demigods, or mythological heroes, as Hercules, Phœbus, Diomede, Perseus, Achilles, Semiramis, or Dido; or else names derived from the place of their birth, as Davus, Lydus, Sirus, Ephesius, Libanus, &c.

Ulpian, the great jurist, classes them with cattle, "a slave or other animal."[2] Gaius and Pomponius use the same expression. It was a disputed ques-

---

[1] Inst. Orat. vii. 3. § 26. All Roman patricians, and in course of time plebeians also, belonged to some *gens*, e.g., *gens Cornelia, gens Virginia,* &c. The *nomen* marked the *gens*. Each *gens* might consist of a number of families, as the *gens Cornelia* comprised the families of the *Scipiones, Lentuli, Sullæ, Cinnæ, Cossi, Dolabellæ,* &c. The *cognomen* distinguished the *familia*. The families were subdivided into households, *stirpes*, and these had each their own *agnomen*. Thus in the case of Publius Cornelius Scipio Africanus, Publius is the *prænomen*, peculiar to the individual, Cornelius is the *nomen*, Scipio the *cognomen*, and Africanus the *agnomen*.

[2] *In Dig.* vi. i. 15, § 3.

tion among Roman lawyers whether the vendor of a slave was bound to declare his vicious propensities, such as being given to run away. Ulpian says, "No, the edict of the curule ediles only speaks of defects of body; it is just the same as with horses who shy and kick, it is the vice of the soul, not of the body; it is not necessary to declare it."[1] Cato advises an economical father of a family "to sell his old oxen, his calves, and his weaned lambs, his wool, his hides, his old carts, his old iron, the old slave, and the invalid slave."[2] The slave was an article of commerce, and there was a tax upon his importation. Sometimes the merchant eluded the tax by dressing a valuable slave in the robe of a free citizen.

The similarity between slaves and animals was carried out into every detail of life. The union between slaves was not dignified even with the name of marriage, *contubernium* it was called, never *matrimonium*. It was as much at the disposal of the master as the pairing of dogs, or horses, or pigs. A *villicus*, a farm slave, or a shepherd, was required to have a wife, to attach him more closely to the property, but a cook, or confectioner, or a butler, was not allowed to marry. It made them idle, Cato observed. Roman law refused to admit that there could be such a crime as adultery in the case of slaves, for there was no marriage. Even incest was only forbidden when the slaves had been liberated. The *contubernium* might at any time be broken, and the husband and

[1] *In Dig.* xxi. i. 4, § 3.   [2] *De Re Rust.* 2.

wife sold to different parties, and each obliged to contract another union. Sometimes a kind master would sell a married couple at a less price, on the condition that the buyer would always keep them together. If a man left as a legacy a plot of land with the slaves upon it, Ulpian thought that such a legacy comprehended also the wives and children of the slaves, unless it was actually expressed that these were to go to some other legatee.[1]

The children of slaves were just as much the property of the master as the fruit of his apple-trees or vines, or of his flocks or herds. *Rex fructificat domino* was true of the female slave just as of the cow. "The heir of a thief could not become the proprietor by *usucapio* of the calf of a cow or the child of a slave stolen by his father," says Ulpian.[2] The *partus ancillarum* and the *fœtus pecorum* stood on the same footing. Slave children did not belong to their parents, but to their master. Sometimes a troop of slaves formed part of the wife's dowry, and they turned out too fruitful; her husband could not be at the expense of supporting them. The lady regarded them as an increase of her capital, and the lawyers decided that she could bring an action against her husband to compel him to maintain them.[3] A testator had the power of leaving as a legacy a child not yet born to one legatee and bequeathing the mother to another. Often a man left a female slave her liberty on condition that she gave birth to a child; but when

---

[1] *In Dig.* xxxiii. vii. 12, § 7.   [2] *In Dig.* xli. iii. 10, § 2.
[3] Julian, *In Dig.* xxiv. iii. 31, § 4.

she had thus obtained her liberty, her baby became the property of her patron's heirs.[1]

Pliny calls slaves *desperati*, the hopeless ones. Aristotle long before had said, "Slaves are not capable of happiness or of free-will."[2] Under ordinary circumstances, a slave had the hope of one day obtaining his freedom. He might have it left him as a legacy by his master; it might be given him as a reward or a favour. He might stint himself for years of his scanty allowance, and thus hoard up a sufficient sum to purchase his liberty; and although these savings, the *peculium* of the slave, strictly belonged to his master, yet it was customary to allow him to deal with it as if it were his own. But the master had it in his power to deprive the slave of this hope by making it a condition of sale, or a condition of a legacy, that the slave thus sold or bequeathed should never be set free. Slaves who attempted to escape, or showed discontent, were often compelled to work in chains, and to sleep in the *ergastulum* or domestic prison. Those who were condemned to the mines were worse off still. Scarcely less fortunate were those condemned to grind flour. Apuleius describes them: "Ye gods, what poor wretched men! their skin livid and all spotted with blows of the scourge; miserable rags cover their bruised backs, some have no clothing save an apron round their loins, none have more than the tatters of a tunic to hide their nakedness. Branded on their brow, with half-shaven head, and feet shackled with a

---

[1] See M. Allard, op. cit. pp. 160, 161.   [2] *Politic.* iii. 7.

ring, their bodies disfigured by the fire, their
eyelids shrivelled by the burning smoke and the
smoky darkness of the steaming heat, their eyes
almost deprived of sight, dusty like athletes with
the pale dust of flour."[1] Plautus speaks from
experience : " There weep the slaves who eat
polenta, there resound the noise of the scourges
and the clanging of chains, there the hide of dead
oxen flays the skin of living men."[2]

Still, even the slaves had their days of festivity,
when their masters encouraged them to forget in
wild brutal orgies the miseries of their lot. We
may take the epitaph of a female slave to express
the general feeling of her class: *Fortuna spondet
multa multis, præstet nemini, vive in dies et horas,
nam proprium est nihil.*[3] Far-sighted men like
Cato preferred drunken or sleepy slaves to men
of thought and moderation. He liked to have
a slave always working or always sleeping, and he
specially liked sleepy slaves, as he thought them
more tractable than wakeful ones.[4] Superior intelligence in a slave was no passport to his master's
favour. The celebrated philosopher Epictetus was
a slave to a freedman. His brutal master, Epaph-
roditus, who had helped Nero to commit suicide,
once amused himself by twisting Epictetus' leg in
an instrument of torture. Epictetus said : " If you

---

[1] *Metamorph.* lib. ix.
[2] Ubi flent nequam homines, qui polentam pransitant,
   Apud fustitudinas ferricrepinas insulas
   Ubi vivos homines mortui incursant boves.
                                    (*Asinar*, I. i. 20, &c.)
[3] Orelli, *Inscr.* 4806.   [4] Plutarc. *Cato Maj.* 20.

go on you will break it." The wretch did go on, and did break it. "I told you that you would break it," said the young Stoic calmly, without a tear or groan.[1] Seneca, the best friend the slaves ever had among the pagans, who went so far as to call them his humble friends, seriously recommended suicide as the shortest remedy for their miseries. He says: "The most ignoble death is better than even the mildest slavery."[2] Suicide often became an epidemic among slaves; and the vendor of a slave with suicidal propensities was bound to declare the fact before the sale could be legal.[3]

Slavery, which thus crushed all vigour out of men, oppressed the weaker sex still more cruelly. If a male slave had no rights, a female slave had no honour in the eye of Roman law.[4] She could not invoke the law for the protection of that which is more precious than life itself. Virtue, which was extolled to the skies in a Lucretia or a Virginia, was denied existence in a slave. No outrage against her could be punished even when committed by a third party, and she was absolutely at her master's disposal. History gives instances of broken-down Roman nobles, who supported themselves by the prostitution of their slaves.[5] Even when she obtained her liberty, her union

[1] This anecdote was thrown in the teeth of the Christians by Celsus, quoted by Origen, *Contra Celsum*, vii. 53.
[2] *Cons. ad Marciam.*
[3] Ulpian, *In Dig.* xxi. i. §§ 2, 3.
[4] "The *lex Julia* protects only the honour of free persons." (Papinian, *In Dig.* xlviii. v. 6.)
[5] Cicero, Orat. ii. *Post Reditum*, 5, denounces the ex-consul Gabinius, "qui cum rem non minus strenue, quam postea publicam, confecisset, egestatem et luxuriam domestico lenocinio sustentavit."

with a free citizen was not admitted to be marriage, and thus the very title of an emancipated slave—*libertina*—became synonymous with that of an abandoned woman. One is surprised that men and women thus oppressed did not instinctively turn upon and slay their oppressors, and that there was only one really serious servile war. But the Roman law had devised a terrible dissuasive against such resistance.

Tacitus tells us, that in Nero's time the whole city was in commotion and the populace wild with indignation. The Imperial troops were leading to execution a long procession of four hundred men, women, and children. What was their crime? Pedanius Secundus, Prefect of Rome, had been murdered by one of his slaves, and by the law all his slaves, without exception, must be put to death. The Senate doubted whether so wholesale an execution should be allowed to take place. The patriot Caius Cassius, insisted that the law should take its course. "Our ancestors," he urged, "suspected the disposition of slaves even when they had been born and bred on our country estates, or in our own households, and had imbibed at once affection for their masters; but from the time that we have been embracing whole nations in our families, who have different religious rites, and foreign religions, or none at all, there is no means of keeping down that seething mass of corruption save by terror." This argument prevailed, and the whole four hundred were put to death.[1]

[1] Taciti, *Annal.* iv. 42, 43.

II. It is refreshing to turn from this hideous picture, of which we have purposely omitted many of the deepest shades, and behold the change that passed over this great Roman Empire before it sank under the deluge of barbarian invasion. The first point that arrests attention is the restoration to the minds of men in the fifth century of the dignity of labour. The crowds that hung upon the lips of St. John Chrysostom heard such words as these: "When you see a man who fells the wood, or rather grimy with soot, who works the iron with his hammer, do not despise him, but rather for that reason admire him. Peter, with his loins girded, dragged the fishing-net even after the Resurrection of the Lord. And why say I Peter? For this same Paul, after traversing so many lands, and working so many miracles, still continued to sit in his workshop, sewing skins together, while angels reverenced him and demons trembled before him; and he was not ashamed to say, 'These hands have furnished necessaries to me and to them that were with me.'"[1] The pagans were ashamed of manual labour: the Christians delighted to inscribe their occupations on their tombs. The same Father cries: "God has given us hands and feet that we might not stand in need of slaves. No race of slaves was created at the same time as Adam: slavery has been the penalty of sin, and the consequence of disobedience. But Christ has come and has destroyed it; for in Christ there is neither slave nor free. This is why it is not neces-

St. Chrys. *In 1 Cor.* Hom. xx. 12.

sary to have slaves; or if one believes it necessary, have but one, or at the most two. . . . I will not be too exacting. We will allow you to keep a second slave. But if you collect many, you do it not for humanity's sake, but in self-indulgence. If it be out of care of them, I exhort you to occupy none of them in ministering to yourself; but when you have purchased them, and have taught them trades, whereby to support themselves, let them go free."[1] Such teaching in the fourth century paved the way for the increase in the number of labourers, and the rapid diminution of slaves in the fifth. Other causes co-operated to this result. When the Roman Empire in its decline was menaced by the barbarians on every frontier, there were no longer conquered cities and provinces to send their crowds of captives to the Imperial slave-markets. The supply of fresh slaves was stopped, and at the same time the emancipations of whole families of slaves went on at an increasing rate.

When the army of Alaric reached the neighbourhood of Rome, forty thousand fugitive slaves came out to meet him, to enter his army, and lead the way to plunder and to revenge. When the feeble hand of the Byzantine Court refused any longer to pretend to defend Rome, and St. Gregory the Great saved the remnant of the Romans from annihilation, slavery had disappeared almost entirely as a domestic institution, and lingered chiefly in the form of serfdom. The last imperial legislation which affected the Western world, the Code

[2] St. Chrys. *In 1 Cor.* Hom. xl. 5.

of Justinian, struck the final blow to slavery by abolishing it as a penalty for crime, *servitus pœnæ*.[1] Justinian says: "We will not change a free condition into a servile one, for we have long ago been eager to be the emancipators of the slaves."[2]

III. Having reviewed the extent and effects of slavery in the Roman Empire, and having noticed its rapid decline and practical abolition, the question forces itself upon us, *what was the agent* which produced so mighty, and yet so noiseless a revolution? It was not science, or philosophy, or political economy, or else we should have seen Seneca or Marcus Aurelius proposing to emancipate the slaves. All thoughtful students of history have recognized one sole agent in this glorious revolution, and that agent was the Christian Church: and if the Church had earned no other claims to the gratitude of the human race, this alone would suffice to win for her the respect of every lover of liberty. But it is more instructive still to study *the means by which the Church effected this bloodless revolution*. Christianity never aroused the passions of the oppressed victims of slavery, by denouncing open war with those who possessed slaves. On the contrary, she never ceased to preach submission and cheerful obedience to the slaves. But she—

1. Permeated the minds of both slaves and

---

[1] Justinian also abolished all distinction between freedmen and freemen, *libertini et ingenui*.
[2] Justinian, *Novell.* xxii. 8. M. Allard, in the last two chapters of his work, enters into a variety of details which prove that free labour had regained its legitimate position before the end of the fifth century, but which it was not possible to condense within the limits of a lecture.

masters with ideas and principles wholly inconsistent with the spirit of slavery. Two of the greatest and earliest Christian teachers, St. Peter and St. Paul, have left letters behind them addressed to their converts, in which the duties of slaves to their masters and of masters towards their slaves are plainly laid down.[1] Now, one can hardly imagine a greater contrast to the slavery in Roman Imperial times than the extremely free and easy independent behaviour of servants in the present day. And yet both masters and servants, now, read those letters of St. Peter and St. Paul, and confess that their own duties are set forth therein, without the thought ever striking one in a hundred that the Apostles were writing to slaves. Christianity called the conscience of the slave out of the moral *ergastulum* into which despair had plunged it, and set before it motives that were stronger than even the terrors on which Caius Cassius relied. In a word, the Church treated the slave as a man, and compelled his master to recognize in him the attributes of a man. Christian masters were told that they were slaves of Christ, while slaves were reminded that they were Christ's freedmen. And both were bound to fulfil their respective duties to each other under the dictates of a conscience enlightened by Christian teaching. A man whose conduct is guided by Christian principles cannot be really a slave. The master's power becomes at once limited by the requirements

---

[1] 1 St. Peter ii. 18, seq. ; 1 Cor. vii. 20—23; Ephes. vi. 5—9; Coloss. iii. 22, iv. 1 ; Titus ii. 9.

of a higher authority. The Christian slave has a range of subjects on which he is able to refuse obedience, nay, on which he is bound to resist his master even to death, and a slave who can say "No," is no longer a slave.

One example from the Egyptian Church in the early part of the third century will suffice to illustrate what has been said. In Alexandria there was a female slave of remarkable beauty. As a matter of course, the eye of her master fell upon her; but she was a Christian, and all his solicitations failed. The persecution of Severus, in which many of Origen's disciples suffered, was raging under Aquila, the Prefect. Potamiæna's master denounced her to the Prefect as a Christian, promising him a large bribe if he could induce her, through dread of punishment for her faith, to yield to his desires. But threats and even tortures proved as ineffectual as the flattery of her master. At last Aquila threatened to have her thrown into a cauldron of boiling pitch, unless she would obey her master. She replied, "God forbid that a judge should be so unjust as to order me to do what is unlawful!" Then the Prefect, in a fury, ordered her to be stripped of her clothes and thrown into the seething cauldron. But the heroic girl cried out, "I conjure you, by the life of the Emperor, not to strip me naked; rather have me let down by degrees into the pitch with my dress, and you shall see what patience Jesus Christ, my God, Whom you know not, gives to me." The judge, somewhat touched by her noble spirit, said that she should have her wish, and for three hours did the torture last, while she was lowered, inch by inch, into the boiling pitch.[1] Eusebius tells us that Basilides, the officer who presided at her execution, and who had defended her from the insults of the rabble, avowed himself a Christian three days afterwards, and sealed his conversion with his blood. The whole city of Alexandria rang with the heroism of this Christian slave, and the name of the virgin martyr, St. Potamiæna, speedily became honoured in every Christian assembly throughout the Roman Empire. Every Christian slave took fresh courage from her example, and felt honoured by her fame.

2. Christianity not only ennobled the slave by giving him spiritual freedom, but the slave, on admission to the Christian Church, found himself associated on terms of equality with free citizens and Roman nobles. Slaves were not considered worthy of admission to the mysteries of Pagan rites, much less to any office in the worship of the gods. Cicero even laid it to the charge of Clodius as a heinous crime that he had permitted slaves to take part in the *ludi megalenses*. But Christian Baptism initiated into one body all alike, Jews and Gentiles, slaves and free. The candidates for Baptism heard St. Cyril of Jerusalem, about the middle of the fourth century, address them thus:

[1] Allies' *Formation of Christendom*, part. i. pp. 231, 232. This account is taken from Paladius (*Hist. Laus.*), who says that he received it from the great St. Antony. Eusebius does not mention the fact of her being a slave, nor of her making this request, but he calls her "the celebrated Potamiæna, concerning whom many traditions are still circulated abroad among the inhabitants of the place," &c. (*H. E.* vi. 5.)

"Be of good courage, O man; the Judge is no respecter of persons. . . . He honours not the learned before the simple, nor the rich before the poor. . . . Though thou be a slave, though thou be poor, be not any whit distressed; He who took the form of a slave despises not slaves. . . . He who brought forth Joseph out of slavery and the dungeon to a kingdom redeems thee also from thy affliction into the Kingdom of Heaven."[1] In Roman law, so rigid were the lines of demarcation between freemen and slaves, that it was considered an *ipso facto* act of emancipation for a master to bid the slave sit at the same table with himself. "In the Christian Church," says St. Chrysostom, "all difference is suppressed. The table of the Lord is the same for the rich and the poor, the slave and the free, . . . the munificence of our God has done the same honour to rich and poor, slave and free; one common gift is offered to all."[2] Nay, sometimes it happened that the slave was of higher rank in the Church than his master, who might be only a catechumen, and, therefore, according to the primitive discipline, not permitted to be present at the Eucharistic Sacrifice. "Often," says St. Chrysostom, "the rich and the poor are assembled together in the same church. The hour for the Divine Mysteries has come. The rich is sent to the door as not being yet initiated; the poor is admitted. . . . See the master going out of the Church, the Christian slave approaching the Holy Mysteries; the mistress withdrawing while her

---

[1] *Catech.* Lect. xv. 23.   [2] St. Chrys. *Hom. in St. Pasch.* 3, 4.

slave remains. God accepteth not persons; in the Church there is neither slave nor free."[1]

Even the ranks of the Christian priesthood were recruited alike from the highest and the lowest classes in society, from the slaves as well as from the free; and servile condition was, during the ages of persecution, no bar to the very highest office in the Church. If among the Popes of the first three centuries we find the patrician names of Clement and Cornelius, we find also that of Callixtus, who is said to have been a fugitive slave. The first Bishop of Ephesus after Timothy is reported to have been that same Onesimus, the runaway slave of Philemon, whom St. Paul sent back to his master, with the exhortation that he should be received "not now as a slave, but, instead of a slave, a most dear brother."[2] The letters of St. Basil and St. Gregory of Nazianzen tell us of the slave of a rich matron, whom these two prelates had, at the entreaty of the people, consecrated Bishop of a country town. Symplicia afterwards claimed her slave, and threatened to prosecute her claim in the secular courts. St. Basil sharply reproved her; but after his death she wrote to Gregory and demanded that the ordination should be annulled. St. Gregory replied: "If you claim as your slave our colleague in the episcopate, I know not how to contain my indignation. Do you think that you honour God by the alms which you scatter, when you bring yourself to rob the Church of a priest? . . . If your

[1] St. Chrys. *Hom. de Resurrect.* 3.   [2] Philem. 16.

claim is inspired, as I hear, by care for your pecuniary interests, you will receive the compensation which is due to you; for we do not think that the kindness and readiness of masters should be to them an occasion of loss. ... If you will accept my advice you will not commit yourself to an action which will be neither just nor honourable; you will not despise our laws in order to ask help from foreign laws; you will pardon our having acted with simplicity in the liberty of grace, and you will prefer an honourable defeat to an unjust victory."[1] Later on, elevation to the diaconate *ipso facto* conferred freedom. In 511, a Council of Orleans decreed that a bishop who knowingly elevated a slave to the diaconate or priesthood without the consent of his master was bound to pay the latter an indemnity equal to double the value of the slave; and another Council in the same city, in 538, suspended a bishop from saying Mass for a whole year for disregarding this canon.

One of the most remarkable differences between the Pagan epitaphs in the *columbaria*, and the Christian inscriptions in the catacombs, is that, while the Pagans rigidly distinguished, even in the grave, the slave and the freedman from his lord, Christianity ignored both these distinctions. After thirty years' close study of these inscriptions, De Rossi says: "I have never yet met with a thoroughly certain instance of the mention of a slave, *servus*, very rarely and exceptionally that

[1] St. Greg. Nazianz. Epist. 79.

of a freedman, *libertus*, while we cannot read Pagan epitaphs of the same period without finding there persons designated as slaves and freedmen."[1] "This rule," says De Rossi, "was nowhere written; it was the spontaneous effect of the religious doctrines of the new society, which reflected itself on its epitaphs as in a mirror."[2]

3. Another effect of Christianity upon slavery was produced by the full recognition by the Church of the marriage of slaves. The degrading *contubernium* of the Roman slave was elevated into the *sacramentum matrimonii* of the Church, equal to, and even higher in its sanctity than the *confarreatio* of the Roman patricians.[3] And when the Empire became Christian, the laws of Rome concerning marriage, and especially the marriage of slaves, had to be changed in order to bring them into conformity with the laws of the Church. The Church went beyond recognizing the validity of the marriage of slaves: she insisted on the validity of the marriage of slaves with persons of free and noble birth.[4] The calumniator of Pope Callixtus urges it against him as a crime that he had sanctioned

---

[1] *Bullett.* 1866, p. 24.
[2] *Roma Sotterr.* tom. i. p. 343.
[3] "In the earliest times of Roman law there were three modes of forming the tie of marriage: first, *confarreatio*, a religious ceremony, in which none but those to whom the *jus sacrum* was open could take part; secondly, *coemptio*, a fictitious sale, in which the wife was sold to the husband; and lastly, *usus*, *i.e.* cohabitation with the intention of forming a marriage." (Sandars on the *Institutes of Justinian*, p. 112.)
[4] See De Rossi, *Bullett.* 1868, pp. 23—26, on the accusations against Pope Callixtus.

such marriages, which were utterly repudiated by the Roman law.

4. This spiritual and moral equality to which the Church had thus elevated the slave could not but attain its legitimate development in actual emancipations. The price of liberty varied from £20 to £25. Petronius makes a freedman value his freedom at £36. The epitaph of a former slave physician and surgeon oculist states that he paid £280 for his liberty.[1] Emancipation was but rarely granted by a master during lifetime. It was more common to leave freedom as a legacy to a valued slave, and usually some condition was attached to the gift.[2] Christianity set forth emancipation of slaves as one of the most meritorious of good works. Even in the first century St. Clement of Rome could say: "We have known many of our people who have cast themselves into chains in order to redeem others. Many have sold themselves into slavery, and have nourished the poor with the price of their sale."[3] The redemption of slaves was one of the objects to which the sums collected in the Christian assemblies were devoted. If the slave's faith or morals were in danger, the Church would charge itself with his freedom. St. Ignatius, the Martyr of Antioch, exhorts the slaves to be "patient, and not to desire to be set free at the expense of the community."[4]

5. The work of emancipation received a mighty

---

[1] 7,000 sesterces. (Orelli, 2983.)
[2] Ulpian, *In Dig.* xl. iv.41, § 13. "Si insulam ædificaverint, si fabricassent navem."
[3] Epist. i. ad Cor. c. 55. [4] *Ad Polycarp*, c. 4.

impulse when the Emperor Constantine proclaimed himself a Christian. One of his first acts was to abolish many of the degrading works of slavery. He forbade slaves to be crucified; and ordered that criminal slaves should no longer be branded on the forehead,[1] but marked by a collar or a bronze plate hung round their necks. He multiplied the opportunities for manumission, especially by making it lawful that this solemn act should be done before the Bishop in the church; in 321 he declared that the slaves they liberated became at once Roman citizens; and in the case of the clergy who owned slaves, he decreed that the simple expression of their wish, without any other formality, should be sufficient to endow the slave with all the rights and privileges of a citizen —*plenum fructum libertatis.*[2] Ennodius gives us the terms in which a Christian master, Agapitus, thus freed his slave in the church. Agapitus says:

"I wish to be for my slave that which I desire God to be for me. And therefore I pray your

---

[1] *Ad Eumelian*, anno 315. The actual decree of Constantine against crucifixion does not appear in Gothofred, who assigns it to this same year.

[2] "Constantinus Imp. Osio Episcopo: Qui religiosa mente in Ecclesiæ gremio servulis suis meritam concesserit libertatem, eandem eodem jure donasse videatur, quo Civitas Romana solemnitatibus decursis dari consuevit. Sed hoc duntaxat iis, qui sub aspectu Antistitum dederint, placuit relaxari. Clericis autem amplius concedimus, ut cum suis famulis tribuunt libertatem, non solum in conspectu Ecclesiæ, ac religiosi populi, plenum fructum libertatis concessisse dicantur, verum etiam cum postremo judicio libertates dederint, seu quibuscunque verbis dari præceperint: ita ut, ex die publicatæ voluntatis, sine aliquo juris teste vel interprete, competat directa libertas." (a. 321). (Gothofred, op. cit. tom. i. p. 396.)

Blessedness to grant the rights of Roman citizenship to Gerontius, whose fidelity, virtue, and honesty, I have well appreciated. I wish to be not so much the author as the witness of his emancipation. The manner in which he has served me makes me see that he has not a slavish nature; I do not grant him his liberty so much as restore it to him. Before possessing the name of free he has merited it. I therefore remit him the services which he owed me, and I restore him his liberty, of which by his life he has shown himself worthy. I demand of this assembly that, by the act of the Church, he may be relieved of all marks of inferiority, and may enjoy for ever the rights of Roman citizenship and of the *peculium* which I allow him without any diminution. It would be unjust to keep back anything from the little fortune amassed by him; I promise, on the contrary, later on, to augment it by my bounty."[1]

How different is all this from the final slap which the Pagan master used to give his slave, even in the act of liberating him!

In the sixth century Justinian decreed: "If a slave has been ordained a cleric, and the master is cognizant of the fact, and does not protest against it, he becomes, by the fact of his ordination, free altogether from slavery."[2] The monastic life became equally a cause of freedom. Justinian laid down: "If a master wishes to claim

---

[1] Ennodius, "Petitorium quo absolutus est Gerontius puer Agapiti." (Migne, *Patrol.*)
[2] *Novell.* 123, c. 17.

as his slave the novice who has been in the monastery for less than three years, the Superior must require from the claimant the proof that the novice is a slave, and that he has taken flight after committing some delinquency, and if the master gives this proof the slave must be given up to him. But if no delinquency is proved, although it be certain that the novice is a slave; if, on the contrary, it is proved by other evidence that his life in the home of his master had been pure and honourable, and if in the monastery his conduct had been good, he must be kept there even though the three years of probation have not expired, and after that time he may be admitted to the monastic profession. He will only fall back under the power of his master if he eventually quits the monastic life."[1]

The Emperor Constantius in 339, and Honorius in 415, forbade Jews to buy Christian slaves.[2] Justinian prohibited Pagans, Jews, or heretics from possessing, on any title whatsoever, a Christian slave.[3] This law was not carried out in the West, but if the Christian slave of a Jew took refuge in the church and demanded redemption, his master was obliged to accept the price of his liberty, which was fixed by one Council at twelve *solidi*.[4] Another Council applies the same principle to all masters.

Thus were multiplied the means of liberty, and the door once opened was never again closed.

---

[1] *Novell.* 5, c. 2.   [2] Gothofred, tom. vi. pp. 271, 272.
[3] *Cod. Justin.* I. iii. 56, § 3.   [4] *Conc. Matiscon.* ann. 581.

Christianity breathed upon the slave in his hopeless bondage, and she emancipated his soul with the new life that she infused into him, and thus made him a man, a Christian, a martyr. She breathed upon his fetters, and upon the cruel laws which riveted them, and she changed those laws and melted those fetters with the noiseless yet powerful force of her charity, until slavery, which had been universally held to rest upon the *jus gentium*, was formally denounced by Justinian, as " barbarous and contrary to natural right." [1]

[1] M. Allard traces most beautifully the action of the Church in rescuing female slaves from compulsory performance in the theatres, and devotes a whole chapter to the interesting subject of the Christian *alumni*.

LECTURE II.

ROMAN SLAVERY AND MEDIÆVAL SERFDOM.

SEVERAL circumstances have combined to bring the subject of slavery prominently before the minds of men. The letter of Pope Leo the Thirteenth to the ~~Emperor~~ of Brazil seems to sound the death-knell of slavery among Christians, while the crusade of Cardinal Lavigerie has stirred up multitudes to do their utmost to compel non-Christian powers to put an end to this odious institution throughout the world at large. At a time when so many are inclined to forget the benefits that Christianity has conferred upon the human race, it is well to recall the action of the Church in the mitigation and subsequent abolition of this wide-spread and degrading custom.

The general history of slavery and serfdom has not yet been written in the English language. With the exception of a very valuable article in Smith's *Dictionary of Christian Antiquities*,[1] there is no English work on the subject; although Mr.

---

[1] The writer, Mr. J. B. Mullinger, is unfortunately possessed with the desire to minimize the influence of Christianity as much as possible.

Seebohm's *English Village Community* has thrown great light on English serfdom. In France the works of Biot, Garsonnet, Wallon, and Guérard give much valuable information on the whole history of serfdom; and M. Paul Allard, the worthy disciple of the great Christian archæologist, De Rossi, has treated the subject with great clearness in his two works, *Les Esclaves Chrétiens*, and *Esclaves, Serfs, et Mainmortables*. Cibrario has brought out an interesting work in Italian, *Della Schiavitù e del Servaggio*. The fact is, that in England serfdom, has ceased to be a practical question ever since the Wars of the Roses; while in Italy slavery existed down to the end of the seventeenth century, in Spain during the first quarter of the eighteenth, and in France serfdom continued to be a real hardship within ten years of the Revolution of 1789.

We have in the last lecture treated of the condition of slaves in the Roman Empire at the Christian era. Guided by M. Allard, we have traced the pernicious effects of slavery on society at large, in the degradation of honest manly labour, the impoverishment of art, and the extinction of all real motive for invention. We followed the slave-holder into the details of his life, and saw how irresponsible power stimulated his passions, enervated his mind and body, and produced such monsters of vice and cruelty as the world had never seen before. We then went on to trace its debasing effect on the slave

himself; how it reduced him to the level of
the lower animals, by crushing out of him all
moral responsibility, and shutting out all hope
from his soul. Into the midst of this dark festering
mass of human corruption Christ came, and
established His Church. The Divine Founder of
Christianity did not stir up a violent revolution by
adopting the *rôle* of Spartacus, and preaching a
Servile War. He did not even denounce slavery as
a crime, or require His followers to manumit their
slaves. And yet the gentle though powerful influence of Christianity effected a greater revolution
than Spartacus had dreamed of. Her voice awak-
ened the conscience of the slave; made him again
a man; and gave strength even to helpless women
to defy, in triumphant martyrdom,[1] the tyranny
of their masters. Christianity taught the master
to recognize a brother-man in his slave, in that
universal brotherhood, where there is neither Greek
nor Jew, barbarian nor Scythian, bond nor free.[2]
The master acknowledged himself the servant of
Christ, while the slave rejoiced that he was Christ's
freedman.[3]

Thus, though Christianity, in the early ages,
never denounced slavery as a crime; never encouraged or permitted the slaves to rise against their
masters and throw off the yoke; yet she permeated the minds of both masters and slaves with
ideas utterly inconsistent with the spirit of slavery.
Within the Church, master and slave stood on an

---

[1] *e.g.*, St. Blandina, St. Potamiæna, and many others.
[2] Coloss. iii. 11.   [3] 1 Cor. vii. 22.

absolute equality. The slave might become a priest
or even a Bishop, perhaps a Pope, like St. Callixtus,
and was often venerated as a martyr. The marriage of the slave was no longer *contubernium*, a
temporary union, dependent on the caprice of his
master, but as valid in the eye of the Church as
the *confarreatio* of the noblest patrician. Then,
when Christianity assumed the Imperial purple,
the Christian Emperors expunged from the legal
code those punishments of crucifixion, branding,
and mutilation formerly reserved for slaves. They
gave legal force to the Canons of the Councils
which multiplied the facilities for the manumission
of slaves. And the result of all this was, that an
enormous number of slaves were enfranchised
during the fourth and fifth centuries. Two or three
examples will suffice. St. Melania the Younger
enfranchised in one day 8,000 slaves;[1] the Consul
Gallicanus, who suffered martyrdom under Julian
the Apostate, set at liberty 5,000.[2] Remember that
the ordinary price of a slave was about £25; so
that Gallicanus's slaves must have been worth
£125,000, and Melania must have sacrificed
£200,000 to set her slaves at liberty. Besides,
the records which tell us of these acts of Christian
generosity add, that the master or mistress not
only allowed the slaves to retain their *peculium* or
little earnings saved up during their time of servitude, but gave them also a sum of money to
prevent their swelling the ranks of that pauper

---

[1] Palladius, *Hist. Lausiaca*, 119.
[2] Bolland. *Acta SS.* Jun. tom. vii. p. 34.

mob which lived on Imperial bounty, and became the pest of Rome and the great cities of the Empire. St. Pelagia, the celebrated penitent actress of Antioch, on her conversion, sent for all her slaves, and gave them their liberty, and also so much of the money and jewels that she had kept back for this purpose, as would enable them to gain an honest livelihood.[1] The Code of Theodosius, and still more that of Justinian, far from consolidating slavery, as some modern authors have asserted, show a continual progress in the course of Roman law, under the influence of Christianity, restricting more and more the power of slavery, and favouring in a variety of ways the liberty of the slave. The Institutes of Justinian lay down as a principle: "Slavery is an institution of the law of nations, by which one man is made the property of another, contrary to natural right."[2] By the Roman law, the children of public actors were bound to follow the profession of their parents, which was in those days quite incompatible with the practice of Christianity. In 380, the Emperor Gratian set them free from this obligation; in 385, Arcadius prohibited the sale of slave-girls as musicians or dancers; and in 394, Theodosius forbade persons connected with the theatres to possess Christian slaves.

Foundlings, who had formerly been regarded as the slaves of those who sheltered them, under the name of *alumni*, were by Constantine and Justinian forbidden to be reduced to slavery.[3] A slave who

---

[1] *Acta SS.* Oct. tom. iv. p. 266. [2] ib. i. tit. iii. 2. [3] *Cod. Just.* viii. lii. 3, 4.

had children by her master was together with them made free by the fact of her master's death. The penalty of slavery for certain offences was abolished by Justinian, who styled slavery "a barbarous institution, and contrary to natural right."[1]

One of the most remarkable effects of Christianity on the Roman world was the re-habilitation of manual labour in public estimation. The ancient Roman respect for labour, as evidenced in the case of Cincinnatus, had long ago given place to utter contempt. Even in the time of Cicero, labouring men were classed with slaves, and with them excluded from the solemn sacrifices. First in cities, and then in the country, slavery drove free labour out of the field, although poets might sing Georgics on the delights of agriculture:

> O fortunatos nimium, sua si bona norint
> Agricolas! si quibus ipsa, procul discordibus armis,
> Fundit humo facilem victum justissima tellus.[2]

The reverse was the fact. The earth itself seemed to resent the indignity of slave-labour, and whole districts became overgrown with forests, destined afterwards to be cleared and cultivated by the labour of Christian monks. And it was through the land that the amelioration of the condition of the slave was mainly effected.

Becker, in his notes to *Gallus*, describes, from

---

[1] *Novell.* xxii. 8.
[2] Virgil, *Georg.* ii. 458. Thus translated by Dryden:

> O happy, if he knew his happy state!
> The swain, who free from business and debate,
> Receives his easy food from nature's hand,
> And just returns of cultivated land.

Varro, Vetruvius, and Columella, the arrangements of a Roman *villa rustica:*

The villa must have had two courts (*cohortes, chortes, cortes*). At the entrance to the first or outer one, was the abode of the *villicus*, in order that he might know who went in or out; also the great common kitchen, where the slaves congregated, and where in winter time different avocations were pursued by the fireside. Near this were the bath-rooms, and also the wine and oil-presses. The oil and wine-cellars were here, the first towards the south, the latter towards the north; but both of them on the ground floor. Columella places the *ergastulum* underground, lighted with a number of narrow windows so high from the floor, that they could not be reached with the hand. The cells of the slaves, which must have been elsewhere in the outer court, were preferred situated to the south. It is best to suppose that the stalls for the oxen, horses, and sheep were around the inner court, although Vetruvius would have them to be near the kitchen.[1]

Columella says of the labourers on an estate:

They are either slaves or *coloni;* and it is pleasanter to deal with the *coloni*, and easier to get out of them *work* than *payments;* they will sooner ask to be let off the one than the other. The best *coloni* are those which are *indigeni*, born on the estate, and bound by hereditary ties to it.[2]

The *colonus*—our "clown"—was originally a free man, a tenant farmer, not merely cultivating as *agricola*, but living on the land.[3] The *colonus*

---

[1] *Gallus*, pp. 58, 59.   [2] *De Re Rust.* i. 7.
[3] "Colonus est qui agrum non excolit, sed incolit." (Gothofred, *Cod. Theod.* tom. iv. p. 114.)

appears originally to have been a barbarian from some conquered country, who had been transplanted to Roman territory, and allowed to have land of his own, for which he paid a yearly rent, but from which he was not allowed to remove. He owed certain duties to his lord, or *patronus;* and the term included *Originarii, Indigeni, Adscriptii, Inquilini,* and *Tributarii,* although these names signified different classes, whose position Gothofred is not always able clearly to distinguish.[1] Part of the difficulty seems to be occasioned by his not taking into consideration the difference that Christianity had effected by the time of Theodosius in the condition of these humble tillers of the soil. The tendency during the first three centuries, from Augustus to Constantine, was gradually to merge together, into one servile class, *coloni* and *servi* of all kinds. The *colonus* became confused with the farm-slave, and lost his liberty and citizenship, in the degradation which was supposed to attach to manual labour. Christianity, whose Divine Founder worked in a carpenter's shop, and whose Apostles were fishermen and tent-makers, restored the dignity of labour; and through the very confusion of the free peasant with the slave-labourer, raised the slave to the privileges of the *colonus,* and thus reduced slavery to serfdom.

In order to prevent the land from falling out of cultivation, the *coloni* had been bound by special laws to the soil. The Christian Emperors

[1] See Gothofred, *Cod. Theod.* v. tit. ix. *Paratitlon de Colonis.*

strengthened these bonds. In 357, Constantius enacted,

If any one wishes to sell his farm, or to give it away, he cannot by a private agreement retain for himself the *coloni* in order to transfer them to some other place, for those who think the *coloni* useful, ought either to keep them with the lands, or else to leave them for the benefit of others, if they themselves despair of getting any profit from the farm.[1]

This was for the West: and Valens made a similar enactment for the East. The commentator Gothofred, summing up the provisions of the Theodosian Code, says, *Coloni prædiis adstricti non hominibus*.[2] They sometimes had land of their own, distinct from that of their lord; and, like the slave, they had their own *peculium*, which they could not alienate without the consent of their lord. Ten years earlier, Constantius had laid down that household slaves (*mancipia urbana*) were to be reckoned with other "moveable property," but that farm-slaves (*mancipia rustica*) ranked with houses and lands, as fixtures to be accounted for to the Imperial Treasury.[3] Thus the farm-slave became a serf, inseparable from the farm. By degrees, in his right to appeal to the law to protect himself, his family and property, he rose to the position of the *colonus*,[4] while the *colonus* attained the privileges of an *ingenuus* or free citizen.

We shall see further on, that in France, in the ninth century, the term *colonus* was employed to

---

[1] *Cod. Just.* De Agricol. l. 2. [2] Tom. i. p. 452.
[3] *Cod. Just.* De Agricol. l. 11, 13. [4] *Ib.* l. 5.

designate one whose holding was described as *mansus ingenualis*, in contradistinction to a *servus* and *mansus servilis*. In the East, where domestic slavery gradually died out, rural slavery long retained the name, but was really serfdom. M. Peyron has discovered a palimpsest MS. of a decree of Honorius and Arcadius, dated 409, concerning a barbarous tribe from the Danube, called the Scyri, who were, on their defeat, transplanted to various provinces and attached to the soil. This decree says:

Let the proprietors know that the labour of these men is free, and that no one can dispose of these individuals as if they had been given to him, so as to cause them to pass from the condition of freedom to the state of slavery, or oblige them to the labour of a slave of the villa.[1]

These regulations show that these Scyri were converted into *coloni*, with all the privileges belonging to such; and yet Sozomen describes these same persons as being sold in Constantinople:

The governors were of opinion that if they were allowed to remain together, they would probably combine and create a sedition: some of them were therefore sold at a low price, while others were given away for nothing, as slaves (δουλέυειν), upon condition that they should never be permitted to return to Constantinople, or to Europe, but be separated by the sea from places that they knew. I have seen several of these scattered about, and cultivating the earth in Bithynia, near Mount Olympus.[2]

[1] *Arcad. de Turin.* t. 28, quoted by Biot, *L'Abolition de l'Esclav.* p. 18.
[2] *Hist. Eccl.* ix. 5.

The Letters of St. Gregory the Great give us an idea of the condition of the servile population in those parts of Europe that still obeyed the Imperial laws in the sixth century. We cannot help remembering the fatherly compassion which this great "Apostle of the English" showed for the fair-haired Angles exposed for sale in the market-place in Rome. His own thoughts about slavery may be easily gathered from the Deed of Manumission by which he sets free Montana and Thomas, two slaves.

Gregory to Montana and Thomas.

Since our Redeemer, the Author of all creation, has been graciously pleased to assume our human flesh, in order that He might by the grace of His divinity, break the bonds of servitude in which we were held captive, and restore us to our original liberty, so it is a salutary act, when men, whom at birth nature brought forth free, and whom the law of nations has put under the yoke of servitude, are restored by the beneficence of their liberator to that liberty in which they were born. And therefore, moved by the instinct of piety, and the consideration of the matter itself, you, Montana and Thomas, slaves (*famulos*) of the Holy Roman Church, which, by the help of God, we serve, we make you free from this day forward, and Roman citizens, and we relinquish all your *peculium*.[1]

The Christian Emperors had enacted that no Jew should possess Christian slaves. St. Gregory writes to the Bishop of Luna, to see that "if any such are found in his diocese, their liberty should

[1] Epist. vi. 12. Constantine had conferred upon Bishops the power of making men Roman citizens.

be secured by the assistance of your guardianship, according to the sanction of the laws." But he distinguishes between the slaves and the *coloni*, and says of the latter:

Although by the strict letter of the law they are free; yet, because for a long time they have stuck to the cultivation of the land, so as to belong to the place, let them remain to cultivate the fields as usual, and let them pay their rents (*pensiones*) to the aforesaid men (*i.e.* Jews), and let them fulfil all that the laws command as regards *coloni* or *originarii;* beyond that, let no further burthen be put upon them. But if any Jew shall want to take any of these, and move them elsewhere, or keep them in his own domestic service, let him remember that he who rashly violates the *jus colonarium*, has by the severity of the law condemned himself to lose his own right of dominion.[1]

It seems that a certain Jew named Nasas had set up an altar to St. Elias, and had tried to induce some Christian slaves, whom he had purchased, to worship before it. St. Gregory desires the Prefect of Sicily to inquire into the matter, and correct the abuse.

But whatever Christian slaves he may have bought, do you restore to liberty, so that there may be no doubt about it, according to the commands of the law, lest, which God forbid, the Christian religion be subjected to the Jews, and be defiled.[2]

Several other instances occur in St. Gregory's letters, which show how vigorously he interfered to protect the rights and liberties of the slave, and of

---

[1] Epist. iv. 21.   [2] Epist. iii. 38.

the *colonus*. It was in this practical way that this glorious Pontiff earned his favourite title of *Servus servorum Domini*.

We do not propose to pursue the subject through the centuries that elapsed after the Byzantine Empire lost its hold upon the West. M. Biot has summed up his investigations in the following conclusions:

1. The ancient right of making a slave of a prisoner of war no longer existed between Christian and Christian, even between Catholic and heretic; but it did exist between Christian and Pagan.

2. The domestic slaves, mentioned in documents of this epoch, are individuals who are not Christians, or at most barbarians become Christian after their captivity.

3. Domestic slavery among Christians seems to have been extinguished slowly by the influence of the dogma, incessantly repeated, of the spiritual equality before God of the master and slave; by that of the equality before the law, granted to all citizens, formerly divided off from each other by the limitations of hereditary rights; finally, by the action of special laws, which prevented the sale of individual liberty, and punished the murderer of a slave just as that of a free man.

4. Rural slavery was entirely, or almost entirely transformed into the *colonatus*, from the time of Justinian, in the sixth century. According to the letter of that legislation, it was real serfdom under another name.[1]

We must now return to the West, and follow the fortunes of the slave through the wild confusion that ensued upon the wreck of the mighty fabric of the Roman Empire.

[1] Biot, *De l'Abolition de l'Esclavage*, p. 249.

Gibbon[1] has traced the strange impulse which set in motion the barbaric invasions, to a Tartar revolution in China; but whatever may have been the cause, a mighty upheaving agitated all the tribes between the borders of China and the Rhine, and from the last quarter of the fourth century to the beginning of the seventh, wave after wave of Goths, Quadi, Marcomanni, Hermanduri, Vandals, Burgundians, Franks, Sclaves, Huns, Sarmatians, Lombards poured across the Danube, the Alps, the Rhine, the Rhone, the Pyrenees, and the Hellespont; while Scots, Picts, Angles, and Danes overran Britain and made descents on the coast of Gaul. As the invading hosts passed along, ruined cities, heaps of corpses, smoking farms marked their course. Brambles grew over the sites of villas, and the land, stripped of its population, returned once more into a forest. Salvian describes what he saw after the third sack of Treves:

The first city in Gaul was but a sepulchre. Those whom the enemy spared succumbed to the calamities which succeeded. Some died of their wounds, others perished of hunger and cold, and thus in different ways all went together to the tomb. I have seen, and my eyes have endured the spectacle of bodies of men and women naked, torn by dogs and birds of prey, lying in the streets which they polluted.[2]

All the foundations of society were rooted up; senators and slaves, nobles and peasants, were involved in one common calamity; the barbarian

---

[1] *Decline and Fall*, c. xxvi. [2] *De Gubernatione Dei*, lib. vi.

conquerors plunged eagerly into the sensual pleasures which the remains of civilization still suggested to them, and trembling captives presented rich wines in jewelled goblets to the murderers of their parents and the insolent possessors of their own inheritance.

The immediate result of the invasions was to aggravate enormously the evils of slavery. The barbarians ignored all the alleviations which the Christian Emperors had introduced into the condition of the slaves, whose numbers were continually recruited by the population of every new province invaded, and every new city captured. St. Gregory of Tours, who lived during the latter half of the sixth century, has given us most graphic accounts of the sufferings of the people under the Salian and Ripuarian Franks, who were perhaps the noblest of all those barbarian tribes. On a slight provocation, the savage master would cause his slave to be buried alive, to be tortured by fire, or cruelly mutilated. The marriage of even a liberated slave with one freeborn was interdicted under the severest penalties. The distinction between slaves and serfs was arbitrarily abolished. We have seen how the Christian Emperors forbade the separation of the serf from the soil which he cultivated. An edict of Theodoric says:

> Every master has the right of withdrawing from the lands rustic slaves of either sex, which he possesses by natural and legal right, even though they be born on the soil, and to transfer them from one place to another on his domain, or to make use of them in the service of

his villa, and they are rightly reckoned among his urban household. No litigation must be allowed on acts and arrangements of this kind, nor on objections drawn from the slave's birthplace. It is permitted to masters to alienate by sale persons of this condition, without any portion of the land, or to make them over, or sell them, or give them away to whomsoever they think well.[1]

St. Gregory gives a touching example of the ruthless way in which this power was exercised on some of the serfs in the royal domains. In 584, when King Chilperic married his daughter Rigontha to the Visigoth King Reccarede,

The King ordered a great number of families to be taken from the houses that belonged to the royal domain and placed in waggons. Many wept and would not go, and he had them put in prison in order to induce them more readily to accompany his daughter. It is said that in the bitterness of their sorrow, and in the fear of being torn away from their relatives, many of them strangled themselves with a cord. The son was separated from his father, the mother from her daughter; they went away sobbing and calling down curses on their oppressor.[2]

But the distinction between serf and slave, though obliterated for a time, reappeared under the beneficent Empire of Charlemagne.

The same power that had undermined and all but destroyed the ancient slavery of the Roman Empire was still at work, the immortal power of Christianity. It worked in various ways; sometimes by its secret influence on the consciences

---

[1] *Edictum Theodorici*, 142; Pertz, *Monumenta Germ.* t. v. p. 166. [2] *Hist. Franc.* l. vi. 45.

of individuals, sometimes through the burning words of preachers, like St. Chrysostom, sometimes through the authoritative letters of Pontiffs, like St. Gregory the Great, and sometimes through the solemn decrees of those great Councils, which in the time of St. Boniface did so much to bring order out of the wild chaos in which he found the whole of Northern Europe. When we examine the Councils of the period, from the fall of the Western Empire to the tenth century, we find decrees continually appearing in reference to slaves; and these decrees were very often in direct opposition to the national customs and laws of the people for whom they were intended. Amongst the Visigoths, Burgundians, Germans, and Bavarians, a great number of crimes involved, as the principal penalty, the being condemned to slavery. Among the Franks, the non-payment of the composition due by a freeman rendered him the slave of the injured party. Failure to render military service, and the inability to pay the *heribann* incurred in this case, made the offender the slave of the King. Even two Councils made use of this barbarous punishment in the interests of morals.

The First Council of Orleans, 511, decreed:

That if a man carried off a woman, and she took refuge in a church, if it be proved that the woman suffered violence, she shall at once be delivered from his power, and he shall be put to death; or, if immunity from punishment be granted him, he shall be either reduced to slavery, or be compelled to redeem himself.[1]

[1] Can. 2.

The Third Council of Toledo, 589, enacted that:

Women of suspicious character who live in the houses of priests and deacons shall be sold by the bishops, and the price given to the poor.[1]

This barbarous penalty was not long allowed to disfigure the legislation of the Church.

The Council of Rheims, in 625, proclaimed:

If any one shall endeavour to reduce to slavery one who is free by birth or emancipation, or if any one has done so, and after being admonished by the bishop has neglected to revoke the act or make amends, let his goods be sequestrated, as if he had been guilty of calumny.[2]

Another Council in the same century deals with the case of men who had sold themselves into slavery:

With regard to freeborn men who have sold themselves into slavery for money or other property, or put themselves in pawn, it is decreed that, as soon as they can find a sum equal to the price that was given for them, they shall, without delay, on payment of the price, be restored to their proper condition, and no more shall be exacted than was given for them; and in the meantime, if a man so situated has a freeborn wife, or a woman a freeborn husband, their children shall continue in the condition of freemen.[3]

The Council of Chalons, 650, declares:

It is the most special aim of piety and religion that the chain of captivity should be altogether redeemed

---

[1] Can. 5. [2] Can 17.
[3] *Synd. incert. loci.* circiter an. 616. Can. 14, quoted by Balmez, *Europ. Civilis.* n. 15, on Slavery.

from Christians: wherefore this holy Synod makes known its decree, that no slave must be sold out of the limits that belong to the kingdom of our Lord, King Clovis, lest by such sale, which God forbid, Christian slaves should be loaded with the chain of captivity, or what is worse, be in bondage to Jews.[1]

St. Batthilda, Queen of Clovis the Second, who had once been a slave herself, is believed to have interested herself especially in having this decree promulgated, since there were at that time merchants, many of them Jews, who travelled through Gaul buying slaves to sell in foreign countries. The Councils forbade the sale of Christian slaves to Jews, and authorized any one to redeem such as were possessed by them. Sales of Christians to Jews or pagans were declared null and void. The Fourth Council of Toledo, 625, after forbidding Jews to possess Christian slaves, either by purchase or gift, decreed that:

If hereafter Jews shall presume to hold Christian men or women as slaves, such slaves shall be removed from their possession and set at liberty by the prince.[2]

The laws of these nations afforded very slight protection to the slave. With the exception of the Visigoths and Burgundians, the rest, down to the time of Charlemagne, left the master with the power of life and death over his slave. The Councils did what they could to supply this defect, by opening the churches as sanctuaries, whither the slave could take refuge from a tyrannical

[1] *Conc. Cab.* Can. 9.   [2] Can. 66.

master, at the same time guarding this refuge against the obvious abuses to which it might lend itself. It was a great evidence of the power of Christianity over these fierce conquerors that they would consent to respect the sanctity of churches, and even listen with patience and deference to the bishop or monk who alone ventured to interpose between them and their victims. The Councils of Orleans[1] and Epône, early in the sixth century, lay down that, when a slave took refuge in a church, and his master demanded that he should be given up to him, the priest or bishop was to hear the case, and if the slave was guilty of some crime, the master had to take an oath that he would not punish him by death or mutilation; and then, on this security, the slave was to be given up, and if he refused to leave the church, the master was to be authorized to take him by force. But if the master broke his oath, and killed or mutilated his slave, he was to be excommunicated. The master was not, however, to be required to swear that he would not crop his slave's hair, or punish him by hard labour. The Council of Epône decrees:

If any one shall put his slave to death without trial before a judge, he shall be excommunicated for two years, and shall expiate the shedding of blood.[2]

The Church had always maintained the validity and sanctity of the marriages of slaves, but the ancient rule was that the consent of the master

---

[1] *Conc. Aurel.* i. Can. 3. [2] Can. 34.

in the first instance was necessary for the validity of such a marriage. It was not until the ~~twelfth~~ century that Pope Adrian the ~~Fourth~~ *(ar)* declared the marriages of serfs valid without their master's consent. In the times we are discussing, the clergy were not allowed to be the upholders of such marriages. Still, there were now and then cases of special hardship, and the clergy did not shrink from braving the anger of unreasonable masters. St. Gregory of Tours tells us of a cruel tyrant who treated his slaves with brutal inhumanity. He would compel them to hold candles, sometimes in their hands, sometimes between their bare shins, while he supped, until the flame burnt down into their flesh, threatening to plunge his sword into them if they moved or screamed. This Frank, whose name was Rauching, had among his slaves a young man and a girl, who fell in love with one another. After two years, during which it may be supposed they had tried in vain to obtain their master's consent, they got married, and took refuge in the church. Their master heard of it and came to the priest of the place, and asked him to give up his two slaves, promising to forgive them. The priest said to him, "You know what respect one ought to have for the churches of God: your servants shall not be given up to you, unless you give me your word that their union shall not be interfered with, and promise me at the same time to exempt them from all corporal punishment." The master hesitated for some time; at last, he said, with an oath, laying his hand upon the altar: "They shall never be separated by me, and I will take care that they shall never be separated by any one else." The priest was satisfied; but the barbarian had no sooner got his slaves into his power, than he had a deep trench dug in the ground, and the trunk of a thick tree hollowed out in the shape of a large coffin. In this coffin he had the unfortunate girl placed, and her husband on the top of her, and both were buried in the trench. As soon as the priest heard of it, he flew to the spot, upbraided Rauching with the violation of his oath, and insisted on the poor young couple being disinterred. The youth was still alive, but the poor girl had died of suffocation, while the brutal master protested that he had only taken the most effectual means of making their union perpetual.[1] It is some satisfaction to know that this wretch came to a bad end, and was assassinated in the King's palace, as he was suspected of treasonable ambition. The whole story gives us a lively picture of the lawlessness of the times, the savage cruelty of some of the chiefs, and the unhappy lot of those who were in their power; but it also shows us the salutary influence of religion in protecting, though not always effectually, the weak from the tyranny of the powerful.

Another point that the Church insisted upon in her Councils was, that the slave should have a day of rest on Sundays and certain other holidays. Thus the Council of Auxerre, 578:

[1] *Hist. Franc.* l. v. c. 3.

It is forbidden on the Lord's day to yoke oxen, or do any other labour except for permitted reasons.[1]

The Council of Rouen, 630, enacts:

Priests must admonish the people who are under their care as to ox-drovers, pig-drivers, and other shepherds or field-labourers, who are constantly employed in the fields or forests, and so live after the manner of cattle, that they make or permit these persons to come to Mass on Sundays and other festivals; for Christ redeemed them as well as themselves with His Precious Blood: and if they neglect to do this, let them know without doubt that they have to render account for their souls.

The next Canon goes on to say:

And let it be understood that the festival-days are to be celebrated with due honour from one evening to the next without any servile work.[2]

The Anglo-Saxon Synods went further still. The Council of Berkhampstead, in 697, enacted:

If, by command of his master, a slave works between the first Vespers of Sunday and those of Monday (*i.e.,* from Saturday evening till Sunday evening) his master shall pay him eighty shillings (*solidi*).[3]

A Council held in Wessex under King Ine, decreed:

If a "theowman" work on Sunday by his lord's command, let him be free; and let the lord pay him thirty shillings as "wite."[4]

The Church also defended to the utmost of her power those who had once been set at liberty,

---

[1] Can. 16.   [2] Can. 14, 15.   [3] Can. 10.
[4] *Laws of King Ine.* Thorpe, *Ancient Laws,* i. 105.

but whom the changing caprice of irresponsible force might attempt to reduce again to slavery. The Fifth Council of Orleans, in 549, decreed:

> By whomsoever this liberty shall be attacked, it may with justice be defended by the Church, except in the case of those offences for which the laws order liberty granted to slaves to be revoked.[1]

Notwithstanding all the direct and indirect influence of the Church in mitigating the hard lot of the slave, and in widening the facilities for his obtaining his freedom, it may not unreasonably be asked, Is not practice more powerful than precept? Why, then, did not the Church begin by emancipating all the slaves and serfs in the possession of Bishops and monasteries? Nay, M. Renan[2] has tried to make out that the condition of the slaves of the Church was more hopeless than that of other slaves; for, as the Bishop or Abbot was only a steward of the property of the Church, and could not sell or alienate it, these slaves were cut off from all hope of emancipation. Hallam takes it for granted that this was the case. The great Councils, however, found a way of meeting the difficulty. The Council of Agde, in 544, laid down:

> Let Bishops hold cottages, or slaves (*mancipiola*), or the sacred vessels, as the ancient authority of the Canons has prescribed, in the light of goods entrusted to them for the purpose of faithful keeping with the full right of

---

[1] Can. 7.   [2] *Marc-Aurèle*, p. 609.

the Church; that is, that they may not presume to sell or alienate by any contract whatsoever the property on which the poor live.

This seems absolute enough, but the same Canon goes on to say:

Indeed, if the Bishop shall have granted freedom to any of the slaves who have well deserved it, this synod has decreed that the freedom so conferred shall be respected by his successors, together with what their emancipator granted them on giving them freedom, and this we prescribe shall be limited to twenty *solidi* in money, and a small plot of land, a cottage, or a homestead. Anything beyond this that has been given the Church will claim back at the death of the emancipator.[1]

The Council of Rheims, in 625, repeats almost word for word the first part of this Canon:

That the Bishop may not presume to sell or by any contract whatsoever to alienate slaves or property belonging to the right of the Church on which the poor live after his death.[2]

This apparently absolute enactment may be interpreted by the latter part of the Canon of the Council of Agde, and we may conclude that, though the Bishop cannot sell his slaves, yet he may emancipate them. In fact, examples are numerous of such emancipation.

St. Aredius, or Yrieix, a Gallo-Roman, who was Chancellor to Theodebert, and greatly esteemed by Chilperic, Abbot of a monastery which he had founded at Limoges, died in 591. Twenty years

[1] *Conc. Agath.* Can. 7.   [2] Can. 13.

before this he had made a will, in which he placed his monastery, monks, and serfs, whose names he mentions, under the protection of St. Martin of Tours, and he enumerates the names of fifty men and women, among whom was a certain Lucy, whom he had redeemed from captivity. He entrusted their freedom to the guardianship of St. Martin.

These are my freed men and women, some of whom have been confided to me by my father of blessed memory by will, and others I have myself enfranchised for the good of my brother's soul. I commend them to thy defence, holy Martin. And if any man shall wish to exact from them more than has been laid upon them as dues, or in any way to disturb or oppress them, thou, O holy Martin, wilt defend them.[1]

In 615, Bertram, Bishop of Mans, liberated by will a great number of serfs, Roman and barbarian, put them under the protection of the Abbey of St. Pierre de la Couture, and laid upon them the obligation of meeting every year, on the anniversary of his death, in the abbey church; and, instead of making an offering they were to recite at the foot of the altar the deed of emancipation, and the list of the gifts that he had made them, and for that day to fulfil the services that they used to render to the abbey before their emancipation. The following day the Abbot was to entertain them at dinner, and then they returned, thus

---

[1] This will is mentioned by St. Gregory of Tours, who gives an epitome of the Life of St. Aredius, *Hist. Franc.* lib. x. 15. See Montalembert, *Monks of the West*, ii. 286.

rendering *obsequium*, or *servitium ingenuile*, as distinguished from *obsequium servile*.

Two centuries later, the Anglo-Saxon Council of Celchyth, in 816, is as strongly opposed to the alienation of church property as any of the French Councils, and yet it prescribes that on the death of a Bishop—

Then for his soul we command that a tenth part of all that he has, whether cattle or herds, sheep or swine, or what is in the cellars, shall be divided and distributed to the poor; moreover, that every Englishman that in his lifetime has been subjected to bondage shall be set at liberty, so that by that he may merit to receive the appropriate fruit of his own labour and pardon of his sins.[1]

Thus the process of emancipation went on even in ecclesiastical establishments. Another avenue of freedom had to be carefully guarded against abuse. The Christian Emperors had, out of respect for the clergy, forbidden slaves to be ordained deacons, or clothed with the monastic habit until after they had been emancipated. The Councils of Gaul and Spain continued the same prohibitions. If a slave had been unwittingly ordained, the Bishop was to pay the price of his emancipation; if he ordained him with knowledge of his servile condition, to pay double his value, but in no case was the sacred minister of God to be made again a slave.

We said that the distinction between slave and serf, obliterated by the Invasions, reappeared under Charlemagne. It came about thus. Under the

[1] *Conc. Celch.* Can. 10.

Merovingians the Franks had seized upon the vast tracts of unappropriated land and divided them by lot, and these were called *allodia*, or freehold. The kings and chieftains took possession of the fisc, or property belonging to the Imperial treasury. They rewarded their courtiers and warriors, *antrustions*, or "trusty ones," by grants of land, detached from these, and called *beneficia*, granted for life, after which they were to return to the original proprietor. The beneficiary, having only the usufruct, was bound to respect the substance of the property; he could not change its character, alienate, or destroy it. Now these *beneficia* were granted with the slave population which cultivated them; and hence, to transfer those slaves elsewhere, or even to remove a single slave from the property, was to abuse the usufruct and endanger its loss. When things became more settled, and especially under the rule of Charlemagne, the great dukes and counts looked sharply after the conduct of their beneficiaries in this respect. By a Capitulary of 794, Charlemagne interdicted the occupant from selling for his own profit any portion of the produce of the soil before having made provision for the subsistence of the serfs on the domain. "Let our Commissioners" (*missi*), said a Capitulary of 812, "draw up with the greatest care the condition of the *beneficia*, and let each of them in the district which he has to inspect make an accurate list of the individuals attached to these *beneficia*." A Capitulary of 806 blames severely the conduct of counts and other retainers of *beneficia*, who were guilty of having employed on their own business the serfs who were dependent on the royal domains which had been granted to them. Some of these followers of Charlemagne brought to his Court slaves belonging to their *beneficia*, but the Emperor ordered them to send them back, each to the place to which he was attached.[1]

Under the Carlovingian dynasty, the hereditary holdings of serfs began again to be recognized. Documents of the ninth century make a distinction between "servi *casati* et *non casati*," serfs who had cottages, and those who had not. The *non casati* were moveables, the *casati* were fixtures. In 806, Charlemagne divided his Empire between his three sons, and laid down: "We ordain that none of the three brothers (Charles, Pepin, and Louis) receive from any man belonging to the kingdom of one of the others, either by gift or sale, any immoveable property, that is to say, lands, vineyards, woods, slaves already *casati*, or any other thing possessed by hereditary titles excepting gold, silver, precious stones, arms, vestments, slaves *non casati*, things which are objects of commerce."

After Charlemagne came another period of anarchy. During the latter half of the ninth century, incessant invasions of the Normans kept the north of France and Germany in continual ferment, while the Saracens again invaded the south. In the general insecurity and the feebleness of Charlemagne's successors, castles grew up on the hills

[1] See Allard, *Esclaves, Serfs*, &c. pp. 173, 174.

and in situations favourable for defence, and the people flocked round them for protection, to the shelter of the chief who proved himself able to help them. Thus the powerful *beneficiaries* ceased to hold their lands of the King by a life-tenure; they became proprietors, holding their own by their strong hand, and transmitting their manor, their borough, or their county to their sons, acknowledging only a military homage to the sovereign. Thus the feudal system sprang out of the circumstances of the time, and was recognized by the Capitulary of Kiersi, 877. The consequence to the servile population was, that there was a great multiplication of serfs attached to the land, and a diminution of personal slaves. As the small proprietor hastened to place himself under the protection of a feudal lord, and in return for his protection became "his man," these petty sovereignties became more and more isolated from the world at large. Journeys became rare, commerce almost ceased. Each district lived on the produce of its own soil, and there was no place for the expensive luxury of personal slaves. Domestic offices were performed sometimes by serfs, sometimes by freemen in the castles and abbeys. And thus it came to pass that, from the middle of the tenth century, there were no more slaves in France, and the Capetian dynasty found slavery entirely absorbed in serfdom.

Sometimes freemen fell into serfdom through the artful tyranny of the powerful. M. Guérard gives an example:

In the borough of Walen (Canton Argau in Switzerland), lived a powerful and rich man named Gontran, who coveted eagerly his neighbours' goods. The freemen of the same borough, thinking him good and kind, offered him their lands, on condition that they should pay him the legal tax, and that they should in return enjoy them peaceably under his protection and *mainbourg*. Gontran accepted their offer with joy, but he went to work at once to oppress them. First, he demanded all sorts of things from them without payment; then he wished to exact everything from them by right of authority; then at last he took upon himself to act towards them as if they were his own serfs. He ordered them to supply *corvées* for the tillage of his fields, the reaping of his harvest, and the mowing of his grass. There was on his part a continual series of vexatious proceedings. When they remonstrated with loud cries, he told them that nothing of what they had should be taken to the market unless they consented to plough his waste land, remove the weeds from his fields and gardens, and cut down trees for him. From each of those who lived near the stream he exacted two fowls every year as forest dues, and one fowl from each of those who lived at a distance. The unfortunate inhabitants without protection were obliged to submit to all these demands. Even when the King came to the Castle of Soleure, and they clamoured to him for redress, the extravagant demands of some of them, and the crowd of courtiers hostile to them, prevented their complaints reaching the King, and they went home in worse plight than they came. It was not for a long time afterwards, in 1106, that the monks of Muri purchased the property from Rudolph, the successor of Gontran, and the inhabitants of Walen obtained more just and equitable treatment.

M. Guérard maintains that, notwithstanding such examples there was a general change for the better in the condition of the serfs from the time of Charlemagne downwards. Mr. Hallam, who speaks with great respect of the deep learning of M. Guérard, yet holds exactly the opposite view. On Mr. Hallam's supposition, the difficulty is to understand how serfdom could have practically died away without a violent revolution.

Further on, we shall endeavour to trace the gradual elevation and emancipation of the serfs, but we may pause to inquire what the life of a serf in France must have been in the ninth century.

When the Franks embraced Christianity, they testified their gratitude to the Bishops and monks in the same way as they did to their comrades in battle, by granting them *beneficia;* but, as the Church never died, but only changed its ruler, these lands remained in perpetual possession, and the estates under the lordship of the abbeys often exceeded in extent those of powerful nobles. Several accounts of these abbey-lands have come down to us, and from them we can form a tolerably correct idea of the ordinary life of a serf. It is true that the serfs on the abbey property were more justly and kindly treated than those on the royal domains, and still more so than on the property of lesser nobles; but the general condition must have been much the same for all.

Mr. Hallam expresses his astonishment that "men were infatuated enough to surrender themselves as well as their properties, to churches and monasteries, in return for such benefits as they might reap by the prayers of their new masters."[1]

The fact is there was less degradation in becoming the serf of a church or abbey than of a secular lord. The Bishop or Abbot was not regarded so much as a living master as the representative of the Saint to whom the church was dedicated. An anecdote related by Montalembert will show how strongly this was felt:

At Perrecy, in Burgundy, a much dreaded knight, named Hugh Bidulphe, had, on the occasion of a riot, beaten a peasant belonging to the Abbey of Fleury so cruelly as to break his arm. The wounded man finding no one to avenge him, entered the abbey church, and approaching the altar, sacred to St. Benedict, laid his arm on it, saying, "My lord St. Benedict, I acknowledge that I am thy serf, and that thou art my master; look now at this broken arm—it was thine, and no one else had any right to it; if thou hadst broken it, I should have had nothing to complain of. But, my lord, why hast thou allowed Hugh Bidulphe, to whom it did not belong at all, to crush it in this manner? Know that in future I shall not be able to do any service to thee or thine, unless, indeed, thou wilt take a just vengeance on him for me." The monks, gathering round the altar, joined their tears and prayers to those of the sufferer. We are not told whether he was cured, but a few days after, the wicked knight began to feel an acute pain in the same arm as that which he had broken for the peasant; the illness spread to his whole body, and he shortly died, a prey to the most terrible anguish.[2]

[1] *Middle Ages*, i. 198.
[2] *Monks of the West*, vi. 125.

It must also be remembered that great numbers of the Frankish nobility, like the victorious Carloman, embraced the monastic state, and the serf of the abbey found himself labouring side by side with the prince or noble, who wore the same rough clothing as himself.

Irmino, Abbot of St. Germain des Prés, in 826, made a *Polypticon* or Register, described thus by Aimo in his *Annals of Hincmar:*

The wise Abbot Irmino has gathered into one MS. the state of the revenues of all the lands of St. Germain, down to an egg or a tile; has regulated the share that the monks should have for their own use, and that which the Abbot ought to reserve for himself, or for the army of the King.

This valuable record was edited, in 1840, by M. Guérard. The property subject to the jurisdiction of the abbey consisted partly of seignorial domains possessed by nobles, in their own right, but who for various reasons chose to become vassals of the abbey, and paid tribute amounting in all to about £14,430 of our money. The portion belonging actually to the abbey consisted of nearly 42,000 acres, producing revenues in specie, in produce, and in serf-labour somewhat over £12,000 a year. This latter property was divided into 25 fiscs or manors, each under one proprietor, though composed of a number of distinct territories, sometimes including a whole village, sometimes part of one, sometimes small plots belonging to separate villages. Each *fisc* consisted of a number of *mansi* or farms, of which 1,430 were *mansi ingenuiles*, or larger farms originally occupied by freeborn tenants, 25 were *mansi lidiales*, smaller farms originally occupied by *lidi*, *leudes*, or *læti*, whose name survives in our "court-leet," and who are supposed to have been Frankish soldiers who took to labouring work; 191 were *mansi serviles*, or lands originally held by serfs. An extract or two from the *Polyptique* will show that these farms were by no means always inhabited by the class whose name they bore:

Alantcus, a *lide*, and his wife a freewoman (*colona*) named Ingberta, vassals of St. Germain, have with them three children, named Ercberta, Adalricus, Antbertus; Hairbert a *lide* and his wife a *lide* also named Godelinde, vassals of St. Germain, have with them three children named Imilgand, Dodo, Hostold. These two families hold one *mansum servilem*, having of arable land about 190 acres, of vineyard 28 perches, of meadow land 42 perches. It does (that is the tenants are bound to do work for the abbey) nearly 3 roods of vineyard, and hand labour (*manoperas*) when ordered; 3 fowls, 15 eggs.

Another manse is thus described:

Ebrulfus a freeman and his wife a serf, named Ermenilda, vassals of St. Germain, have with them four children, named Merulfus, Bertha, Dominica, Murna; Ermenold a serf, and his wife a free-woman, named Martha, vassals of St. Germain, have with them four children, named Ermenbert, Ardegar, Ermenard, Ingalsinde; Teutgarda a serf, has with her one child, named Teutgaria. These three families hold one *mansus ingenuilis*, having of arable land about 120 acres, about 142 perches of vineyard, and 56 perches of meadow. They do in the vineyard (of the abbey) about an acre and a half; they pay of wine 128 gallons (*modios II.*), 3 lbs. of mustard (*sextarios II.*).[1]

It will be seen that the farmer and his wife were by no means always of the same condition. Out of 248 households, where the heads of the family are of different conditions, in 190 the condition of the wife is superior to that of the husband, and only in 58 is she inferior. There was a very practical inducement for a serf to marry a free-woman, because in France and Germany his children then were freeborn. Beaumanoir, in the thirteenth century, lays down:

It should be known, that there are three conditions of men in this world; the first is that of gentlemen, and the second is that of such as are naturally free, being born of

---

[1] These measurements are translated under correction. The original is subjoined:

Polypticon: n. 14. "Alanteus lidus et uxor ejus colona nomine Ingberta, homines S. Germani, habent secum infantes iii, his nominibus, Ercamberta, Adalricus, Antbertus; Hairbertus lidus et uxor ejus lida, nomine Godelindis, homines S. Germani, habent secum infantes iii. his nominibus, Imilgardus, Dodo, Hostoldus. Isti duo tenent mansum servilem I. habentem de terra arabili bunnaria vi et dimidium, de vinea aripennum i, de prato aripennum i et dimidium. Facit in vinea aripennos iiii, manoperas, quantum ei jubetur; pullos iii, ova xv."

"38. Ebrulphus colonus et uxor ejus ancilla, nomine Ermenildis, homines S. Germani, habent secum infantes iiii, his nominibus Merulphus, Berta, Dominica, Murna; Ermenoldus servus et uxor ejus colona nomine Marta, homines S. Germani, habent secum infantes iiii, his nominibus Ermenbertus, Ardegarius, Ermenardus, Ingalsindis; Teutgardis, ancilla S. Germani, habet secum infantem i, nomine Teugaria. Isti tres tenent mansum ingenuilem i, habentem de terra arabili bunnaria iiii et antsingam i, de vinea aripennos iiii, de prato aripennos ii. Faciunt in vinea aripennos viii; solvunt de vino in pascione modios ii, sinapis sextarios ii."

a free mother. All who have a right to be called gentlemen are free, but all who are free are not gentlemen. Gentility comes by the father, and not by the mother; but freedom is derived from the mother only; and whoever is born of a free mother is himself free, and has free power to do anything that is lawful.[1]

In England, on the contrary, as Hallam points out, "the father's state determined that of the children."[2] This was embodied in the laws of Henry the First. The *villani* in France were free *coloni* attached to a villa, the *villeins* in England were serfs.

In the Capitularies of the Carlovingian Kings are many curious enactments about the circulation of the royal coinage. One of these, bearing the date of 864, lays down that if after the 1st of July in that year, any one refuses to take the new denarius in exchange, if a freeman (*liber homo*) he shall pay a fine of 60 solidi. But if he is serf of the Church or of the counts, or one of our own vassals, they shall whip him with sixty strokes.

And that indiscreet men may observe moderation in this discipline, we ordain, with the consent and counsel of our trusty ones, that they shall not beat *coloni* or serfs who have thus offended with their thick clubs, but on the bare back with twigs. And in cities, towns, and villages, the Bishops shall provide by their officials or priests, in concert with the State officers, that the punishment be not excessive.

[1] Beaumanoir, *Coûtumes de Beauvoisis*, c. 45.
[2] *Middle Ages*, i. p. 199.

The serf, as we gather from the *Polypticon* of Irmino, knew perfectly well his position and its obligations. He was secure on his little holding, he occupied his farm-house, either alone with his family, or jointly with one or two other families. He had his out-houses for his beasts, pigs, and poultry, part of his land was under tillage for crops of wheat or barley, part was devoted to the vineyard, and part laid out for the cultivation of mustard, flax, &c., besides the little meadow for his cattle. On certain days, sometimes two or three days in each week, sometimes only at particular seasons of the year, he had to perform his *corvée* or labour for his lord. He had to present himself at the fiscal mansion, with his horses or oxen, his spade, pick, shovel, axe, shears, or whatever might be the implement of his work, and then to go into the hayfield, cornfield, or vineyard, and fulfil his task; after which there was generally a feast at the expense of the lord, and the serf returned to labour for his own benefit on his own farm. If his wife was a serf, she had to do some weaving or other female labour, and to take care of the fowls, whose eggs were an important part of the rent that was paid for the manse.

On Sundays and holidays the family could not be bidden to work for their lord, and the thirty-five churches scattered over the lands of the Abbey of St. Germain, each with its little manse for the support of the priest, show that the spiritual wants of the ten thousand persons who lived on the property were not neglected. Charlemagne had all the village churches on his royal domains decorated with paintings on the walls. Wherever there was a monastery, there was a school for the children; and, though the records of those days tell us doleful stories of the whippings poor boys got when they were slow at their lessons, the good monks had some tenderness for the little ones, for among the rents paid to the Abbey of St. Peter at Corbey, one item is "six pounds of honey for the infants' school."[1]

If the serf had no legal rights against his master, he had for his protection that vast body of unwritten law called "custom," and this could be appealed to with success. In 906, the serfs of the Monastery of St. Ambrose at Milan complained that the new Abbot had increased their burthens. His overseer had taken away their cattle at his will, obliged them to gather the olives, contrary to custom, to work at the wine-press, to prune the vines, to thresh the corn, &c. The Abbot said, "But the Emperor gave you to the monastery as slaves, therefore I can command you what I choose." "No," said the serfs, "when we belonged to the Emperors, neither we, nor our fathers before us, had any other obligations than these," and they enumerated them. Witnesses were called and heard, and sentence was pronounced in favour of the serfs.[2] In 858, the Bishops of Rouen and Rheims wrote to Louis le Debonnaire: "Let not

---

[1] *Statut. Corbeiens.* Cited by Guérard in *Polyptique d'Irminon*, t. ii. Append. p. 356, and quoted by Allard; see *Esclaves, Serfs*, &c. chap. xii. "Vie d'un Serf au neuvième siècle."

[2] Allard, *Esclaves*, &c. p. 221.

the judges oppress the slaves of the royal domain, and not exact from them rents exceeding those which they were accustomed to pay in the life-time of your father; let them not impose *corvées* at inconvenient times." These customs protected the serf against much oppression, secured him from being turned out of his house and farm, and gave him the hope, always dear to a father's heart, of seeing his children rise to a condition above his own. Although he was ordinarily excluded from the honour of fighting for his country, yet in times of extreme danger the serfs were armed, and we may suppose them animated with the thoughts which Sir Walter Scott places on the lips of the Scotch "bondsmen and serfs" at Bannockburn:

> To us, as to our lords, are given
> A native earth, a promised Heaven;
> To us, as to our lords, belongs
> The vengeance for our nation's wrongs;
> The choice, 'twixt death or freedom, warms
> Our breasts as theirs—to arms, to arms![1]

Later on we hope to show how serfdom like slavery also passed away, and under the same beneficent influences, but we must give a hasty glance to other countries besides France.

In Germany almost the same distinctions prevailed as in France. The wars that were necessary for two centuries to repel the invasions of the Bulgarians, Hungarians, and other Oriental tribes, terminated by the victories of Henry the Fowler in the middle of the tenth century, brought a vast multitude of those barbarians into a state of sub-

[1] *Lord of the Isles,* canto vi. 30.

jection and serfdom, so that their very name of *Sclave*, which originally meant glorious, became the common appellation of servitude—*slave*. Personal slavery seems to have died out in Germany at a very early period, but serfdom has lingered there longer than in any other part of Europe except Russia.

In Italy and Spain personal slavery, and even the slave-trade, continued down to the sixteenth or seventeenth centuries. In Spain this was owing to the constant struggle with the Moors, and in Italy to the conflict between the Algerine and other corsairs, and the fleets of the merchant cities of Genoa and Venice. Cibrario, a learned Milanese author, has brought out a work full of curious facts on this subject, drawn from the Public Records. There was a slave-market at Venice in the eighth century, and Lombard slaves were sold in Naples in the ninth century. In 836, the slave-trade was prohibited in Naples, and in Venice at the same time. But, notwithstanding the prohibition, it was still carried on privately. Two sales of slaves took place at Genoa in 1677. Most of those in the fourteenth and fifteenth centuries came from Spain, then under the Moors. Of one set, 30 were white, only 6 black, 33 olive, 18 brown; none over 40, most under 25; out of 29 female slaves, one was a baby 3 months old. At Venice, in 1429, a Russian girl of 17 was sold for 87 gold ducats, or £84. In 1407, a Circassian slave-girl of 18 was given in pledge for a loan. In Genoa, in 1481, the *podestà* obtained authority to torture a slave beyond the legal extent, because she was suspected of poisoning her mistress, and it was urged that this was a grave danger in a *città piena di servi*. The ravages of Mahomedan pirates on the coasts of Italy hardened the hearts of Italians, so that although the traffic was forbidden, it did not excite much disgust. It was different when Christians and Italians were the victims. In 1386, Leonardo Vidal took on board his ship, on the coast of Apulia, an Italian, his wife, and two children. At Zara, he contrived to induce the man to land, and then carried off the wife and children to Venice and sold them as slaves. He was in course of time brought to justice, and he had to refund the money he had received for the sale, the woman was to give him two blows (*due ferite*), his right arm was cut off between the two Pillars, and fastened round his neck. He was then led to the Rialto, where his crimes were proclaimed, and he was driven into perpetual banishment.[1]

It ought to be remembered that all this was in spite of the protests of the Bishops and the explicit condemnations of slavery by the Popes. In 1482, Pope Pius the Second denounced the Portuguese in Africa for reducing the natives to slavery; and in 1537, Pope Paul the Third, in reply to an appeal made to him by Las Casas and the Dominicans of New Spain, declared that "it is an invention of the devil to affirm that the Indians may be reduced to slavery," and adds :

---

[1] Cibrario, *Della Schiavitù e del Servaggio*, towards the end of the work.

The Indians, as well as all other people, even those who are not baptized, ought to enjoy their natural liberty, and the proprietorship of their goods; and no one has the right to trouble them, or to disturb them in that which they hold from the liberal hand of God.

He pronounced excommunication against those who should enslave them. In both Spain and Italy serfdom disappeared at the same time with personal slavery.

Although Spain had not the commercial interests which brought Italy into conflict with the Turkish corsairs, yet her long and deadly struggle for independence against her Moorish conquerors produced similar results with regard to slavery and serfdom. Under the Visigoths, two classes of slaves are mentioned, domestic and rural; but so far from the rural slaves being regarded as in a higher condition, they are designated as *viles*, while the domestic slaves are called "fit and good"—*idonei, boni*. The domestic slave was allowed to bear arms, and sometimes attained to high honour and fortune, without being enfranchised, although he was severely punished if he married a free-woman. Consequently when, in 713, the country fell under the yoke of the Moors, the lot of the slaves changed but little. As Spain began by degrees to recover itself, and regain possession of its own soil, the feudal system became established in the several kingdoms of Navarre, Aragon, Castile, and Leon. Serfdom, or the binding of the peasant to the soil, followed as in other countries with something of the same varieties. The *abadengos*, or serfs on the church lands, were, as usual, the best off. The yoke pressed most heavily upon the *solariegos*, or those under lay lords. The former had the disposition of the property that they might have acquired, while the latter had to render the labour dues, differing in amount, and also to give free quarters to their lord or his followers for thirty days in the year. This was in Navarre. In Aragon, they distinguished the *villanos de parada*, who had no proprietorship in their lands, nor fixity of rent, but who could, from the tenth century, appeal to a court of justice against a lord who claimed more than his due. Next, there were the *mudjares*, Saracen prisoners, who were attached to the soil, except on church lands. Lastly, there were the *villanos*, or *pecheros*, who were free as to their persons, could dispose of their property, and free themselves from all dues by giving up their holdings, but who had not the power of marrying without the permission of their lord, and in case of their dying intestate, he came into all their property. In Castile and Leon, the serfs or *solariegos*, from the tenth century, enjoyed fixity of tenure and rent, and in 1258 they obtained the right of marrying their daughters without the consent of their lord. In the same provinces, in the middle of the fourteenth century, it was strictly forbidden to make slaves of Christian prisoners, but it was not forbidden to enslave infidels. The law, however, protected the slave in a variety of ways. If his master did not feed him properly, he could demand to be sold to some one else. If a husband and wife were slaves to two different masters, they could demand a fresh sale to take place, that they might be together: or else the Bishop could purchase both.[1] The last mention of slavery in Spain was as late as 1712, when Philip the Fifth expelled the Moors from Spain, but excepted the Moorish slaves.

[1] Allard, op. cit. p. 328.

LECTURE III.

SLAVERY AND SERFDOM IN THE BRITISH ISLES.

1.—England.

IN treating of the transition from Roman Slavery to Mediæval Serfdom in Europe generally, we purposely omitted to trace this transition in these islands. The subject deserves fuller treatment than we were able to give to it then. Lord Macaulay says: "How great a part the Roman Catholic ecclesiastics had in the abolition of villenage we learn from the unexceptionable testimony of Sir Thomas Smith, one of the ablest Protestant Counsellors of Elizabeth."[1] Sir Thomas Smith was Secretary of State both to Edward the Sixth and Queen Elizabeth, and therefore cannot be suspected of a desire to over-estimate the benefits of the Catholic religion, so we may safely accept anything that he says to the credit of the Church. His position gave him the best opportunities of knowing the condition of the country; and, though his desire to make England look well in the eyes of the French, to whom he was Elizabeth's Ambassador when he wrote his *Commonwealth of England*, may have coloured his

[1] *Hist.* i. 24.

statements somewhat favourably, yet in the main they will be borne out by the testimony of other writers of the period. The edition from which we shall quote was published in 1633, and we are not aware that the work has been republished since the seventeenth century. It gives a complete picture of the political and social condition of England in the reign of Elizabeth. He says:

We in England divide our men commonly into four sorts: gentlemen, citizens, yeomen, artificers. Of gentlemen, the first and chief are the king, the prince, the dukes, marquises, earls, viscounts, barons, and all these are called lords and noblemen: next to these are knights, esquires, and simple gentlemen. Next to gentlemen be appointed citizens and burgesses. . . . Those whom we call yeomen, next to the nobilitie and squires, have the greatest charge and doings in the commonwealth. . . . I call him a yeoman, whom our lawes doe call *legalem hominem*, which is a freeman borne English, and may dispend of his owne free land in yeerely revenue to the summe of forty shillings sterling. . . . This sort of people confesse that they be no gentlemen, and yet they have a certain pre-eminence and more estimation than labourers, and commonly live wealthily, . . . and daily do buy the lands of unthriftie gentlemen. The fourth sort or classe amongst us is of those whom the old Romans called *capite censi proletarii*, day labourers, poor husbandmen, yea, merchants or retailers, which have not free land, copyholders, and all artificers. These have no voice nor authoritie in our commonwealth, and no account is made of them, but only to be ruled, and not to rule others, and yet they be not altogether neglected. For in cities and corporate townes for default of yeomen, enquests and juries are impannelled of such manner of people. And in villages they may be commonly made church-wardens, ale-cunners, and many times constables, which office toucheth more the commonwealth, and at the first was not imployed upon such low and base persons. (Bk. i. cc. xxii.—xxiv.)

After that we have spoken of all the sorts of freemen according to the diversitie of their estates and persons, it resteth to say somewhat of bondmen, which were called *servi*. . . . The Romans had two kinds of bondmen, the one which were called *servi*, and they were either which were bought for money, taken in warre, left by succession, or purchased by some other kind of lawful acquisition, or else borne of their bondwomen, and called *vernæ:* all these kind of bondmen bee called in oure lawe *villains in grosse*, as you would say, immediately bound to the person and his heires. Another they had which they called *adscriptitii glebæ*, or *agri censiti*. These were not bound to the person, but to the manor or place, and in our lawe are called *villaines regardants*, because they be as members, or belonging to the manor or place. Neither of the one sort nor of the other have we any number in England. And of the first, I never knew any in the realme in my time. Of the second, so few there be, that it is almost not worth the speaking, but our lawe doth acknowledge them in both those sorts.

He goes on to explain how slavery and serfdom were gradually abolished :

Since our realme hath received the Christian religion, which maketh us all in Christ brethren, and in respect of God and Christ *conservos*, men began to have conscience to hold in captivitie and such extreame bondage, him whom they must acknowledge to bee their brother, and as wee used to term him, a Christian. Upon this scruple, in continuance of time, and by long succession, the holy fathers, monks, and friers, in their confession, and specially in their extreame and deadly sicknesses, burdened the consciences of them whom they had under their hands: so that temporall men by little and little, by reason of that terror in their conscience, were glad to manumitte all their villaines: but the said holy fathers, with the abbots and priors, did not in like sort by theirs, for they had also conscience to impoverish and despoile the Church so much as to manumitte such as were bound to their churches, or to the manors which the Church had gotten, and so kept theirs still. The same did the bishops also, till at last, and now of late, some bishops (to make a peece of money) manumitted theirs, partly for argent, partly for slanders, that they seemed more cruell than the temporality: afterwards monasteries coming into temporall men's hands, have been occasion that now they be almost all manumitted. I think that both in France and England, the change of religion to a more gentle, humane, and more equall sort (as the Christian religion is in respect of the Gentile), caused this old kind of servile servitude and slavery to be brought into that moderation, for necessity, first to *villaines regardants*, and afterwards to servitude of landes and tenures, and little by little finding out more civill and gentle means, and more equal, to have that done, which, in time of heathenesse, servitude or bondage did, they almost extinguished the whole. (Bk. iii. c. x.)

Sir Thomas Smith explains the transition from personal servitude to servile tenure of land, saying:

Some would not have bondmen, but *villaines regardants* to the ground. . . . Others found out wayes and meanes, that not the men, but the land, should be bond, and bring with it such bondage and service to him that occupieth it, as to carry the lord's dung unto the field, to plow his ground at certaine dayes, sow, reape, come to his court, sweare unto him faith, and in the end to hold the land, but by copy of the lord's court rolle, and at the will of the lord. (*Ibid.*)

We have quoted such long extracts from this curious treatise because it shows a period when slavery had come to an end, and serfdom had become little more than a legal fiction. Strong Protestant as Smith was, his testimony that this abolition of slavery was owing principally to the appeal to men's consciences made by priests, monks, and friars, is valuable. And none the less so, because he has a fling at them for not having emancipated their own serfs. We may discover a more probable reason for this than the one that he suggests. But at present we will go back another two hundred years in the history of England, and see what the state of slavery and serfdom was before the destruction of more than half the population by the Black Death in the fourteenth century, and before the Peasant Revolt under Wat Tyler, which two events immediately succeeded each other.

Mr. Seebohm, in his invaluable book on *The English Village Community*, gives us an accurate account of the state of the manor of Winslow, in Buckinghamshire, in the reign of Edward the Third. He shows from the manor rolls, a complete set of which is in the Cambridge University

Library, that the fields were "open fields," divided into furlongs, and cut up into half-acre strips, the names of the holders of each half-acre being identified. The land was divided into the demesne of the lord, in this case the Abbot of St. Albans, and land in villenage. The former was partly farmed by the lord, and other portions let out to tenants for longer or shorter terms, at money rents in free tenure. The land in villenage was also let out, but held in villenage, at the will of the lord, and at customary services. An idea may be formed of the extent of these holdings from a single instance where the virgate, or yard-land, of one John Moldeson, had reverted to the lord, and was again let out in parcels to a number of persons. It consisted of a messuage in the village of Shipton, no less than 68 half-acre strips, scattered over the fields, 3 rood strips of arable land, 2 doles of meadow-land, 1 acre of pasture, 3 half-acres of pasture, and 1 half-acre of meadow. The virgate, or yard-land, of a villanus thus consisted of about 30 acres of land, with a messuage in the village, and a half-virgate of half the number of strips of land scattered about over the great open fields. Out of 43 jurymen who had served in 1346, 1347, and 1348, 27 died of the Black Death in 1348 and 1349. Out of these 27, 16 held virgates, 8 held half-virgates; and, of the other 3, 1 held a messuage and 2 cottages, another a messuage and 15 acres, and the third, 8 acres arable and 2½ acres of meadow. Those who were *nativi*, or villeins by descent, were *adscripti glebæ;* they held their holdings at the will of the lord. If they allowed their houses to get out of repair they were guilty of waste, and the jury were fined if they did not report the neglect. Yet the entries in the rolls prove that their holdings were hereditary, passing by the lord's grant from father to son by the rule of primogeniture, on payment of the customary heriot or relief. The heriot of a virgate was generally an ox, or money payment of its value. The holders could make wills, which were proved before the cellarer of the abbey, and had been so time out of mind. Thus far they were free. But, if they married without the lord's consent, they were fined; if they sold an ox without leave, again they were fined; if they left the manor without licence, they were searched for, arrested as fugitives, and brought back; if their daughters lost their chastity, the lord had his fine. And in all these cases the whole jury were fined if they neglected to report the delinquent.

Their services [Mr. Seebohm says] were no doubt limited and defined by custom, and so late as the reign of Edward the Third mostly discharged by a money payment in lieu of the actual service, but they rested nominally on the will of the lord; and sometimes, to test their obedience, the relaxed rein was tightened, and trivial orders were issued, such as that they should go off to the wood and pick nuts for the lord. In cases of dispute, a court was held under the great ash tree at St. Albans, and the decision of this superior manorial court at head-quarters, settled the question. This villenage of the Winslow tenants was, no doubt, in the fourteenth century, mild in its character; the silent working of economic laws was breaking it up; but it was villenage still. It was serfdom, but it was serfdom in the last stages of its relaxation and decay.[1]

Going a century further back, we have, in the Hundred Rolls of Edward the First, a minute description of the land held by free tenants, and that held in villenage, with the services required of the latter, in 1279. We will take one example from Oxfordshire, cited by Mr. Seebohm. A *villanus*, holding a virgate, of about 30 acres, owes:

	s.	d.
82 days' work (about two days a week) between Michaelmas and June 24th, valued at ½d.	3	5
11½ days' work (rather more than 2 days a week) between June 24th and August 1st, valued at 1d.	0	11½
19 days' work (2½ days a week) between August 1st and Michaelmas, valued at 1½d.	2	4½
1 *precaria* (or "boon-days," extra services which the lord had the right to require), with two men, for reaping, with food from the lord, valued at	0	2
6 *precariæ* with one man, valued at	1	0
Half a carriage for carrying the wheat	0	1
Half a carriage for carrying the hay	0	1
The ploughing and harrowing of an acre	0	6
One ploughing called *graserthe*	0	1½
1 day's harrowing of oatland	0	1

[1] Op. cit. pp. 22—31.

1 horse (load) of wood	0	0½
Making 1 quarter of malt, and drying it...	0	1
1 day's work at washing and shearing sheep, valued at	0	0½
1 day's hoeing valued at	0	0½
3 days' mowing	0	6
1 day's nutting	0	0½
1 day's work in carrying to the stack	0	0½

Tallage once a year at the lord's will.
The value in money at that time was about 9s. 7d.

A *cotarius*, or cottager, in the same county, holds one croft, and owes:

From Michaelmas to August 1st, each workable week, one day's work of whatever kind the lord requires.

At Martinmas (*i.e.* Nov. 11th, half-quarter day) he gives one cock and three hens for churchshot, and ought to drive to certain places, and to carry writs, his food being found by his lord; also to wash and shear sheep, receiving a loaf and a half, and being partaker of the cheese with the *servi*; and to hoe. In the autumn, to work and receive like as each *servus* works and receives for the whole week.[1]

It may be noticed that while the *villanus* had his services valued at so much money, no such commutation is reckoned in the case of the *cotarius*, and here we have mention of a grade lower than that of the lowest kind of serf, viz., the *servus*, or actual slave.

In some counties, as appears from the *Liber Niger* of the Abbey of Peterborough, the lower class of *villani* were called *bordarii*, from the Saxon

---

[1] Op. cit. pp. 42—45.

bord, a cottage. These seem not to have possessed oxen, as the *villanus* generally did, but they sometimes had five or even eight acre-strips of land, as allotments in the open fields.

We may sum up the condition of England from the eleventh to the thirteenth century thus: The country was covered with manors. Each of these manors consisted of the lord's demesne (*i.e.*, the home farm belonging to the manor-house), and the land held in villenage. The demesne of the lord was cultivated chiefly by the services of the village community, or tenants in villenage, and partly by the slaves of the lord, the *villeins in gross*. The land of the serfs or *villani* lay in open fields round the village, where the homesteads of the community were clustered together. The holdings of the *villani* were generally in half-acre strips scattered over the open fields. This system of holding bundles of separate strips of land, which seems to us so inconvenient, appears to have originated, as Mr. Seebohm shows by the minute enactments of the Welsh laws, in a custom of co-operative farming, under which a number of different occupiers each contributed two or more oxen to the team of eight, which was considered requisite for ploughing the land. The virgate was the normal extent of the holding of a *villanus*. Four virgates made a hide of land, and the occupier was sometimes called a *hidarius*. The half-virgate was in some places called a *bovate*, or oxgang. The plough was driven by four oxen yoked abreast, and often four more in front of them. And thus the plough was called a *caruca*, or four-horsed chariot ; and hence the land ploughed by this team of eight was styled a *carucate*.

These holdings of the *villani* were indivisible bundles of land ; passing, with the homestead, which formed part of them, by re-grant from the lord, from one generation of serfs to another in unbroken regularity, and always to a single successor, whether the eldest or the youngest son, according to the custom of each individual manor. They

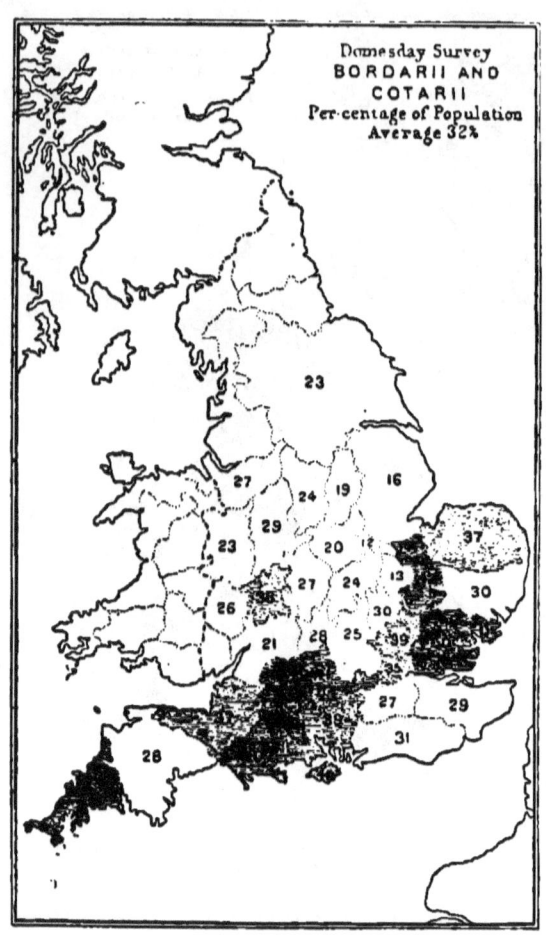

possessed all the unity and indivisibility of an entailed estate, and were sometimes held for generations by the family name of the holders. But the reason underlying all this regular devolution was

not the preservation of the family of the tenant,
but of the services due from the yard-land to the
lord of the manor.

Below the *villani* proper were the smaller
tenants of the cottier class, the *cotarii* and *bordarii*,
who had generally no oxen, and therefore took no
part in the common ploughing. And below the

villeins or cottiers were in some districts remains of a class of *servi*, or slaves, fast becoming merged in the cottier class above them, or losing themselves

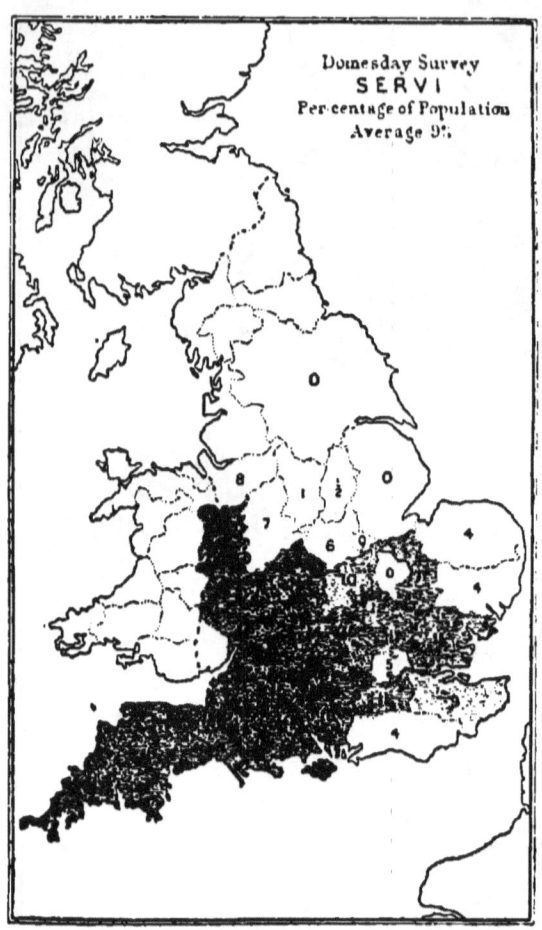

among the household servants or labourers upon the lord's demesne.

We may now come to the great survey of England contained in Domesday Book. The various manors were divided into hides, or *carucates*, the hide being the unit of taxation, the *carucate* marking the number of plough-teams on the manor. Originally they were different words for the same piece of land, but the number of hides often fell short of the number of *carucates*.

The four maps of England, in Mr. Seebohm's work, give a clear idea of the proportions to the population in each county of the various classes of freemen, or *sochmanni, servi*, or slaves, *bordarii* and *cotarii*, and *villani*, at the time of the Domesday Survey. We are able, by the author's kind permission, to reproduce them here. The figures in each county represent the percentage of the population of the county consisting of these different classes. It will be seen that the free-tenants only existed in the eastern counties most completely under Danish influence. The *sochmanni*, according to Sir Henry Ellis, "were those inferior land-owners, who had lands in the soc or franchise of a great baron; they could not be compelled to relinquish their tenures at their lord's will, nor against their own." The *liberi homines* sometimes included all ranks of society, even those holding on military tenure. The survey of Domesday mentions 23,000 *sochmanni*, and 12,000 *liberi homines*. The *villani* were 108,407 in number; and the *bordarii* and *cotarii* about 89,000. The *servi* formed only 9 per cent. of the population, and were most numerous in the south-western counties, the Bristol slave-dealers raising the average of Gloucestershire to 24 per cent., and Cornwall coming next with 21 slaves to every hundred men in the county. The population of Devonshire is given as 17,434, but this is with one exception only the male population, and leaves out both women and children. There were—

Tenants in capite	77
Under-tenants	402
Villani	8070
Bordarii	4847
Cotarii, in some way distinguished from them	19
Coscez, who paid rent as well as service	70
Coliberti, who held their freedom of tenure	32
Buri, under condition of certain works	4
Porcarii	294
Burgenses, citizens, in Barnstaple	67
,, ,, Lideford	69
,, ,, Luperige (N. Huish)	1
,, ,, Exeter	13
,, ,, Okehampton	4
,, ,, Totenais (Totnes)	110
Homines, including Feuditories	3
Francigenæ, Normans, as distinguished from Angli	3
Ferrarii, iron-workers, not carpenters	4
Fabri, smiths either in wood or iron	2
Salinarii, salters	48
Servi, slaves who tilled the land	3294
Ancilla, or female slave	1

Mr. Seebohm calculates that at the time of the Domesday Survey about five millions of acres were under the plough in England, and this is from one-third to one-half the arable acreage now.

An example or two from our own neighbourhood[1] may serve to enable us to realize the condition of Devonshire 800 years ago. The Exeter Domesday says:

Bishop Osbern has a manor called St. Mary Church, which Bishop Leofric held on the day on which King Edward was (alive) and dead, and it rendered geld for two virgates. These can be ploughed by three ploughs. There the Bishop has in demesne one virgate and one plough, and the villeins have one virgate and two ploughs. There the Bishop has four villeins, and four bordars, and 64 sheep; and it is worth yearly 15 shillings; and this (manor) is part of the sustenance of the Canons.

As Leofric was the first Bishop of Exeter, we may presume that this manor of St. Mary Church was the origin of the vicarage being in the gift of the Chapter of Exeter. The remains of the Bishop of Exeter's manor-house at Paignton still exist. We find

Bishop Osbern has a manor called Paignton (Peintona), which Bishop Leofric held on the day on which King Edward was alive and dead, and it rendered geld for twenty hides. These can be ploughed by 60 ploughs. Of them the Bishop has in demesne six hides and eight ploughs; and the villeins have 14 hides and forty-two ploughs. There the Bishop has 52 villeins, and 40 bordars, and 36 *servi*, and five swineherds who render 50 swine, and four pack-horses, and a salt-work which renders ten pence, and 20 head of cattle, and 16 pigs, 350 sheep, and 41 acres of wood, and 18 acres of

---

[1] The author was living at St. Mary Church, near Torquay, when this paper was written. It would be easy to find examples from any other locality.

meadow, and 40 of pasture; and it is worth yearly fifty pounds; and when he received it, it was worth thirteen pounds.

The Committee of the Devonshire Association, in their reprint of the Devonshire Domesday, have translated *servi* by the word "serfs." But it must be remembered that the *villani*, and *bordarii* were also serfs, though not slaves. The *servi* were perhaps slaves holding land, and thus in the process of becoming serfs. The Saxons called the *villani* by the name of "gebur," and the land held in villenage was called "geneat-land," and sometimes "Gafol-land." The *servi*, or slaves, were called "theows."

Mr. Seebohm quotes from a Saxon MS. dialogue of Aelfric a passage which sheds much light on the condition of a "theow" in the tenth century. The "theow" is a ploughman, or "yrthling:"

"What sayest thou, ploughman? How dost thou do thy work?"

"Oh, my lord, hard do I work. I go out at daybreak driving the oxen to field, and I yoke them to the plough. Nor is it ever so hard winter that I dare loiter at home, for fear of my lord, but the oxen yoked, and the ploughshare and coulter fastened to the plough, every day must I plough a full acre or more."

"Hast thou any comrade?"

"I have a boy driving the oxen with an iron goad, who also is hoarse with cold and shouting."

"What more dost thou in the day?"

"Verily then I do more. I must fill the bin of the

oxen with hay, and water them, and carry out the dung. Ha! ha! hard work it is, hard work it is! because I am not free."[1]

"Perhaps," Mr. Seebohm remarks, "some day his lord will provide him with an outfit of oxen, give him a yard-land, and make him into a 'gebur' instead of a 'theow.' This at least seems to be his yearning."

The *Rectitudines*, or "the services due from various persons," a Saxon work of the tenth century, gives details of the services due to the king from the "thane," who held his land by military tenure, which included (1) the obligation to attend the king in his military expeditions, (2) to assist in building his castles, or "burh-bot," (3) to maintain the bridges, or "brig-bote." The "geneat's" services are very similar to those of the villein under Edward the First. The cottiers' services are like those of the bordar in the later times. From passages in King Alfred's works, Mr. Seebohm is able to give a fairly complete idea of the way in which the Saxon manors were formed out of the "folk-land," originally held by the king as conqueror:

The young thane, with his lord's permission, makes a clearing in the forest, building his log hut and then other log huts for his servants. At first it is forest game on which he lives. By-and-by the cluster of huts becomes a little hamlet of homesteads. He provides his servants with their outfits of oxen, and they become his "geburs." The cleared land is measured out by

[1] Op. cit. p. 166.

rods into acres. The acres ploughed by the common plough are allotted in rotation to the yard-lands. A new hamlet has grown up in the royal forest, or in the outlying woods of an old *ham* or manor. In the meantime the king perhaps rewards his industrious thane, who had made the clearing in his forest, with a grant of the estate with the village upon it, as his boc-land for ever, and it becomes a manor; or the lord of the old manor, of which it is a hamlet, grants to him the inheritance, and the hamlet becomes a subject manor held of the higher lord. (p. 172.)

Sir Thomas Smith has told us in general terms how the emancipation of slaves was affected, but it is interesting to mark the actual process, in the ancient records of England.

The Penitential of Archbishop Theodore (670—690) enacts :

If a man leads astray his slave-girl, he shall set her free, and do penance for six months.

A whole section is devoted to regulations on slaves,[1] from which it appears that—

1. A father compelled by necessity has the power of giving into slavery his son for seven years, after which he has no power of doing so without the consent of the son.

2. A youth of fourteen can make himself a slave.

3. It is not lawful for a man to take away from his slave the money which he has acquired by his own labour.

A little later, about 692, one of the Dooms of Ine King of Wessex enacts :

---

[1] Lib. ii. c. xiii. *De servis et ancillis.*

If a theowman work on a Sunday by his lord's command, let him be free; and let the lord pay xxx. shillings as wite. But if the theow work without his knowledge, let him suffer in his hyde, or in hyde-gyld. But if a freeman work on that day without his lord's command, let him forfeit his freedom, or sixty shillings; and let a priest be liable two-fold.[1]

These laws show that slavery was deeply engrained in the habits of the Saxons. They had enslaved the whole population of Britain, and they used even to sell their own children into slavery. In time the firm though gentle pressure of Christian influence first mitigated the evil, and then gradually obliterated it. A letter of Archbishop Brihtwald, Theodore's successor in 709, to Forthere, Bishop of Sherborne, shows how tenaciously even a monk could maintain his right to a slave, though pressed by an Archbishop to surrender it:

My request, by which I besought in your presence the venerable Abbot Beorwald, to grant the redemption of a captive girl, who is proved to have relatives in our neighbourhood, has come to nothing, though I hoped it would have been granted. I am now again moved by their entreaties, and have deemed it most advantageous to send this letter to you by a cousin of the same girl, named Eppa. Hereby I implore you yourself to obtain without fail from the aforesaid Abbot, his acceptance for the same girl of 300 solidi from the hand of the bearer of these presents, and hand her over to him that she may pass the rest of her life with

---

[1] Thorpe, vol. i. p. 105. See also p. 403, where this is repeated under Canute.

her own kindred, not in the sadness of slavery, but in the gladness of liberty. And when your benevolence shall have brought this affair to pass, you will have a reward from God, and from me hearty thanks. And even our brother Beorwald loses by it, in my estimation, none of the rights which he justly possesses in her. What I ought to have done before, I now beseech you, that when in your frequent prayers you make mention of yourself, you would at the same time deign to make mention of me. May our Lord Jesus Christ preserve your Reverence safely in a prolonged life!¹

This letter, so full of Christian charity, is a pleasing memorial of the first Archbishop of Canterbury who was an Englishman.

In 681, the indefatigable St. Wilfrid, who had once narrowly escaped slavery at the hands of the still pagan inhabitants of Sussex, nobly repaid them good for evil by preaching to them the Gospel, and teaching them how to make fishing-nets. The South Saxons and their King were converted, and bestowed on their Apostle a considerable tract of land, on which St. Wilfrid found 250 slaves of both sexes. Bede says, "He not only saved them by baptizing them from the slavery of the devil, but by giving them all their liberty he also delivered them from the yoke of slavery to man."² Five years later, Ceadwalla, the warlike young King of Wessex, who though not yet a Christian, conceived a great veneration for St. Wilfrid, vowed, when he rushed to the

---

¹ Inter *Epist. S. Bonif.* n. 7 : Jaffé, *Monum. Moguntin.*
² *H.E.* iv. c. 14.

slaughter of the Jutes, who inhabited the Isle of Wight, that he would give a quarter of the island to the God of Wilfrid. He kept his vow, and Wilfrid found himself the owner of 300 families, whom he emancipated, and instructed in the Faith, appointing one of his clergy to be their pastor. Mr. Green, in his *Short History*, thus sums up the chief steps by which slavery was uprooted from its tenacious hold on the Saxons:

Slavery was gradually disappearing before the efforts of the Church. Theodore had denied Christian burial to the kidnapper, and prohibited the sale of children by their parents after the age of seven. Egbert of York punished any sale of child or kinsfolk with excommunication. The murder of a slave by lord or mistress, though no crime in the eye of the State, became a sin for which penance was due to the Church. . . . Athelstan gave the slave-class a new rank in the realm by extending to it the same principles of mutual responsibility for crime which were the basis of order among the free. Manumissions became frequent in wills, as the clergy taught that such a gift was a boon to the soul of the dead. At the Synod of Calcuith, the bishops bound themselves to free, at their decease, all serfs on their estates who had been reduced to serfdom by want or crime. Usually the slave was set free before the altar or in the church-porch, and the Gospel-book bore written on its margins the record of his emancipation.[1]

The Book of the Bodmin Gospels, now in the British Museum, a MS. of the ninth century, bears on its fly-leaves the records of some fifty of these manumissions, extending from A.D. 941 to 1043,

[1] *History of English People*, p. 54.

granted at the altar of St. Petroc. Here are a few examples at random:

These are the names of those people: Huna and his sister Dolo, whom Byrhtflaed set free for the redemption of her soul on the Altar of St. Petroc, before these witnesses: Leofric, priest; Budda, priest; Morhaytho, priest; Devi, priest; Hresmen, deacon; Custentin, layman; Wurlowen, layman: that they may have their liberty with their seed for ever. And cursed be he who shall infringe this liberty.

Bishop Wulfsige set free Inaprost with his sons for the soul of King Edgar, and for his own soul, before these witnesses: Byrhsige, priest; Electus, priest; Abel, priest; Morhatho, deacon; Canretho, deacon; Riol, deacon.

These are the names of the sons, Wurcon, Æthan, Junerth, Worfothu, Guruaret, whose sons, and grandsons, and all their posterity, defended themselves upon oath, by permission of King Edgar, because, by the accusation of evil men, their fathers were said to have been villeins (*coloni*) of the King: Comoere, the Bishop, witness; witness, Ælfsie, priest; witness, Dofagan; witness, March; witness, Ælfnoth; witness, Byrhtsie, priest; witness, Mitcuuth, priest; witness, Abel, priest.[1]

Lingard gives some examples of freedom being purchased:

Elfry the Red bought himself out for one pound. Brightmær purchased the freedom of himself, his wife Ælgiva, their children and grandchildren, for two pounds. Siwin bought Sydefleda into perpetual freedom for five shillings and some pence. Ægilmær bought Sethfryth for three mancuses, to be free after the death of himself and his wife.[2]

---

[1] Oliver, *Monasticon Exon.* pp. 431—433.
[2] Lingard, i. c. vii. p. 418, note.

On the other hand, slaves were sold during the whole of the Saxon period like cattle. A slave was usually valued at four times as much as an ox.

John bought Gunilda from Gada for half a pound of silver, and gave her to the Church of St. Peter. Wulfric bought Elfgitha for half a pound. Egilsig bought Wynric for an yre of gold.[1]

The Danes carried away into slavery numbers of the inhabitants of the countries they ravaged; but it is remarkable that the Danish settlements in England are precisely those districts in which, at the time of the Doomsday Survey, there were extremely few slaves and a large proportion of freemen. William of Malmesbury tells us that the mother of the celebrated Earl Godwin "was in the habit of purchasing companies of slaves in England and sending them to Denmark; more especially girls, whose beauty and age rendered them more valuable, that she might accumulate money by this horrid traffic." He says that she "paid the penalty of her cruelty, being killed by a stroke of lightning."[2] He also mentions that the Saxons made money by their female slaves, by selling them for infamous purposes.[3] So inveterate was the habit of slavery in the Saxon race, that as late as 1102, in a Council held in London under St Anselm, it was necessary to pass a canon, expressly forbidding—

That any one presume henceforth in any way to carry on that nefarious merchandise, in which up to this time

[1] Lye, App. v.   [2] *Chron.* ii. c. 13.   [3] *Ib.* iii.

men in England have been accustomed to be sold like brute animals.[1]

The Bristol merchants were the worst offenders in this respect; their agents travelled all over the country, giving the highest price for pregnant women, and shipping them off to Ireland, where they were sure of a ready market. In vain did the magistrates strive to repress this infamous trade. At length, St. Wulstan, Bishop of Worcester, one of the greatest preachers of his day, visited Bristol year after year, and used all his efforts to induce them to give up the practice. He then took up his abode in the town for some months, and preached every Sunday against the barbarity and wickedness of the dealers in slaves. At last the merchants were convinced, and in their guild solemnly bound themselves to renounce the traffic. One of the members soon afterwards violated his engagement, and was punished by the loss of his eyes.

William the Conqueror not only confirmed the laws already cited in favour of the slaves, but facilitated their manumission. Thus:

We forbid that any one sell a man out of the country. But if any one wishes to make his slave free, let him lead him by the hand to the sheriff in full session, and hand him over to him, and by manumission grant him quit-claim from the yoke of servitude, and show him free ways, and gates, and hand him the arms of freedom, viz., a lance and sword; then shall he be made a freeman.

[1] Can. 28.

The next law opens another door for freedom:

Also, if slaves shall have remained without denunciation for a year and a day in our cities, or boroughs, or walled towns, or castles, from that day forward they shall become free, and shall be for ever freed from the yoke of bondage.[1]

It thus appears that, as far as it is possible to go back in the history of the Anglo-Saxons in this country, we meet with the same distinctions between slaves and serfs that we saw in Gaul, when the Franks and Germans had settled themselves in the land. Those distinctions existed all over the Roman Empire; and as these barbarians established themselves permanently in the countries that they conquered, they learned to admire and adopt the wise legislation of the Roman law, as reformed by Christianity, and preserved in the Codes of Theodosius and Justinian. Britain, in the fourth and fifth centuries, formed no exception to the rest of the Roman Empire; although, during the period that elapsed between the departure of the Roman legions and King Vortigern's fatal invitation of the Saxons, the orderly condition of a Roman colony must have given place to a state of considerable confusion. The Romano-British villas, which became the manors of later times, were exposed to the plundering inroads of Picts, and Scots or Irish, who carried off into slavery many of the inhabitants. Before examining the social

[1] Thorpe, *Laws*, i. pp. 493, 494.

condition of the British, or Welsh as they were afterwards called, it will be useful to consider the condition of Ireland with regard to slavery.

2.—*Ireland.*

About twenty years before the Saxons came, Pope Celestine sent Germanus, the saintly Bishop of Auxerre, to assist the Bishops of Britain to withstand the inroads of Pelagianism; and he was accompanied, in 430, by a monk, commissioned by the same Pope to preach the Gospel to the Irish. This monk had been himself carried into slavery in his youth, either from the greater or the lesser Britain; but was now returning good for evil, and was to be known throughout all time as St. Patrick, the Apostle of Ireland. Ireland had never been conquered by the Romans. Its laws were enshrined in the memories and traditions of an hereditary caste of lawyers, called the Brehons; and it is one of the greatest wonders that St. Patrick worked, that within a few years of his arrival, the whole Irish nation should have allowed a stranger Missionary Bishop to revise and correct their ancient laws, and bring them into conformity with the laws of Christ. The most ancient Code of Brehon Law, the *Senchus Môr*, says:

Every law which is here was binding until the two laws were established. The law of nature was with the men of Erin, until the coming of the Faith in the time of Laeghaire, son of Nial. It was in his time that Patrick came to Erin. . . . Dubhthach Mac Ua Lugair, the poet, exhibited the law of nature; it was Dubhthach that first gave honourable respect to Patrick; he was the first who rose up before him at Temhair. . . . There are many things that come into the law of nature which do not come into the written law. Dubhthach showed these to Patrick; what did not disagree with the Word of God in the written law, and with the consciences of the faithful, was retained in the Brehon law-code by the Church and the poets.[1]

The account given of the revision by St. Patrick of the ancient laws of Ireland in the *Senchus Môr*, is so picturesque that we do not like to paraphrase it:

Patrick requested of the men of Erin to come to one place to hold a conference with him. When they came to the place of conference the Gospel of Christ was preached to them all; and when the men of Erin heard of the killing of the living and the resuscitation of the dead, and all the power of Patrick since his arrival in Erin; and when they saw Laeghaire with his druids overcome by the great signs and miracles wrought in the presence of the men of Erin, they bowed down, in obedience to the will of God and Patrick. Then Laeghaire said: "It is necessary for you, O men of Erin, that every other law should be settled and arranged by us, as well as this." "It is better to do so," said Patrick. It was then that all the professors of the sciences in Erin were assembled, and each of them exhibited his art before Patrick, in the presence of every chief in Erin.

It was then that Dubhthach was ordered to exhibit the judgments and all the poetry of Erin, and every law which prevailed among the men of Erin, through the law of nature, and the law of the seers, and in the judgments of the island of Erin, and in the poets. They had fore-

---

[1] *Senchus Môr*, vol. iii. p. 32.

told that the bright word of blessing would come, *i.e.* the law of the letter; for it was the Holy Spirit that spoke and prophesied through the mouths of the just men who were formerly in the island of Erin, as He had prophesied through the mouths of the chief prophets and noble fathers in the Patriarchal law; for the law of nature had prevailed where the written law did not reach.

Now the judgments of true nature which the Holy Spirit had spoken through the mouths of the Brehons and just poets of the men of Erin, from the first occupation of this island, down to the reception of the Faith, were all exhibited by Dubhthach to Patrick. What did not clash with the Word of God in the written law and in the New Testament, and with the consciences of the faithful, was confirmed in the laws of the Brehons by Patrick and by the ecclesiastics and the chieftains of Erin; for the law of nature had been quite right, except the Faith and its obligations, and the harmony of the Church and the people. And this is the *Senchus Môr*. (Vol. i. pp. 16, 17.)

The very first statement of this Christianized Brehon Code is:

The enslaved shall be freed, and plebeians shall be exalted by receiving Church grades (*i.e.* Holy Orders), and by performing penitential service to God (*i.e.* pilgrimages); for the Lord is accessible; He will not refuse any kind of person after faith, either among the noble or the plebeian tribes; so likewise is the Church open for every person who goes under her rule. (*Ibid.* vol. i. p. 31.)

A story, which formed an important precedent in Brehon law, is related in the *Senchus Môr*, and gives an idea of what Irish slavery was before St. Patrick came :

There were three principal races in Erin, the Feini, the Ulaidh, and the Galeoin. And there was a great dissension among the Feini, between Conn of the hundred battles and Eochaidh Belbuidhe, grandson of Tuathal Techtmar. Eochaidh Belbuidhe, after having committed great ravages, was expelled by Conn, and fled to Fergus, son of Leidi, King of Uladh, and remained some time with him. One day Eochaidh set out to go to his tribe to demand justice, but was met at Sliabhfuait by Asal, son of Conn, and by the four sons of Buidhe, and by Fotline, the son whom Dorn, the daughter of Buidhe, brought forth to a stranger, and they slew Eochaidh Belbuidhe, who was under the protection of Fergus. Fergus went with forces from the north to demand satisfaction, and justice was ceded to him, *i.e.* three times seven *cumhals:* seven cumhals of gold, and seven cumhals of silver, and land of seven cumhals, for the crime of the five natives; and Dorn, the daughter of Buidhe, was given as a pledge for the crime of her son. After this, Fergus made a perfect covenant respecting this *eric-fine*, and returned to his own country, having his bondmaid with him in bondage.

Fergus had obtained from the fairies the power of passing under water, but they had forbidden him to enter the Lough Rudhraidhe in his own territory. One day Fergus took it into his head to enter Lough Rudhraidhe, and as he went into the Lough, he saw in it the Muidris, a frightful sea-monster. One moment it used to contract, and then dilate like a smith's bellows. On his beholding it his mouth became distended to both his ears, and he fled out of the Lough from fear, and he said to his charioteer: "How do I look?" The charioteer replied: "Thy aspect is not good, but it shall not be so long; sleep will restore thee." Upon which Fergus went into his chariot and slept.

Now while he slept, the charioteer went to the wise men of Ulster, who were at Emhain-Macha, and told them the adventures of the King, and what was the matter with him. And he asked them what King they would have after him, for it was not easy to keep a king with a blemish at Emhain. The advice of the wise men was that the King should return to his house, which should be cleared before him of rabble, that there might be no fools or idiots in it, or persons who would reproach the King with the blemish on his face, and that a muddy bath should be prepared for him, that he might not see his shadow in the water. And so they kept the King in this manner for three years ignorant of his own blemish. At last one day he bade his bondmaid make a bath for him. He thought that the woman was making the bath too slowly, and he gave her a stroke of his horsewhip. She became vexed, and reproached the King with his blemish; whereupon he gave her a blow with his sword and divided her in twain.

He then went off and plunged into Lough Rudhraidhe, where he remained a day and a night, and fought the sea-monster. He afterwards appeared on the surface of the Lough, having the head of the sea-monster in his hand, so that all the Ulster men saw him, and he said to them: "I am the survivor, O men of Ulster!" He then descended into the Lough, and died.

After this the Feini demanded eric-fine for their bondmaid and the restoration of their land. A balance was struck between the crimes. Eochaidh Belbuidhe was killed while under the protection of Fergus, who, being the king of a province, was entitled to eighteen cumhals, both as irar-fine and honour-price for the violation of his protection; there were also due to him nine cumhals for his half irar-fine and half honour-price, in compensation for Dorn having reproached him with his blemish, so that this was twenty-seven cumhals due to Fergus. Honour-price was demanded by the Feini for the killing of the pledge, and for that twenty-three cumhals were payable by him. Buidhe was entitled to honour-price for the killing of his daughter, six cumhals, for his rank was that of an Aire-forgill of the middle rank. Her brother was entitled to four cumhals, so that the men of the South demanded thirty-three cumhals and the men of the North demanded twenty-seven; and a balance was struck between them, and it was found that an excess of six cumhals was due by the men of the North, for which the land of Inbher Debline was again restored.[1]

This curious story throws much light on the state of slavery in Ireland before that nation received the Christian faith. In the first place, the word *cumhal* means a female slave, and this being the unit of currency shows that slavery was deeply rooted in the ancient institutions of the people. Then, Dorn being given as a bondmaid, as a compensation for the crime of her son, shows that free persons might easily be reduced to slavery. Her duties were simply those of a household slave, and she was by no means detained as a hostage in honourable captivity. Her master beats her with his horsewhip when he thinks her lazy; and, though her spirit resents this treatment, yet the blow is not mentioned as an injustice. Even her death is held to be deserved for her rude speech to the King, and compensation is only due for the wrong done

[1] *Senchus Mór*, vol. i. pp. 71—77.

to her father and brother. The system of compensation for every kind of injury to life or limb, which runs through the Brehon laws, was common to all ancient nations. The minute and complicated distinctions and refinements of the fines, and exemptions of the Brehon laws, is what might be expected, when there was a caste of professional lawyers, by whose decisions every dispute had to be settled.

There is very little in those laws relating to slaves, but incidental notices show that they were regarded as chattels. Thus:

Distress of three days [by which is meant that the person injured could retain for three days any property of the injured that he could lay his hands on, without incurring any counter-claim for damages], for cutting thy wood, for breaking thy land, for injury caused to thy fence, thy ploughed land, thy weir, for scaring thy horses, for carrying off thy pet animals, for grinding in thy mill, for taking possession of thy house, for stripping it, burning it, or opening it, for carrying off thy bondman, thy bondmaid. (p. 163.)

In the *Cain-Lanamna*, or Law of Social Connections, eight of such connections are legislated for: "The chief with his 'aigillne-tenants;' the Church with her tenants of ecclesiastical lands; the father with his daughter; a daughter with her brother; a son with his mother; a foster-son with his foster-mother; a tutor with his pupil; a man with a woman." The respective rights of these various parties are minutely laid down, for instance: "The woman may entertain half the company of the man, according to the dignity of the man." That is, if a lady give a party to her friends, she can only give them half the quantity of food that she has to provide for her husband's guests. Again, we learn that: "The corn is divided into three parts, *i.e.*, one-third for the owner of the land, one-third for the owner of the seed, and one-third for the person who has done the work." But in all these regulations there is no mention whatever of the relations between a slave and his master.

In Ireland there was no place for serfdom.[1] Each sept or clan possessed in common the land belonging to it, and the occupants held it under certain conditions from the "tanist," or chief, who alone had property out of which he could not be ousted. "On the death of the tanist, or head of a sept, his successor (who was not necessarily his son, but elected and adopted during his lifetime) assembled all the males of the sept, and divided the lands at his discretion between them." The English lords in the sixteenth century, to whom were granted the confiscated land of the Irish tanists, took the place of the chieftain, and kept the occupiers still tenants at will; but, as the sept no longer elected him, they had no sort of voice in the matter, and practically sank into a worse position than the medieval serfs. The English and Scotch farmers

---

[1] This statement may be thought too absolute, especially after Professor W. K. Sullivan's learned Introduction to O'Curry's *Lectures on Irish Antiquities*, in which he tries to identify the various classes of *daer-ceilles* with the classes of Saxon serfs. Space will not admit of a discussion of the question here, but the reader is referred to Dr. Sullivan's treatise.

who settled in Ulster refused to hold land on these terms, and obtained the extension of the English system to that province, or the "Ulster Tenant Right." This survival of the worst part of the tribal system, even to our own day, has been the chronic source of difficulty in the relations between landlord and tenant in Ireland. In ancient times, the absence of a class of serfs bound to the soil, and not liable to be removed from it, probably delayed the emancipation of the slaves; for it left no middle condition between slavery and freedom, such as we have seen in countries under the operation of the modified Roman law. There does not seem to be any solid ground for supposing, as some writers have done, that the distinction between the *saer-tenant* and *daer-tenant* can rightly be rendered by the terms "free-tenancy" and "servile-tenure." In both cases the chief supplied stock to the occupier of the land. The *saer-tenant* had his stock without giving any security for it, but he was bound to attend his chief on military expeditions. The *daer-tenant* was required to give security for the stock, but was not eligible for military service.

The true distinction between *saer-tenant* and the *daer-tenant* seems to be, that certain Irish tribes have been conquered by others, and reduced to the position of tributaries; and when land in their possession, but which they did not cultivate, was occupied by members of a non-tributary tribe, the occupants had to pay the tribute levied on the land. These were *saer-tenants*, while the members of the tributary tribe were *daer-tenants*. In this sense the learned Mr. John O'Donovan styles them "serfs" in his treatise on the *Tribes and Customs of the Hy-Many:*

The O'Mailfinnains were originally a noble Scotic or Milesian family, who were banished from their own territory, and were obliged to settle in Hy-Many, as serfs to the O'Kelly. The celebrated antiquary, Duald MacFirbis, in his interesting Preface to his smaller genealogical work, compiled in 1666, gives us the following account of the six classes of plebeian families in ancient Ireland:

1. The remnant of the Firbolgs and Tuatha De Dannanns.

2. The descendants of the Scotic or Milesian nobility, who left their own territories and were obliged to enslave themselves under other tribes.

3. Those tribes whose lands were converted into sword-lands, or who were enslaved by enemies.

4. Descendants of the Milesian nobility, who lost their dignity and lands for their crimes, according to the law.

5. Those who were descended from common soldiers and foreigners.

6. The descendants of the slaves who came with the sons of Milesius into Ireland, and who were never able to get beyond their caste. (Op. cit. p. 85, note.)

In his "Introductory Remarks," Mr. O'Donovan gives some extracts from the *Life of St. Grellan,* by the same Duald MacFirbis, which show how the territory was occupied by the conquerors:

It was at this period the race of Colla da Chrioch meditated to migrate from Oirghialla, and they said: "Numerous are the heroes and great is our population, our tribe having multiplied, and we cannot all find room in any one province without quarrelling among ourselves, for nobles cannot well bear to be confined;" and they also said: "Let us see which province of Banba is thinnest in population, and in which most Firbolgs remain; and let us narrow it on them. The province of Connaught is in the possession of these Attacots, excepting that they pay tribute to our relative, and let us attack it." (Op. cit. p. 9.)

It is rather sad to read that St. Grellan sided with the invaders, and by his prayers gained them the victory and the destruction of the unfortunate Firbolgs.

Some extracts from another work of Mr. O'Donovan, will explain what has been said above concerning the *saer-tenants*.

> Of the same tribute, it was heard,
>   Without injustice, without tyranny,
>   Thrice fifty oxen on a day hither
>   To supply the ploughing.
> Although the Luighne bring hither
>   Their tribute for their territory,
>   It is not the tribes here are ignoble,
>   But the grass and the land (are liable).[1]

The territory of Luighne, or Gaileanga, anciently belonged to an enslaved tribe of the Firbolgs, who inhabited this country down to the third century. The same work shows how completely slaves were regarded as chattels in ancient Ireland.

> Entitled is the rapid King of Laeghaire (a territory in E. Meath)
>   To ten strong steeds in his territory,
>   Ten bondmen, ten large women,
>   Ten hounds, ten horns for drinking.

[1] *The Book of Rights*, p. 105.

The stipend of the noble King of Ardgha (is)
    Seven shields, seven steeds out of Alba (Scotland),
    Seven large women, seven bondmen,
    And seven hounds (all) of the same kind. (Op. cit. p. 179.)

Eight steeds to the Ui Bairrche (near Carlow) for their vigor,
    'Twas but small for a man of his (their chieftain's) prowess,
    Eight drinking-horns, eight women, not slaves,
    And eight bondmen, brave (and) large. (*Ib.* p. 213.)

Further on the chronicler distinguishes between the free tribute (*saer-chisa*), and the tribute exacted from the *daer-clanna*:

The free-tributes, as I have heard,
    Are they which we have above mentioned,
    Of the noble tribes these are due,
    Who are upon lands external (to the mensal lands).

The unfree tribes—a condition not oppressive,
    That are on his (the King of Leinster's) own lands:
    Servile rent by them, it is the truth,
    Is to be supplied to the palaces of the chief King.

The tribute which is due of these
    (Is) of fire-bote and wood;
    (Also) the renewing of his cloaks, constant the practice,
    A tribute in washing and in cleansing.

There is due of the best party of them
    Ruu and purple of fine strength,
    Red thread, white wool, I will not conceal it,
    Yellow blaan and binnean.

From the unfree tribes of ignoble countenance,
    Who fly with the rent from the land,
    Twice as much is due
    As they carried off from their father-land.
                        (*Ib.* pp. 223—225.)

We have seen how St. Patrick obtained the modification of the old law, so as to have it enacted that a slave obtained freedom by becoming a cleric, or a monk or a nun; and we may be sure that other modes of facilitating enfranchisement were encouraged by him and his successors. We have preserved to us a powerful letter of remonstrance which he addressed to "the Christian subjects of the tyrant Caroticus," King of the Welsh, complaining bitterly of the savage inroad of a band of his soldiers, who had slain and carried into captivity a great number of his recent converts :

On the very day after they had received as neophytes the Chrism of Confirmation, while it shone on their foreheads, and they still wore their white robes, they were mangled and slain with the sword by the above-mentioned. And I sent a letter by a holy priest, whom I taught from his infancy, with some clerics, begging that they would restore us some of the prey or the baptized captives, whom they had taken, but they laughed at them. . . . I beseech you, therefore, earnestly who are holy and humble of heart, that you will not flatter these wicked men, and that you will neither take food nor drink with them, nor receive their alms, until they do penance with many tears, and liberate the servants of God, and the baptized handmaids of Christ, for whom He was crucified and died. . . . It is the custom of the Christians of Rome and Gaul to send holy men to the Franks and other nations, with many thousand solidi, to redeem baptized captives. You who slay them, and sell them to foreign nations who know not God, deliver the members of Christ, as it were, to a den of wolves . . . The Church laments and wails over her sons and daughters, not slain by the sword, but sent away to distant lands, where sin is more grievous and abounds more shamelessly.[1]

He conjures whoever receives this letter to read it before Caroticus and all the people, "that they

---

[1] See original, given in Miss Cusack's *Life of St. Patrick*, vol. ii. p. 646.

may liberate the baptized captives, and repent for their murder of the Lord's brethren."

These unfortunate captives, who were sold into slavery to the Pagan Picts, may perhaps have prepared the way for the subsequent conversion of the Picts by St. Columba and the monks of Iona. Long afterwards, in the year 684, Bede tells us that—

Egfrid, King of the Northumbrians, sent Beort, his general, with an army, into Ireland, and miserably wasted that harmless nation, which had always been most friendly to the English.[1]

The Irish Annalists add that the Saxons—

Spared neither the people nor the clergy, and carried off to their ships many captives and much booty.[2]

Bede attributes the misfortunes that fell upon the Northumbrians to this atrocious outrage, and the Irish historians say that when Egfrid was succeeded by his brother Aldfrid, who had studied for many years in Ireland,

Adamnan, the saintly Abbot of Iona, was sent to that country for the purpose of recovering the captives and property carried off by Egfrid's pirates.[3]

The monks of Iona had, before this, been zealous in the mitigation of the evils of slavery, both among the Picts and Saxons. Thus, it is related of St. Aidan, the Apostle of Northumbria, a monk

---

[1] *H. E.* iv. p. 26. [2] *Four Masters*, p. 385.
[3] Lanigan, iii. p. 96.

of Iona, in the interesting sketch of him by Bede, that—

> He never gave money to the powerful men of the world, but only meat if he happened to entertain them; and, on the contrary, whatsoever gifts of money he received from the rich, he either distributed them to the use of the poor, or bestowed them in ransoming such as had been wrongfully sold for slaves.[1]

Still, it is sadly true that slavery remained in Ireland to a very late period, and the Bristol merchants drove a thriving trade in slaves with the Irish. Even towards the end of the twelfth century many English slaves were in bondage in Ireland, until St. Laurence O'Toole, Archbishop of Dublin, moved a Plenary Synod at Armagh, in 1170, to recognize the invasion of Strongbow as a sign of Divine anger with the Irish for their slaveholding, and the whole clergy issued a peremptory admonition, that all the English throughout Ireland who might happen to be in a state of slavery, should be restored to their original liberty. We do not hear of slavery again in Ireland, until Oliver Cromwell sold thousands of the people and shipped them off as slaves to Barbadoes, and it is a strange thing to read that the Bristol merchants were the agents in this detestable traffic, and revived the ill-fame of their predecessors in the twelfth century. Even in the present century, when Edmund Burke took part with Wilberforce in the abolition of the slave trade, the Bristol merchants ejected him from his seat for that city.

[1] *H. E.* iii. p. 52.

3.—Wales.

We have seen the Welsh, or, if we prefer to call them so, the Britons of the fifth century, carrying Irish Christians into slavery, and selling them to the Picts. In the following century, Gildas draws a dark picture of the state of corruption into which both princes and people had fallen, and slavery appears to have been very prevalent among them. An ancient Canon, which Mr. Haddan ascribes to the sixth century, ordains:

> If a man commit murder intentionally, let him give three men-slaves and three women-slaves, and let him receive assurance of safety.[1]

Similar penalties are exacted for other crimes. In one case, where the penalty is "half a bondmaid," it is added, "that is, half the price of a slave." This is the penalty for cutting off a man's thumb. Another Canon says:

> If a man has bought a male or female slave, and within the year some unsoundness is found in them, we order the slave to be handed back to the former master; but if a year has elapsed, whatever defect may be found in the slave, the buyer has no claim.[2]

A Canon exactly similar follows with regard to a horse; only the time is a month instead of a year. Another Canon relates to runaway slaves. A later Canon provides:

---

[1] *Councils*, &c., Stubbs and Haddan, vol. i, p. 127.
[2] *Ib.* p. 131, Can. 28.

If a man wish to marry his female slave, he has also power over all that she has. But, if afterwards he should wish to sell her, he cannot be allowed. And if he makes up his mind to sell her, we command him to be condemned, and the bondmaid to be placed under the protection of the priest.[1]

On the margin of an Irish MS. of the Gospels, formerly at Llandaff, afterwards at Lichfield under the name of the Book of St. Chad, is the record of the manumission of a slave and his family on payment of a sum of money which cannot now be ascertained.

An ancient Welsh MS., called the "Brut y Tywysog, Gwent," tells us—

In the year of Christ 926, Howel the Good, son of Cadell, King of all Wales, went to Rome, and three Bishops with him. . . . The reason they went there was, to consult the wise in what manner to improve the laws of Wales, and to ascertain the laws of other countries and cities, and the laws in force in Britain during the sovereignty of the Emperors of Rome. And after obtaining information of these things, and the counsel of the wise, they returned to Britain, where Howel convoked all the heads of tribes of the country and their assistants, and all the wise and learned, ecclesiastical and lay, in a combined session at the White House upon Tav (near the site of Whitland Abbey in Carmarthenshire), in Dyved (or West Wales); and after the laws had been all made and completely written, Howel the Good, accompanied by Princes of the Welsh, and three Bishops, and the Archdeacon of Landaff, went again to Rome, to Pope Anastasius, to read the law, and to see if there

---

[1] *Councils*, &c., Stubbs and Haddan, p. 137, Can. 60.

were anything contrary to the law of God in it. And as there was nothing militating against it, it was confirmed, and was called the law of Howel the Good from that time forward.[1]

In these laws, of which three versions are extant, the Venedotian, Dimetian, and Gwentian Codes, little mention is made of slavery. But a few instances will show that it was a practical reality in Wales in the tenth century. Thus:

Three persons who are not to receive "galanas" (blood-fine), ... the third is a bondman, there is no galanas for him; only payment of his worth to his master, like the worth of a beast.[2]

From the *Anomalous Welsh Laws*, published by Thorpe, it appears that if a bondman's son become a cleric, or a bard, or a smith, he thereby gains his freedom; but his sons are bondmen, unless they belong to one of these privileged classes.[3]

There were certain privileges belonging to every true born Welshman, which are thus enumerated:

Three original privileges of every native Cymro, the grant and fruition of five free erws (acres), under the privileges of his origin as an innate Cymro; and the issue of an aillt (alien) and stranger obtain this in the fourth person (generation) by legitimate marriages, that is, in the degree of scisor; the privilege of bearing defensive arms, with their emblems, for that is not allowed but to an innate Cymro of warranted descent; and the privilege of raith (or verdict) under the protection of

---

[1] *Councils*, &c., Stubbs and Haddan, vol. i. p. 209.
[2] Thorpe, vol. i. p. 599.   [3] Op. cit. ii. p. 327.

his chief of kindred; and at the age of growth of beard they are bestowed upon a Cymro, and upon a Cymraes (Welshwoman) when she shall marry.[1]

There are several laws relating to "Tacogs," as the *villani* were called. One of these enacts:

There are three arts which a taeog is not to teach his son without permission of his lord, scholarship, smithcraft, and bardism; for if the lord be passive until the tonsure be given to the scholar, or until the smith enter his smithy, or until a bard be graduated in song, he cannot afterwards enslave them.[2]

Three persons whose privileges increase in one day: the first is, where a church is consecrated in a taeog-trev with the permission of the King, a man of that trev (*i.e.* villein-township), who might be a taeog in the morning, becomes on that night a free man. The second is, where the King confers one of the twenty-four offices of a privileged court on a person, who, before the office was given him, was a taeog, and after it was given, becomes a free man. The third is a cleric, who, on the day before he receives the tonsure, being the son of a taeog, is on that night a freeman.[3]

If a church be built by permission of the King within a taeog-trev, and there be a priest offering Mass in it, and it be a burying-place, such a trev is to be free henceforward.[4]

There are two laws which seem to hint at slavery in penal form. One of which prescribes that "There are three thieves liable to be sold." And another enacts:

---

[1] Thorpe, op. cit. vol. ii. p. 504.
[2] Op. cit. i. p. 437.   [3] *Ib.* p. 445.   [4] *Ib.* p. 543.

Whoever draws blood from an Abbot of any of those principal sees before-mentioned, let him pay seven pounds; and a female of his kindred to be a washerwoman, as a disgrace to the kindred, and to serve as a memorial of the payment of the fine.[1]

The Brut y Tywysog states:

A.D. 1030. . . . That year Joseph, Bishop of Teilaw (Llandaff), ordered that no work or occupation should take place on the Sundays and holidays, and obliged the priests to teach to read the Holy Scriptures without payment or gift, and to abandon controversies.[2]

This law would principally affect the serfs, who were thus exempted from servile work on these days. The Welsh system was a curious mixture of the primitive tribal system, such as we have seen in Ireland, and the Saxon manorial, or the Roman villa. There were aliens, or *aillts*: and, like them, but yet distinct from them, there were *taeogs*, a class who could not claim tribal blood, and had not the rights of free-born Welshmen, while on the other hand they were not *caeths*, or slaves. These two classes were sworn men of some lord, on whose land they were placed, and they remained his tenants at will. Each of these *taeogs*, or *aillts*, had his homestead, or *tyddyn*, with corn and cattle-yard. In South Wales these were grouped together into a *taeog-trev*. In this trev (or township) all the adults took equal shares, except the youngest sons who had no tyddyn of

---

[1] *Ibid.* p. 559. [2] *Councils*, p. 291.

their own, until their father's death, when they succeeded to their father's tyddyn. With this exception, there was nothing hereditary about the holdings. The tacogs had no true Welsh blood, and therefore they were considered to have no family rights. They shared *per capita*, and not *per stirpes*. The tacog might not bear arms; he might not, without his lord's permission, become a scholar or cleric, a smith, or a bard, nor sell his swine, honey, or horse. Even if he were to marry a free Welshwoman, his descendants till the ninth degree remained tacogs. But after that, his descendant might claim his five free acres, and become the head of a new kindred. Yet the tacog had no menial services to pay. He had to pay his dues in food for the chief's table. In Gwent, these were in winter a sow, a salted flitch, sixty loaves of wheat bread, a tub of ale, twenty sheaves of oats, and pence for the servants. In summer a tub of butter and twelve cheeses and bread.[1] In North Wales four crws or Welsh acres went to a tyddyn, sixty-four tyddyns composed a trev, and fifty trevs made a cymwd, or half-hundred, which had its court, with a "maer" and "canghellor" as officers over it, each of whom had four trevs free for his support. Honey was a very important item in the food-rents of the tacog. His lord could buy it all up if he chose. The wax was valuable for candles at the altar and for the chief's household. A swarm of bees was equal in value to an ox ready for the yoke. The "Law

[1] Seebohm, *English Village Community*, p. 108.

of Bees" in the Gwentian Code has a separate section to itself. It begins as follows:

The origin of bees is from Paradise; and on account of the sin of man they came from thence, and they were blessed by God, and, therefore, the Mass cannot be without wax.[1]

The tacog, though not free, was yet more like the Roman *colonus* than the Saxon *villein*, and when Wales was conquered finally, the tacogs became the *villani* of the Prince of Wales, without being subject to any intermediate lord. In fact they were free, only not holding tribesmen's land.

The ancient Welsh laws supply the key to that curious system of which remnants are to be found in many parts of England at the present day, and which seem to have been universal in mediæval times, viz., the land of a *villanus* being composed of a number of small strips of half an acre each, scattered over the whole parish, or manor. This system was the result of co-tillage, or co-operative farming, by which a number of tenant-farmers clubbed together to get their ploughing done by a combined team of oxen, generally eight.

The Venedotian Code traces back the measures of length to the time of King Dyvnwal, who is supposed to have reigned over Britain six hundred years before Christ.

They made the measure of the legal erw by the barley-corn. Three lengths of a barley-corn is an inch; three inches in the palm breadth; three palm breadths

[1] Thorpe, *Ancient Laws of Wales*, vol. i. p. 739.

in the foot; four feet in the short yoke, and eight in the field yoke; and twelve in the lateral yoke, and sixteen in the long yoke; and a rod, equal in length to that long yoke, in the hand of the driver, with the middle spike of that long yoke in the other hand of the driver, and as far as he can reach with that rod, stretching out his arm, are the two skirts of the erw, that is to say, the breadth of the legal erw; and thirty of that is the length of the erw.

Four such erws are to be in every tyddyn. Four tyddyns in every randir (shareland). Four randirs in every gavael (holding or farm). Four gavaels in every trev (township). Four trevs in every maenol (manor). And twelve maenols and two trevs in every cymwd (province).[1]

Applying this to English measure, it would seem that the pole or perch, which is five yards and a half, was the length of the long yoke of the carruca, or team four abreast. Forty times the length of this rod makes a furrow-long, or furlong. A strip one pole wide and a furlong in length is a rood; and four of these roods make an acre. The half-acre strip is two roods side by side. The Welsh laws say:

Whoever shall engage in co-tillage with another, it is right for them to give surety for performance, and mutually join hands; and after they have done that, to keep it until the tye be completed; the tye is twelve erws.

The first erw belongs to the ploughman; the second to the irons (*i.e.*, the man who contributes them); the third to the outside sod ox; the fourth to the outside

[1] Thorpe, vol. i. pp. 185—187.

sward ox, lest the yoke should be broken; and the fifth to the driver; and so the erws are appropriated, from best to best, to the oxen, thence onward unto the last; and after that the plough erw. . . .

Every one is to bring his requisites to the ploughing, whether ox or irons, or other things pertaining to him; and after everything is brought to them, the ploughman and the driver are to keep the whole safely, and use them as well as they would their own.

If there should be a dispute about bad tillage, let the erw of the ploughman be examined as to the depth, length, and breadth of the furrow, and let every one's be completed alike.[1]

The erws were divided from each other by balks two furrows in breadth. The tenth strip, set aside for tythe, was easily calculated. The strips being ploughed successively would all have a fair start for the harvest, while another tye of a similar number of strips would all be a little later; whereas, if all the land of one farmer were ploughed before any of the land of another co-tiller, he would have an unfair advantage of his neighbour, who had an equal right with himself in the combined team.

4.—Scotland.

This account of "Slavery and Serfdom in the British Isles" would not be complete without some notice of Scotland. Mr. William Skene has brought much varied erudition to prove that the Highlanders of Scotland are descended neither

[1] Thorpe, vol. i. pp. 315—319.

from the Saxon Lowlanders, nor from the Dalriadic Scots who came from Ireland, but from the aboriginal Caledonians mentioned by Tacitus.[1] The Lowlanders followed the manorial system of the Saxons, which the latter found established by the Romans. The Scots carried their tribal system with them from Ireland. Both were modified by the circumstances of the parts of the country they inhabited. But, according to Mr. Skene, the Highlanders appear to have differed very slightly from the Irish and Welsh in their domestic institutions. The Irish system of Tanistry prevailed, and the Tanist was not generally succeeded by his son, but by one of his brothers chosen by the clan. There was another chieftain, the head of the most powerful house of the clan, who was called the Toisich, or "first in battle," because in the absence of the chief he had to take the command, and when the chief was present, he commanded the van, and the right wing in battle. Mr. Skene says:

We must be careful to draw a proper distinction between the *nativi* or native men of Highland properties, and the *servi fugitivi* or *cumerlach*, the latter of which were slaves, and the same as the Welsh *caeth*, . . . and might be bought and sold either with or independent of the land. . . . The native man was the tenant who cultivated the soil, and who possessed, all over Scotland, but especially in the Highlands, a definite and recognized estate in the soil. So long as he performed his services

[1] *The Highlanders of Scotland.* By William F. Skene, F.S.A., 2 vols. 1837.

he was not to be removed from his land, nor could his lord exact from him a higher rent or a greater proportion of labour than what was due, and of right accustomed to be given. Their great privilege, therefore, was that they held their farms by an inherent right which was not derived from their lord, and from which he could not remove them. And in this way we find that all old Highland alienations of land included the *nativis ad dictas terras pertinentibus*. The *servi* and *fugitivi* were the cottars and actual labourers of the soil, who were absolute slaves, and possessed no legal rights of station or property.[1]

Mr. Skene says that when a Norman baron obtained possession of a Highland property, the Gaelic *nativi* remained in actual possession of the soil under him, but at the same time paid their *calpis*, or tribute to the head of the clan, and followed him to war. Mr. Skene states that there were no *servi* among the Highlanders, and infers from this that they were not a conquered race. Even if the fact were admitted, the analogy of other countries would not lead us to this inference. In England many of the *nativi* were doubtless descendants of the conquered Britons; and the rest, Saxons or Angles, were conquered in their turn.

We have already seen what a large proportion of the population of England were in serfdom at the time of the Domesday Survey. The condition of the serfs, whether *villani* or *bordarii*, had already been much ameliorated, though emanci-

[1] *Ibid.* i. pp. 171, 172.

pation had scarcely begun. One of the laws of William the Conqueror, as cited by Ingulph, the Abbot of Croyland, was—

> They who hold the land by customary rent shall not be troubled for anything beyond their proper payment; nor shall it be lawful for the lords to remove the cultivators from their lands so long as they pay the proper service.[1]

This gave them fixity of tenure, though that fixity was not voluntary on their part, for the next law runs:

> The *nativi* (*i.e.*, those born on the property in a state of villenage) who depart from their land, ought not to change their quarters nor to seek reception before doing the proper service which appertains to their land. The native who departs from the land where he is born, and comes to another land, no one shall retain him or his goods, but shall cause him to return to do his service, as it appertains to him. (*Ib.*)

But another law of the Conqueror, probably intended to increase the importance of the towns, became the cause of emancipation to many of the more enterprising villeins. It was this:

> If *servi* (and a fortiori *villani*) shall have dwelt without reproach for a year and a day in our cities, or our boroughs which are fenced with a wall, or in our fortified places, they become from that day free, and they may be free from the yoke of their servitude for ever. (lxvi.)

Blomefield, in his *History of Norfolk*, quotes a case of appeal to this law as late as 1312, when—

[1] Thorpe, vol. i. p. 481.

Sir John de Clavering sued William Fitz and seventeen others, villanes of his manor of Cossey, for withdrawing themselves, their goods and chattels, out of his manor, and dwelling in other places, to his and the King's prejudice, upon which a writ was directed to force them to come and dwell in the manor, and bring all their goods with them. Upon execution of this writ, six of them pretended to be freemen, and came to their trial, and pleaded that they came by their freedom in this manner, viz., by being citizens of the city of Norwich, having lived there and paid scot and lot for above thirty years with the free citizens there; and two of them pleaded that they were born in the wall of the city, and as such produced the Conqueror's Charter, in which it was contained, that if any slaves or villanes lived without claim of their lords (*i.e.*, without paying chevage, or a fine for licence so to do) for a year and a day, in any of the King's cities, walled towns, or in the camp, from that day they should be freemen, and their posterity for ever; upon which these six were declared freemen, and an appeal from the King's Charter was not admitted; and two more pleaded and obtained their freedom, by proving that Edward the First granted their fathers houses and lands in Norwich, to hold of him and his heirs, according to the custom of the city, and that they were their father's heirs; but all the rest were forced to return and live in villenage under their lord.[1]

Such narratives as these show us that down to the fourteenth century, the *villanus*, who was in France a free peasant, was still in the eye of the English law a serf. His tenure of land had, however, during the eleventh and twelfth centuries,

[1] Sir H. Ellis, *Introd. Domesday*, vol. i. p. 65.

advanced from a mere tenancy at will into what is still called "copyhold." Many of the villeins had no doubt followed their lords to the Crusades and other wars, and having borne arms became free. Villeins "became free," says Mr. Reeves, in his *History of English Law*, "if their lords grant or give them any free estate of inheritance to descend to their heirs." The Courts of Law, as we have just seen, "throw the onus of proof upon the man who claimed another as his slave or serf."[1] Emancipation was facilitated in a variety of ways. A villein could not indeed purchase his own freedom, but he might get some one else to buy him from his lord in order to set him free. Sometimes the lord would liberate at once all the bondmen on a particular estate, in return for a fixed rent to be yearly assessed on the inhabitants. But, as Lingard says—

The progress of emancipation was slow; the improved condition of their former fellows served only to embitter the discontent of those who still wore the fetters of servitude; and in many places the villeins formed associations for their mutual support, and availed themselves of every expedient in their power to free themselves from the control of their lords. In the first year of Richard the Second's reign (1377) a complaint was laid before Parliament that in many districts they had purchased exemplifications out of the Domesday Book in the King's Court, and under a false interpretation of that record had pretended to be discharged of all

---

[1] Reeves, op. cit. Edit. Finlayson, vol. i. p. 152.

manner of servitude, both as to their bodies and their tenures, and would not suffer the officers of their lords either to levy distress or to do justice upon them.[1]

When we come to trace the abolition of serfdom in these islands, we shall see the various causes that combined to put an end to both kinds of servitude.

[1] Lingard, *Hist.* vol. iii. p. 285.

LECTURE IV.

THE ABOLITION OF SERFDOM IN ENGLAND.

SERFDOM disappeared in this kingdom earlier than in any other country in Europe. Therefore, in tracing the process of the abolition of serfdom, it will be most convenient to begin with England. We say England, and not the British Isles; for, as we have shown, although slavery existed in Ireland until the twelfth century, yet we do not find in Irish history any evidence of that middle state between slavery and freedom which we call serfdom. It may be said, and with much truth, that practical serfdom has existed in Ireland down to our own days in the shape of forced labour, restrictions upon marriage, and uncertain rents, under the penalty of eviction. But these conditions, however tyrannical, differ essentially from serfdom; for the serf could not be evicted, except from one part of the manor to another, nor had he the power of giving up his holding if he wished. We may therefore dismiss Ireland altogether from our present inquiry. It is not easy to obtain any accurate information about serfdom in Scotland. In all probability Northern Scotland, being a colony from Ireland, planted there Irish customs, and the land was held by the clan in the same way as by the Irish sept. Slavery existed from early times, but it is doubtful whether serfdom ever obtained, except in the southern part. Though even here the Scotch system of tribal occupation seems rather to have invaded the northern counties of England, than to have allowed serfdom to be borrowed from England. Domesday Book tells us nothing about *servi*, or *bordarii*, or *cottarii*, or *villani* either in Lancashire, Westmoreland, Durham, Cumberland, or Northumberland. Northumbria extended from Edinburgh down to Derbyshire, and the parallel province of Strathclyde included Cumberland, Westmoreland, and Lancashire.

In the absence of exact information, we may leave the question of serfdom in Scotland. Mr. Seebohm quotes[1] the *Rotulus Redituum* of the Abbey of Kelso, a few miles from the border of Northumberland, which proves that in the thirteenth century the abbey-lands there were reckoned by virgates, or, as they were there called, "husband-lands," composed of two bovates, or ox-gangs. The services for these lands are set out in the *Rotulus*, and it is stated that each "husband" took with his land his outfit, viz., two oxen, one horse, three chalders of oats, six bolls of barley, and three of wheat. "But when Abbot Richard commuted that service into money, then they returned their *stuht* (or outfit), and paid each for his husband-land 18s. per annum." It does not appear from this quotation whether these "husbandmen" were serfs or

[1] *English Village Community*, p. 61.

free-tenants; indeed, from the fixed amount of the rent, one would be disposed to think that they were free-tenants.

Now, to confine ourselves to England, we need not recapitulate the evidence already given of the existence of serfdom from the earliest Saxon times to the Norman Conquest, and of the disappearance of serfdom in the sixteenth century; so that, though legally not abolished until the time of Charles the Second, it had practically ceased to exist at the time when Sir Thomas Smith wrote, as the Ambassador of Queen Elizabeth in Paris, his work on the Commonwealth of England. We saw also, from the comparison of the *Rectitudines Singularum Personarum* of the tenth century, with the various services of the *gebur* and *cotzes*, all in labour or kind, with the corresponding services of the *villanus* and *cottarius* in the thirteenth century, when the services of the *villanus* were commuted for so much money, that this commutation marks the gradual improvement in the condition of the *villein*, and his approach to the status of a free tenant.

But here we are stopped by a question which it is important to have satisfactorily answered before we pass on to the abolition of serfdom. We have assumed that all holders of land except those described as *sochmanni*, or *liberi tenentes*, were serfs. This has, however, been sometimes indignantly denied; and the question deserves a more complete investigation. We shall, therefore, give the grounds upon which we maintain the real serfdom of the

English *villani*, and it will be seen how some modern writers have not unnaturally been led into the mistake of supposing them freemen.

Let us then, first of all, ascertain what position the *villein* held in the eye of English law, and our first authority shall be Blackstone's *Commentaries*. Blackstone was by no means inclined to admit the rights of slavery, or to restrict the liberties of the subject; yet, when he comes to treat of the tenure of land, and the history of copyhold, he says:

Now with regard to the folk-land, or estates held in villenage, this was a species of tenure neither strictly feudal, Norman, nor Saxon; but mixed and compounded of them all. . . . These villeins, belonging principally to lords of manors, were either *villeins regardants*, that is, annexed to the manor or land; or else they were *in gross*, or at large, that is, annexed to the person of the lord, and transferable by deed from one owner to another. They could not leave their lord without his permission; but if they ran away, or were purloined from him, might be claimed and recovered by action, like beasts or other chattels. They held, indeed, small portions of land by way of sustaining themselves and families; but it was at the mere will of the lord, who might dispossess them whenever he pleased, and it was upon villein services, . . . and their services were not only base, but uncertain both as to their time and quantity. . . . In many places also a fine was payable to the lord, if the villein presumed to marry his daughter to any one without leave from the lord; and, by the common law, the lord might also bring an action against the husband for damages in thus purloining his property. For the children of villeins were also in the same state of bondage with their parents;

whence they were called in Latin *nativi*, which gave rise to the female appellation of a villein, who was called a *neife*. . . . The law, however, protected the persons of villeins, as the King's subjects, against atrocious injuries of the lord: for he might not kill or maim his villein, though he might beat him with impunity, since the villein had no action or remedy at law against his lord, but in the case of the murder of his ancestor, or the maim of his own person. (Bk. ii. c. vi.)

It is very clear from this that Blackstone held that all the various grades of villeins were just as much serfs as those recently emancipated in Russia. But, it may be urged, Blackstone may not have examined the ancient records with that critical acumen that is the especial glory of modern research. Now there is a certain self-sufficiency about some of our modern critics, which often misleads them in examining an ancient record. They discover a sentence, apparently inconsistent with the generally received ideas upon the subject, and jump to the conclusion that older writers have all been in the dark until they revealed this new light. Whereas it often turns out that they have overlooked the context of the passage on which they have founded their novel theory. We will, therefore, go back to the most ancient of commentators upon English law, the learned Archdeacon of Barnstaple, Henry de Bracton, who composed his great work on *The Laws and Customs of England* about the year 1270, towards the end of the long reign of Henry the Third. The system of villenage was in full swing at this time, and Bracton must have been thoroughly acquainted with all the phases of it. In the first chapter of his First Book, on the Primary Division of Persons, he lays down :

Every man is either a freeman or a bondman (*servus*). But to this an objection may be made from the case of the *ascripticius* (as he is called, that is the man bound to the land), because he is really a freeman, although he be bound to a certain service.

Now, one can easily understand a man looking into Bracton, and, after reading this sentence, going away with the idea that Bracton regarded the villeins, who were bound to the land, *ascripticii*, as not serfs, but freemen. But Bracton continues:

The brief solution of this difficulty is, that, from him who is free, the villenage or service takes away nothing of his freedom, if the distinction be maintained whether such persons are *villani* and held in villein socage of the demesne of our lord the King, concerning whom we shall treat further on. (fol. 1.)

Turning to the passage referred to, we read :

In the demesne of our lord the King, there are many sorts of men. There are bondmen (*servi*), whether *nativi* before the Conquest, at the Conquest, and after, and they hold villenages and by villein and uncertain services, and whatever may be required of them, so long as it be lawful and honest. Also, there were at the Conquest free-tenants, *liberi homines*, who freely held their tenements by free service, or by free customs; and when they were ejected by more powerful persons, they afterwards came back, and received again those same tenements of theirs to be held in villenage, doing henceforward servile works, but fixed and specified. And these are called *glebæ ascripticii*, and nevertheless they are freemen, because, although they do servile works, yet they do not do them by reason of the (servile) condition of their persons, but on account of the condition of their holdings (*ratione tenementorum*). . . . And so they are called *glebæ ascripticii*, because they enjoy such privilege that they cannot be removed from the glebe, so long as they pay the pensions due, to whomsoever the demesne of our lord the King shall pertain, nor can they be compelled to hold that tenement unless they choose. There is also another sort of men on the manor of our lord the King, and these hold of the demesne, and by the same customs and villein-services, as those just mentioned, and they are not in villenage, nor are they bondmen (*servi*), nor were they at the Conquest, but they hold by a certain agreement which they have made with the lords, and so some of them have charters and some not. . . . There are also other sorts of men who hold freely and in free socage and by military service by new feoffment, and this since the Conquest. Also, under the dominion of lords, there are freemen possessed as serfs (*servi*), and who sometimes proclaim their liberty, and who may be said to be in the state of bondmen (*servi*), though they are free, on the same ground that bondmen may be said to be in the state of freemen when they are fugitives, and out of their lords' power. (fol. 7.)

Further on again, he says:

The holding does not change the status of the freeman any more than that of the serf. For a freeman may hold a simple villenage, doing whatever belongs to the villenage, and nevertheless he will be free, since he does this on account of the villenage, and not on account of his own person, and so he can desert the villenage when he pleases, unless he has been ensnared by a serf-wife (*nativam*) to do this, and had gone in to her in villenage, and she could prevent his departing. For there is simple villenage, to which belongs a service uncertain and unspecified, in which a man cannot know in the evening what service must be done the next morning, as where one is bound to do whatever is commanded him. Again, villein-socage does not alter the status of a freeman any more than free-socage. But, although the services of the villein-socage become fixed, the tenant will not on this account have a free holding, because he does this service on account of the holding, and not on account of his own personality. However, he may hold it by fixed and stipulated services, yet by agreement and consent of the lords, for life or in feof, and in this case, the agreement and consent of the lords make it free for him, since the works are fixed and specified, although the works done, tallage, &c., are servile. But to give merchetum for a daughter, among other things, does not belong to freemen, on account of the privilege of free blood; and hence on the demesnes of our lord the King, a distinction will be made between freemen and villein-sochmanni, who are born on the demesne, and from ancient times have held their land in villenage. Also between simple villeins and those who are so by circumstances, and hold by fixed and stipulated services stipulated by agreement, although they resemble the villein-sochmanni; yet their condition is not the same, because in the person of the one there is a free holding, and in the person of the other there is villenage. (*Ib.*)

It will be seen that the distinctions drawn out in these passages of Bracton, show clearly that villeins, properly so called, were real serfs; while the case he mentions, of freemen holding land in villenage, and doing for it villein-services, while they themselves were free, readily accounts for the mistake that has been made by those who have regarded the villein as not a serf but a freeman. The fact that the villein in France, in the later middle ages, was a freeman, has doubtless assisted to confirm this mistake. But it was much more easy to obtain freedom in France than it was in England, because there the offspring of a serf and a free-woman was free; whereas, in England, if, according to Bracton, "a *villanus* lives with a free-woman in a free tenement the offspring will be a serf (*servus*)." And "he is called a serf, who is begotten of one of a free nation who has united himself with a *villana* living in villenage, whether that union be a marriage union or not."

Again, it is supposed by many modern writers that in early Saxon times the villeins were freemen, but that as the royal power increased, the condition of these tenant-farmers became more and more grievous, until from freemen they sank into serfs. Thus, Mr. Charles Elton, in his valuable work, *The Origins of English History*, says:

> The whole country passed in time under the power of the King, the Church, and the Thanes; and as the jurisdiction of the lords was gradually converted into ownership of the lands in their districts, the descendants of freemen fell under onerous rents and services, and in many cases became serfs and bondmen. (p. 403.)

In proof of this he adds a note, giving an extract from the Record of the Court of Common Pleas in the eighteenth year of Edward the First, in which it is stated that:

T. R. is the villein of one Folliott, therefore the latter can tax him high and low (*de alto et de basso*), and he must pay a fine of *merchetum* for his flesh and blood (at his daughter's marriage).

Now the investigations of Mr. Seebohm prove that, in the time of Edward the First, the services of the villeins were much less servile, and less onerous than they were in the twelfth century; and that these again were not so heavy as they had been in the tenth century, in Saxon times. And, comparing the tenth century with the times of King Alfred, and even with those of King Ine of Wessex, the further back we go, the more hard and servile do we find the condition of the villein. In Edward the First's time, nearly all the villein's services could be commuted for a money payment, but in the earlier times they had to be worked out, without any such alternative. Mr. Seebohm sums up the result of his inquiry in the following words:

Throughout the whole period, from pre-Roman to modern times, we found in Britain two parallel systems of rural economy, side by side, but keeping separate and working themselves out on quite different lines, in spite of Roman, English, and Norman invasions—that of the *village* community in the eastern, that of the *tribal* community in the western districts of the island. Neither the village nor the tribal community seems to have been introduced into Britain during a historical period reaching back for two thousand years at least.

On the one hand, the village community of the eastern districts of Britain was connected with a settled agriculture; which, apparently dating earlier than the Roman invasion, and improved during the Roman occupation, was carried on at length, under that three-field form of the open-field system, which became the shell of the English village community. The equality in its yard-lands and the single succession which preserved this equality we have found to be apparently marks, not of an original freedom, not of an original allodial allotment on the German "mark system," but of a settled serfdom under a lordship—a semi-servile tenancy, implying a mere usufruct, theoretically only for life, or at will, and carrying with it no inherent rights of inheritance. But this serfdom, as we have seen reason to believe, was, to the masses of the people, not a degradation, but a step upward out of a once more general slavery. Certainly during the twelve hundred years, over which the direct English evidence extends, the tendency has been towards more and more of freedom. In other words, as time went on during these twelve hundred years, the serfdom of the old order of things has been gradually breaking up under those influences, whatever they may have been, which have produced the new order of things.[1]

We have already attempted to describe the daily life of an English serf in the middle ages. The value of his labour, and the cost of the necessities of life, have been carefully calculated and compared with modern equivalents by Mr. Thorold Rogers in his interesting volumes, *Six Centuries of Work and Wages*. Mr. Rogers says, that "except that the thirteenth century villager was greatly better

[1] *English Village Community*, pp. 437, 438.

off, there was little change induced on the rustic's condition in many parts of England from the middle of the thirteenth to the beginning of the nineteenth century."[1] He sums up the income and the expenditure of a man farming twenty acres of land, and computes that "he might be supplied abundantly from the produce of his farm, debiting himself with the cost of his own produce, and laying aside 20s. a year (equivalent to at least £12 of our present money), with which hereafter, as opportunity might arise, he might increase his holding, portion his daughters, provide for his widowed mother, or put forward his son in the Church, or any similar advantageous calling. Such may be fairly taken to represent the receipts and expenditure of those small landowners, who were, as I have frequently stated, so numerous in the thirteenth century."[2] "All the necessities of life in ordinary years, when there was no dearth, were abundant and cheap. . . . Meat was plentiful; poultry found everywhere; eggs cheapest of all. The poorest and meanest man had no absolute and insurmountable impediment put in his way on his career, if he would seize his opportunity and make use of it."[3] It is perhaps well for us, who talk complacently of the advantages of civilization, to be reminded by Mr. Rogers, "that there is collected a population in our great towns which equals in amount the whole of those who lived in England and Wales six centuries ago; but whose condition is more destitute, whose homes are more

[1] Op. cit. p. 84. [2] Ibid. p. 177. [3] Ibid. p. 184.

squalid, whose means are more uncertain, whose prospects are more hopeless, than those of the poorest serfs of the middle ages and the meanest drudges of the mediæval cities."[1]

We cannot agree with Mr. Rogers in thinking that the English serf was better off than the French peasant in the middle ages. The French serf always maintained his hold on the land, which the English serf lost when he became emancipated, and this seems to be the origin of our present pauperism; while the French peasant is the proprietor of the soil which he cultivates, and has been so from the time of his emancipation. But it is time that we should pass on to the occasion of the cessation of serfdom in England.

We have seen how, in the reign of Edward the First, money payments in lieu of labour dues, had become the practice for the villeins, though not for the bordars or cottiers. The money compensation was more easy to collect than the labour dues to enforce; and ready money was often more useful to the lord than the forced labour of the serf. Thus we may say safely that, in the time of Edward the Third, the compensation was generally in use, except on the monastic lands. But while Edward was gaining his victories in France, a more formidable foe had invaded England. Edward's daughter, the Princess Joan, died of the plague on her way to be married to Don Pedro of Castile; and in the same year, 1348, the Black Death made its appearance at Bridport, and

[1] P. 186.

travelled slowly westwards and northwards, through Devon and Somerset to Bristol. In vain the authorities strove to isolate Bristol, the plague spread to Oxford, and then to London by the 1st of November. At the beginning of 1349, it reached Norwich, and travelling further north, it was caught by a Scottish army ravaging the borders, and they spread the contagion through Scotland. The mortality was appalling. It is probable that more than one-third of the population perished. All classes suffered from its devastations. The immediate consequence was a great dearth of labour, an abnormally high rate of wages, and a serious difficulty in the collection of the harvests of those who depended on a supply of hired labour. We are told that the crops often rotted in the fields for want of hands; cattle wandered at large over the country for lack of herdsmen, and much land went out of cultivation. Many of the lords excused their tenants' rent, lest they should quit their holdings, sometimes reducing the rents by one half, sometimes remitting it for a term of years. Knighton says:

They who had let lands on labour-rents to tenants, such rents as are customary in villeinage, were compelled to relieve and remit such labour, and either to utterly excuse them, or to rehabilitate their tenants on easier terms and less payments, lest the loss and ruin should become irreparable and the land lie utterly uncultivated.[1]

---

[1] Quoted by Mr. Rogers, op. cit. p. 227.

This shows that the lords found themselves compelled to make new compositions with their tenants in villenage, and that they accepted a less money compensation than heretofore. In fact, to use the expression of Mr. Rogers, "The plague had almost emancipated the surviving serfs."[1] In vain did the King, by proclamation through the sheriffs of each county, forbid the payment of higher wages than usual. In vain did he punish by heavy fines those who disobeyed his mandate. The labourers were the masters of the situation. At last, when Parliament assembled, a statute was passed, enacting :

1. No person under sixty years of age, whether serf or free, shall decline to undertake farm labour at the wages which had been customary in the King's twentieth year (1347), except they lived by merchandise, were regularly engaged in some mechanical craft, were possessed of private means, or were occupiers of land. The lord was to have the first claim to the labour of his serfs, and those who decline to work for him or for others are to be sent to the common gaol.

2. Imprisonment is decreed against all persons who may quit service before the time which is fixed in their agreements.

3. No other than the old wages are to be given, and the remedy against those who seek to get more is to be sought in the lord's court.

4. Lords of manors paying more than the customary amount are to be liable to treble damages.

5. Artificers are to be liable to the same conditions,

[1] Op. cit. p. 227.

saddlers, tanners, farriers, shoemakers, tailors, smiths, carpenters, masons, tilers, pargetters, carters, and others.

6. Food must be sold at reasonable prices.

7. Alms are strictly forbidden to able-bodied labourers.

8. Any excess of wages taken or paid can be seized for the King's use, towards the payment of a fifteenth and tenth lately granted. Summer and winter wages may differ; but town population is not to migrate to the country in summer.[1]

It was found practically impossible to prevent evasions of this "Statute of Labourers." Taking the period from 1350 to 1400, it appears that the value of agricultural labour of all kinds was fifty per cent. higher than in the first half of the century, while the price of agricultural produce remained what it was before. The price of everything on which labour was expended increased enormously; so that the landlord had to pay dearly for everything that he wished to buy, and could only obtain an extremely low price for what he had to sell. On the other hand, the serf, as well as the free labourer, found everything that he needed was as cheap as ever, while his labour was daily rising in value. He had bargained for his labour-rent, and was free to choose his market. If the bailiff would give him his price, well; if not, there were plenty of hands wanted in the next village, or a short distance off. Besides, the agricultural population were no longer in scattered manorial groups, each

---

[1] Stat. 23 Edw. III. was made more stringent two years afterwards, and still more so by 34 Edw. III. c. x. See Reeves' *History of English Law*, vol. ii. pp. 272—276.

isolated from the other; there was an active band of agitators, who kept the peasants in one locality acquainted with what was going on elsewhere, and thus enabled the serfs and free labourers of the fourteenth century to resist successfully all attempts to carry out the Statute of Labourers. The more we study the subject, the more convinced we become that Mr. Thorold Rogers is right in saying that "Wycliffe's poor priests had honeycombed the minds of the upland folk (as the peasantry were described) with what may be called religious socialism."[1]

We cannot be accused of unfairness towards Wycliffe if we take our estimate of his political ideas from Mr. Reginald Lane Poole, who has carefully edited his treatise, *De Civili Dominio*, or "On Civil Lordship," which contains his theory of government and the rights of property. Mr. Poole says:

Wycliffe begins his book by the proposition, of which the latter part was already noted as dangerous by Gregory the Eleventh in 1377, that no one in mortal sin has any right to any gift of God, while, on the other hand, every man standing in grace has not only a right to, but has, in fact, all the gifts of God. . . . All lordship of man, natural or civil, is conferred on him by God, as the prime Author, in consideration of his returning continually to God the service due unto Him; but by the fact that a man, by omission or commission, becomes guilty of mortal sin, he defrauds his Lord-in-Chief of the said service, and by consequence incurs forfeiture. Where-

[1] *Work and Wages*, p. 254.

fore ... he is rightly to be deprived of all lordship whatsoever. ... By means of this ... the way is prepared for Wycliffe's second main principle, namely, that the righteous is lord of all things, or, in precise terms, every righteous man is lord over the whole sensible world. ... He is not afraid to pursue his doctrine to the logical conclusion that, as there are many righteous, and each is lord of the universe, all goods must necessarily be held in common. ... Any objections to the doctrine he dismisses as sophistical.[1]

Mr. Poole thinks that,

If we are startled by the premature socialism of the thesis, we have to bear in mind that Wycliffe had yet to learn its effects in practical life, as displayed in the excesses of the rebels in 1381. Such application, indeed, was never in his mind. (p. 299.)

We may be permitted to doubt this. Whatever else he was, John Wycliffe was no fool. He zealously indoctrinated a numerous band of "poor priests" with his socialistic theories, and—under the protection probably of John of Gaunt, the Princess of Wales, and other powerful friends, whose jealousy of the Bishops blinded them to the danger—sent them into all parts of the country, with the Bible, as Mr. Poole puts it, "translated into the language of feudalism." Mr. Poole sees clearly enough that,

However ideal the principle on which Wycliffe goes, it has none the less a very plain meaning when applied to the circumstances of the religious organism in the writer's own time. (p. 300.)

[1] *Illustrations of the History of Mediæval Thought*, pp. 293—295.

It is true that Wycliffe made a reservation. He stated it in his famous paradox, "God ought to obey the devil;" by which, Mr. Poole says, he meant "that no one can escape from the duty of obedience to existing powers, be those powers never so depraved."

It is difficult to imagine that Wycliffe was so ignorant of human nature as to suppose that men would be deterred, by this reservation, from putting into practice his fundamental principles, as soon as they got an opportunity. The very paradoxical form in which the reservation was made, rendered it all the more certain to be rejected, as in fact it was. Mr. Thorold Rogers says:

> By Wycliffe's labours the Bible men had been introduced to the new world of the Old Testament, to the history of the human race, to the primeval garden and the young world, where the first parents of all mankind lived by simple toil, and were the ancestors of the proud noble and knight, as well as of the down-trodden serf and despised burgher. They read of the brave times when there was no king in Israel, when every man did that which was right in his own eyes, and sat under his own vine and under his own fig-tree, none daring to make him afraid. . . . But most of all, the preacher would dwell on his own prototype, on the man of God, the wise prophet who denounced kings and princes and high priests, and, by God's commission, made them like unto a potter's vessel in the day of His wrath; or on those bold judges, who were zealous even to slaying. . . . And when they told them that the lords had determined to drag them back to their old serfdom, the preacher could discourse to them of the natural equality of man,

of the fact that all—kings, lords, and priests—live by the fruits of the earth and the labour of the husbandman, and that it would be better for them to die with arms in their hands than to be thrust back, without an effort on their part, into the shameful slavery from which they had been delivered.[1]

There seems great probability in Mr. Rogers' theory, that the rising of the peasants was precipitated by attempts, on the part of the landlords, to insist upon the serfs performing their labour services, instead of paying the very inadequate money compensation which had by this time become general. The popular account connects the rising with an insult to the daughter of Wat Tyler by the collector of the obnoxious poll-tax; but there must have been some deeper and more general cause to have occasioned so wide-spread a rising.

Bishop Stubbs, in his *Constitutional History*, says:

The rising of the commons is one of the most portentous phenomena to be found in the whole of our history. The extent of the area over which it spread, the extraordinary rapidity with which intelligence and communication passed between the different sections of the revolt, the variety of cries and causes which combined to produce it, the mystery which pervades its organization, its sudden collapse and its indirect permanent results, give it a singular importance both constitutionally and socially. North and south, east and west, it broke out within so short a space of time as makes it impossible to suppose it to have arisen, like an

[1] *Six Centuries of Work and Wages*, p. 255.

accidental conflagration, from mere ordinary contact of materials.[1]

The rustics of Essex were the first to rise. Walsingham, a monk of St. Albans, tells us that they were "those whom we call *nativi* or *bondi*," that is, serfs, together with the *accoli*, perhaps free labourers. They flocked up to London, crying that all were to be lords, and there were to be no more serfs. As soon as the peasants of Kent, where serfdom had died out, heard of it, they too assembled in large bands, and filled the roads towards the metropolis, seized upon all pilgrims to Canterbury, and compelled them to swear loyalty to the King and the Commons. The Princess of Wales was stopped by them on her way to London, and the "Fair Maid of Kent" had

---

[1] "Norfolk, Suffolk, Cambridge, Essex, Hertford, Middlesex, Hants, Sussex, Kent, and Somerset, are mentioned in the Rolls of Parliament; Huntingdon, in the Records of Evesham Monastery. For Kent, Devon, Cambridge, and Herts the presentments of the juries are extant in the Archives of Canterbury. At Cambridge the townsfolk burned the charters of the University before May 1, 1381; the mayor and bailiffs seem to have joined the revolt in June, or to have taken advantage of it to attack the Colleges. Besides the southern seats of rebellion, Froissart (c. 76) mentions Lancashire, York, Lincoln, and Durham as ready to rise." (Op. cit. vol. ii. p. 450.) Bishop Stubbs mentions Devon, and cites the Canterbury Archives, which the present writer has not been able to consult; but he also says, "Knighton describes the rising in Devonshire." (c. 2639). Now, I have looked carefully through Knighton's account of the rebellion, and cannot find the faintest allusion to Devonshire, so that this usually most accurate historian must either have made a clerical error, or have trusted to the reference of some other author on this point. I have been unable as yet to find any proof of Devonshire having taken part in this rebellion.

to allow herself to be kissed by the leaders before she was permitted to proceed. Their animosity was especially excited against Simon Sudbury, Archbishop of Canterbury and Lord Chancellor of England. Froissart tells us:

A crazy priest in the county of Kent, called John Ball, every Sunday after Mass, as the people were coming out of church, used to assemble a crowd around him in the market-place and preach. His favourite text was a popular rhyme:

> When Adame dalve, and Eave span,
> Who was then a gentleman?

And he would say: "My good friends, matters cannot go on well in England until all things shall be in common, when there shall be neither vassals nor lords, when the lords shall be no more masters. How ill do they behave to us? For what reason do they thus hold us in bondage? Are we not all descended from the same parents, Adam and Eve? And what can they show, and what reason can they give, why they should be more masters than ourselves? They are clothed in velvet and rich stuffs, ornamented with ermine and other furs, while we are forced to wear poor clothing. They have wines, spices, and fine bread, while we have only rye and the refuse of the straw, and when we drink it must be water. They have handsome seats and manors, while we must brave the wind and rain in our labours in the field, and it is by our labour they have wherewith to support their pomp. We are called slaves, and if we do not perform our service we are beaten, and we have no sovereign to whom we can complain, or who would be willing to hear us. Let us go to the King, and remonstrate with him; he is young, and from him we may obtain a favourable answer, and if not we must ourselves seek to amend our condition."[1]

The Archbishop heard of these inflammatory harangues, and had John Ball arrested and imprisoned for three months; but as soon as he was released he returned to his old courses, and soon had to be imprisoned again. When the rising took place, he was in prison at Maidstone; but the mob speedily released their favourite orator, who joined them on Blackheath, where about one hundred thousand ill-clad and half-armed peasants were assembled under the leadership of Wat Tyler. John Ball preached on his usual text, and proceeded to exhort this undisciplined crowd to "shorten by the head" the lords spiritual and temporal, the judges, the lawyers, and all pen and inkhorn men who belonged either to Westminster Hall or to the Courts Christian. These fellows, said he, are all of them enemies to the liberty of the Commons, and are not to be endured. When they are despatched, servitude and poverty will die with them.

Hitherto they had observed a certain degree of moderation. But now they declared Ball to be a prophet sent to them from Heaven, and that he was the only person fit to be at once Archbishop of Canterbury and Lord Chancellor. A council of war was held, in which it was decided that the way should be cleared for Ball by the Archbishop

[1] *Chronicles*, c. ix.

being put to death, and that certain other obnoxious persons should be executed without the formality of a trial. Having done this, they issued a proclamation in the name of the King and the Commons, making no mention of the Bishops or the Temporal nobility. This was on Thursday, June 12, 1381, being the feast of Corpus Christi. The lowest part of the London mob fraternized with the rustics, and the following morning they entered the city, the citizens being terrified at their numbers. They burnt to the ground the stately palace of the Duke of Lancaster in the Savoy—the Duke was then in Scotland—and threw his gold and silver plate and jewels into the river. One, who was secreting a piece of plate for himself, was flung with his booty into the fire, for they professed to be reformers and not thieves. But they were not so scrupulous about liquor, for they drank so much of John of Gaunt's good wine, that thirty-two of them were unable to escape from the burning palace, and perished in its ruins. They destroyed the Temple, as the head-quarters of the lawyers, and burnt all parchments, deeds, rent-rolls, and papers that they could lay their hands on. Reinforcements came in from Barnet and St. Albans, and then they sent a message to the King in the Tower, demanding to have the Archbishop and the Lord Treasurer and other obnoxious persons handed over to them. The King was a youth of fifteen, and though he had twelve hundred well-armed soldiers, yet such terror seemed to have seized upon all, that on

Friday morning, when the King had ridden out to Mile End, they actually invited the drunken, brutal mob to enter the fortress and search for themselves.

They rushed across the moat, pushed one another through the corridors, and swarmed all over the palace. Passing from room to room, they reached the royal apartments, and did not even respect the bed-room of the Princess of Wales. They treated the highest of the nobles with the most terrific familiarity, stroked their beards with their filthy hands, and greeted them in terms of jocular endearment. They seated themselves on chairs of state and even on the King's bed, and asked the Princess for a kiss. They probed her bed with their pikes on pretence of searching for their enemies, so that she fainted with terror.

At last they found the Archbishop. Simon de Sudbury had prepared for his fate with the calm courage of a martyr. He had spent the night in prayer and penitential exercises, and was making his thanksgiving after Mass when the yells of the mob sounded nearer and nearer the chapel. They dragged him from the Tower, and carried him with shouts of triumph to Tower Hill, where the main body of the rioters were assembled. The Archbishop attempted to reason with his murderers. He reminded them that murder was a heinous sin, that he was a priest and an archbishop, and that his murder would compel the Pope to lay England under an interdict. But the men of Kent laughed him to scorn. He was a sinner, said these followers of Wycliffe, and therefore could be no true priest or archbishop; and what cared they for Pope or interdict? He prepared for death; but, before he laid his head on the block, he forgave the wretch who was about to despatch him, and who did his business so clumsily that it was not until the eighth blow that the head of Simon de Sudbury fell to the ground, and after being exposed to numerous indignities, was finally fastened up on London Bridge, and no one dared to bury the mutilated corpse. Sir Robert Hales, the Prior of St. John's, and several others were next despatched, and many were executed at hap-hazard, without any definite reason. No church or sanctuary was respected, and the very altars were defiled with blood.[1]

The young King seems to have been the first to regain his courage; and we need not repeat the well-known story of how he met the rioters at Smithfield, how the Lord Mayor struck down the insolent Wat Tyler, and how Richard by his presence of mind and tact appeased and dispersed the mob, and recovered his all but lost royal authority. But we cannot pass over the demands of the peasants at Mile End. They were:

1. That all men should be free from servitude and bondage, so that from henceforth there should be no bondmen.
2. That the King should pardon all men, of what state soever, all manner of actions and insurrection committed, and all manner of treasons, felonies, transgressions, and

[1] See Walsingham, *Hist. Angl.* i. pp. 460—463.

extortions, by any of them done, and should grant them peace.

3. That all men from henceforth might be enfranchised to buy and sell in every county, city, borough, town, fair, market, or other place within the realm of England.

4. That no acre of land, holden in bondage or service, should be holden but for four pence; and if it had been holden for less in former times, it should not hereafter be enhanced.[1]

The King had at first granted these demands, and gave charters signed and sealed, with one of his banners, to the representatives of each county; but when Tyler declared that he was not satisfied, and threatened further outrage, the King revoked the charters.

When the peasants of St. Albans had obtained their demands from the King they returned home, and were met by a band of villeins and servants sent by the Abbot of St. Albans to appease them. But the villeins betrayed the Abbot's cause, and fraternized with the mob; and, under the guidance of one William Grindecobbe, approached the abbey, saying that they were no longer serfs, but lords. They compelled the Abbot to give them all the rolls and charters of the abbey, which they committed to the flames, broke in pieces the millstones, as the tokens of their servitude, threatened to destroy the whole abbey and massacre the monks, unless a certain charter were produced, which the Abbot declared was at Westminster.

[1] Stowe, *Survey of London*, p. 288.

During the next three days they extorted letters of manumission for all the serfs of the abbey. When the insurrection had been suppressed, the King sent officers to restore order at St. Albans; and, after some difficulty, the villeins surrendered the deeds of manumission, and pledged themselves to pay a fine for the damage they had done to the abbey. Grindecobbe and others were executed.

Similar scenes, only with more bloodshed, were enacted at Bury-St.-Edmunds, and other places in the counties of Suffolk, Norfolk, Cambridge, Lincoln, and Stafford. One of the leaders, called Jack Straw, before his execution, made the following confession of the designs of the rebels to the Lord Mayor of London:

At the same time as wee were assembled upon Blackheath, and had sent to the King to come up to us, our purpose was to have slaine all such knights, squires, and gentlemen as should have given their attendance thither upon him. But as for the King, wee would have kept him among us to the end, that the people might more boldly have repayred to us. Sith they would have thought that whatsoever wee did, the same had been done by his authority. Finally, when wee had gotten power enough, that wee needed not to fear any force which might be made against us, wee would have slaine all such noblemen as might either have given counsell, or made any resistance against us; especially wee would have slaine the Knights of Rhodes of St. John's; and lastly wee would have killed the King himself, and all men of possessions, with bishops, monks, canons, and parsons of Churches; only friars and mendicants wee would have spared, that might have sufficed for ministration of the sacraments. When wee had made a riddance of all those, wee would have devised lawes, according to which laws the subjects of the realme should have lived. For wee would have created kings, as Watt Tyler in Kent, and others in other counties. (Stowe.)

The contemporary collector of the *Fasciculi Zizaniorum*, or Bundles of Tares, tells us that, when the insurrection had been quelled, and the King was at St. Albans,

The aforesaid John Balle, of Coventry, was there condemned by Robert Tresilian as guilty of treason, to be drawn, hanged, and quartered. And when he saw that he was condemned, he called to him William (Courtenay), Bishop of London, and afterwards of Canterbury, and Sir Walter Lee, knight; and mr. John Profete, notary; and there confessed publickly to them that for the space of two years he was a disciple of Wycliff, and from him had learned the heresies which he taught. . . . He also said that there was a certain organized band (*comitiva*) of the sect and doctrine of Wycliff, who had conspired together a kind of confederation, and had bound themselves to go round the whole of England preaching the matters of the said Wycliff, which he had taught them, so that thus all England together would agree in his perverse doctrine. And then he named the said Wycliff as the principal author of the plot, and in the second place Nicolas Herford, and John Aston, and Laurence Bedenam,[1]

---

[1] See Prebendary Hingeston-Randolph's *Episcopal Registers.—Stafford*, p. 241. Prebendary Randolph adds: "Laurence Bedeman [Bednam is a corrupt form of the name: which was also spelt 'Bedmond,'] was a west-countryman, a 'Cornish Fellow,' of

Masters of Arts. And he further added, that, unless resistance were made to the aforesaid conspirators, they would destroy the whole kingdom within two years. (Op. cit. p. 273.)

In the following year the same author says:

Anno Domini 1382, a certain son of iniquity, Nicolas Hereford, master in theology, maintained and favoured master John Wycliff in all things; and said openly, that Symon, Archbishop of Canterbury, was put to death, and that justly, because he wished to correct his own master, and he said that no falsity could be found in any doctrine of master John Wycliff. Master John Wycliff went wrong in many things, but this most proud Nicolas said in his sermons things intolerable and most abominable; and was always stirring up the people to insurrection. (p. 296.)

In the face of all this testimony, I cannot see

Exeter Coll., Oxford, from some unrecorded date up to 16 April, 1380, when he resigned (or, perhaps, was 'removed,' as many of the Fellows were at that time). He was Rector of the College during his last year. He was sometimes called 'Stevyn.' Embracing the doctrines of the Wycliffites, he went about Cornwall preaching. In 1382 Bp. Brantingham determined to stop him, and issued his mandate to the Priors of Launceston and Bodmin and the Provost of Glasney, to make inquisition as to his doings and teachings. This step seems to have had a very remarkable result; for, before 1382 came to an end, Bedeman renounced his errors, and soon afterwards settled down quietly as a Devonshire country parson. He was for many years Rector of Lifton, and at least eleven times served as Penitentiary for his Deanery. The character of his preaching must have been completely changed, for in 1410 he was licensed by Bp. Stafford as a Publick Preacher in the Diocese. Nevertheless, he was, probably, of a turbulent turn of mind, for Lifton Churchyard had to be reconciled in 1418, having been polluted (by bloodshed) by Walter Hardeby and John Huntyngford, on the one side, and the Rector, Laurence Bedman on the other." *See* Boase's *Register of Exeter College.*

how it is possible to acquit Wycliff of the most direct complicity with the Rebellion. There were no laws against heresy at that time in England, and the strong Court influence of the Duke of Lancaster protected him from anything beyond spiritual censures.

When Parliament met, the King informed them that he had revoked his charters, but urged upon them the question, whether it was not advisable to enfranchise their villeins by common consent. But the Lords and Commons declared that "this consent they would never give, not to save themselves from all perishing together in one day."

Ten years afterwards, in 1391, Richard refused his assent to the petitions of the Commons that the sons of serfs should not be allowed to frequent the Universities, or that fugitive serfs should be seized without regard to the freedom of the city or borough where they were harboured. Although rejected by Parliament, the work of emancipation went rapidly forward; and, though still acknowledged by the law, villenage was silently dropping out of the life of England. In the later years of Edward the Third we find "villein-tenants by copy of court roll."[1] In the reign of Henry the Fourth they are called "tenants by the verge,"[2] but in the reign of Edward the Fourth, Sir Robert Danby, Chief Justice of the Common Pleas, and his successor, Sir Thomas Brian, afterwards laid down, "that the copy-holder doing his customs and services, should, if put out by his lord, have

---

[1] Littleton, 73.　[2] *Tenants per le verge*, 14 Hen. IV. 34.

an action of trespass against him."[1] Thus distinctly establishing his perfect freedom. The three volumes of the Paston Letters extend from 1422 to 1509, and contain, among the letters, leases of land, accounts of rents, distraints, reports of stewards or bailiffs, wills, and marriage settlements; yet in none of them can we find a single mention of, or allusion to, any bondman, villein, or serf, as a living person. There are bequests to servants, male and female, but no mention of manumission. The mention of the witnesses in the case of Sir John Fastolf's will being "of free condition," shows that the idea of "servile condition" was fresh in the minds of the people, or at any rate of the law.[2] Sir John Paston was accused of having had a serf for his grandfather; but he proved, before Edward the Fourth in Council, that his ancestors had been gentlemen since the Conquest, and that his mother possessed "bondmen, whose ancestors have been bondmen to the ancestors of the said John Paston sithen the time that no man's mind is to the contrary."[3] Grandisson, Bishop of Exeter, who died in 1369, emanci-

---

[1] Reeves' *History of English Law*, ii. p. 565.

[2] We take at random five specimens of these witnesses: "John Dawson, husbandman (agricultor), literatus, liberæ conditionis. John Gyrdynge, . . . a cook, illiterate, and of free condition. Robert Ingbys of London, gentleman, illiterate, and of free condition. Henry Clarke of Blowfield, husbandman, illiterate, and of free condition. John Tovy of Caistor, agricultor, literatus, and of free condition. His mother was Sir John's washerwoman." (vol. ii. p. 283.) It is curious that while the gentleman and the cook can neither read nor write, two out of three of the husbandmen are lettered persons. [3] Vol. ii. p. 281.

pated all his serfs, who were (*custumarii*) holders of a ferling of land, on his manor of Ottery St. Mary. The Registers of Bishop Stafford contain five charters of manumission, ranging from 1405 to 1418, that is, in the reigns of Henry the Fourth and Fifth. Littleton, who was Chief Justice of the Common Pleas under Edward the Fourth, and whose decisions have still great weight, lays down the law about villenage, both as to the tenure and as to the persons of villeins, as an existing institution. In the time of Richard the Third, one John Huston, brought an action against the Bishop of Ely for claiming him to be his villein. In the reign of Henry the Seventh, Chief Justice Frowike gave a reading upon villenage, which showed that it was not then obsolete. In another case it was held that if the lord granted the villein a lease for even one year or half a year, the villein was enfranchised. Henry the Eighth executed at Knoll a deed of manumission *et ab omni jugo servitutis liberasse* "to Henry Knight, a tailor, of Stoke Climsland, Cornwall, and John Erle, of the same parish."[1]

In 1574, Elizabeth granted a commission to William Cecil, Lord Burghley, the High Treasurer, and Sir Walter Mildmay Chancellor of the Exchequer, "to accepte, admitte, and Receive to be Manumysed, Enfranchesed, and made Free, sucche and so many of our Bondmen and Bondwomen in Blood, with all and every their children and Sequelism, theire Goodes, Landes, Tenements and

[1] Rymer, *Fœd.* xiii. p. 470.

Hereditaments, as are nowe apperteynynge or regardaunte to all or any of our Mannors, Landes, Tenements, Possessions or Hereditaments within the several counties of Cornwall, Devon, Somersett, and Gloucester." Hallam observes on this deed, that it is the last unequivocal testimony to the existence of villenage; though it is highly probable that it existed in remote parts of the country some time longer.[1]

Sir Thomas Smith says in Elizabeth's reign that he hardly knew an instance; but in the last year of Elizabeth, 1602, villenage comes into court. In the case of Dighton v. Bartholomew, "a writ *de nativo habendo* was brought, claiming the defendant as a villein, and judgment was given that he should be enfranchised for ever. This was the last claim of the kind."[2]

This is the last instance of villenage that appears; and we may assume that it had then died out of the life of England, although its formal legal abolition was not effected until the beginning of the reign of Charles the Second, when a statute was passed abolishing all services both military and base. "A statute," says Blackstone, "which was a greater acquisition to the civil property of this kingdom than even *Magna Charta* itself."[3] A similar statute was passed for Scotland in the twentieth year of George the Second.

It is, however, instructive to inquire, What was

---

[1] *Middle Ages*, iii. p. 182. 10th Ed.
[2] Reeves' *History of English Law*, iii. 590.
[3] *Commentaries*, bk. ii. c. 5.

the effect of the abolition of serfdom? In the case of those villeins who held their land "by copy of the Court Roll," they had already become free-tenants. But comparatively few of the serfs were in this position; and, for the rest, emancipation, indeed, freed their persons, but it did not secure to them a single rood of land. Probably this was not much felt at first; for the fifteenth century was the golden age of the English labourer, though Mr. Rogers says that he lost in the sixteenth all that he had gained in the two preceding centuries. The "Statute of Labourers" laid down that any villein unemployed could be taken and put to labour by any one, on pain of being put in gaol. Under Richard the Second no servant could depart out of the hundred where he dwelt without a testimonial, and, in default of such testimonial giving the causes of his wandering and the date of his return, he was to be put in the stocks till he gave security to return to his service. No child of either sex, who had been employed in husbandry up to twelve years of age might be apprenticed to any other craft; and no child could be apprenticed unless his or her father had land to the value of 20s. a year, attested by two Justices of the Peace.[1] In the eleventh year of Henry the Seventh it was enacted that vagabonds, and idle and suspected persons, should be set in the stocks three days and three nights, be sustained only on bread and water, and then put out of the town, with a forfeiture of 1s. on those who gave them more.[2] In 1530, under Henry

---

[1] Reeves, op. cit. ii. 465.   [2] *Ib.* iii. 134.

Abolition of Serfdom in England. 179

the Eighth, a vagabond taken begging "was at the first time to be whipped out of the place at the end of a cart until his body was bloody: and he was to take an oath to return to the place where he was born, and there labour as a true man ought. Those found a second time in a state of vagrancy were not only to be whipped, but to have the upper part of the gristle of the right ear clean cut off. For a third offence he was to be committed to prison by a Justice, and then indicted for wandering and loitering; and if found guilty, he was to suffer death as a felon and enemy of the commonwealth."[1]

Even these savage laws failed to suppress vagrancy; and the clique that governed England in the name of Edward the Sixth, in 1547, passed a law, the preamble of which "laments the increase of vagabonds, and declares them to be more in number than in other regions," and then goes on to ordain—

That any person may apprehend those living idly, wandering and loitering about without employment, being servants out of place, or the like, and bring them before two Justices, who, upon proof by two witnesses or confession of the party, were to adjudge such offender to be a vagabond, and to cause him to be marked with a hot iron on the breast with the mark of V, and adjudge him to be a slave to the person who brought him and presented him, and to his executors, for two years. The person was to keep him upon bread, water, or small drink, and refuse meat, and cause him to work, by beating,

---
[1] *Ib.* iii. pp. 259, 260.

chaining, or otherwise, in any work or labour he pleased, be it ever so vile. If such slave absented himself from his master within the two years, for the space of fourteen days, then he was to be adjudged by two Justices to be marked on the forehead, or the ball of the cheek, with a hot iron with the sign of an S, and farther adjudged to be a slave to his master for ever; and if he run away a second time, he was to be deemed a felon. Any person to whom a man was adjudged a slave, had authority to put a ring of iron about his neck, arm, or leg. . . . Any child of the age of five years, and under fourteen, wandering with or without such vagabonds, might be taken, and adjudged by a Justice to be servant or apprentice to the apprehender till twenty years of age, if a female, and twenty-four if a man-child; the child to be treated as a slave, and punished with irons or otherwise, if he run away. The master might assign and transfer such slaves for the whole or any part of their time.[1]

This is perhaps the most atrocious law that ever disgraced the Statute-Book of a Christian country, and it is some consolation to know, as Blackstone tells us, that "the spirit of the nation could not brook this condition, even in the most abandoned rogues, and therefore this Statute was repealed in two years afterwards."[2] The Statute of Henry the Eighth was substituted for it. In the reign of Queen Elizabeth, several laws of a similar kind were passed. Sir Thomas Smith gives the practical scope of them in these words:

And if any young man unmarried be without service, he shall be compelled to get him a master, whom he must serve for that yeare, or else he shall be punished

---

[1] Reeves, op. cit. iii. 462, 463.   [2] *Comment.* bk. i. c. 14.

with stockes and whipping, as an idle vagabond. And if any man married or unmarried, not having rent or living sufficient to maintain himselfe, doe live so idly, hee is enquired of, and sometimes sent to the jayle, sometimes otherwise punished as a sturdie Vagabond; so much our policy doth abhorre idleness. This is one of the chief charges of the Justices of Peace in every shire. . . . As England is governed at this day, the eight and twentie of March, Anno 1565, in the seventh yeare of the Raigne and Administration thereof of the most religious, vertuous, and noble Queene Elizabeth, Daughter of King Henry the Eighth, and in the one and fiftieth yeere of mine age, when I was Ambassadour for her Majestie in the Court of France.[1]

Now, how came England to be "more than other regions" overrun with these "sturdie vagabonds"? Lord Bacon tells us in his *Life of Henry the Seventh:*

Inclosures at that time began to be more frequent, whereby Arable Land (which could not be manured without people and families) was turned into pasture, which was easily rid by a few Herds-men; and Tenancies for Years, Lives, and At Will (Whereupon much of the Yeomanry lived) were turned into Demesnes. This bred a decay of People. . . . The King's wisdom . . . and the Parliaments . . . Took a course to take away depopulating Inclosures. . . . The Ordinance was, That all Houses of Husbandry, that were used with twenty acres of Ground, and upwards, should be maintained and kept up for ever; together with a competent proportion of land to be used and occupied with them; and in no wise to be severed from them. . . . This upon Forfeiture

---

[1] *Commonwealth of England, circa finem.*

to be taken ... by seisure of the Land itself, by the King and Lords of the fee, as to half the profits, till the Houses and Lands were restored. By this means the houses being kept up, did of necessity enforce a Dweller; and the proportion of Land for occupation being kept up, did of necessity enforce that dweller not to be a Beggar or Cottager, but a man of some substance, that might keep Hinds and Servants, and set the Plough on going.[1]

Bacon's idea was that it was most important to keep up the English yeomanry, as the main strength of the army. For he says presently:

To make good Infantry it requireth men bred, not in a servile or indigent fashion, but in some free and plentiful manner. Therefore if a State run most to Noblemen and Gentlemen, and that the Husbandmen and Plough-men be but as their work-folks and labourers, or else meer Cottagers (which are but housed Beggars), you may have a good Cavalry, but never good stable bands of Foot.

This passage shows that land was falling out of cultivation, that there was a difficulty in keeping up the farms of twenty acres and more, once held in villenage, but now enclosed as part of the domain of the lord. That the cottager class had no longer their five acres of land for their own use, but were mere "housed beggars." The poor had already begun to drift into the towns. The dissolution of the monasteries by Henry the Eighth must have aggravated these evils enormously. Godwin says of the dissolution of the smaller monasteries,

[1] *History of Henry the Seventh*, pp. 43, 44. Edit. 1676.

These things of themselves were distasteful to the vulgar sort. Each one did as it were claim a share in the goods of the Church. . . . But the commiseration of so many people, to the number of at least ten thousand, who were, without any warning given, thrust out of doors and committed to the mercy of the world, was a more forcible cause of general distaste.[1]

It is very doubtful whether even the copy-holders on the abbey lands could make good their claims, and the lesser serfs found themselves "free" indeed from serfdom, but ejected from the land on which their forefathers had lived, and handed over to the tender mercies of the greedy courtiers of Henry, or to the operation of those new-fangled laws which punished poverty as a crime. Froude shows that under Edward the Sixth these evils became worse and worse.

Leases as they fell in could not obtain renewal; the copy-holder, whose farm had been held by his forefathers so long that custom seemed to have made it his own, found his fines or his rent quadrupled, or himself without alternative expelled. The Act against the pulling down of farmhouses had been evaded by the repair of a room which might be occupied by a shepherd; a single furrow would be driven across a meadow of a hundred acres, to prove that it was still under the plough. The highways and the villages were covered with forlorn and outcast families, now reduced to beggary, who had been the occupiers of comfortable holdings; and thousands of dispossessed tenants made their way to London, clamouring in the midst of their starving children at the

---

[1] *Annals*, p. 84. Edit. 1675.

doors of the courts of law for redress which they could not obtain.[1]

Mr. Thorold Rogers, after reviewing the history of the last six hundred years, says, that to his mind, "England was at its lowest degradation during the twenty years which intervened between the destruction of the monasteries and the restoration of the currency."[2]

Thus the immediate consequence of the abolition of villenage or serfdom in England, inasmuch as the emancipated serf was ejected from his holding on the land, was the creation of that frightful amount of pauperism, which is at once the disgrace and danger of the British Empire.

When Henry the Eighth, and the guardians of Edward the Sixth had destroyed, under the pretext of superstitious uses, all the institutions by which poverty had hitherto been relieved in England, it was found necessary to provide some substitute. Accordingly, we find several Statutes of Queen Elizabeth, resulting at length in that celebrated Statute of 1600, which directed the appointment of "overseers of the poor," and workhouses for each parish or district; and authorized them to assess the inhabitants for the maintenance "of the lame, impotent, old, and blind, and such other among them being poor and not able to work." This Act, the foundation of our present Poor Laws, is variously estimated by many of us. Mr. T. Rogers says:

---

[1] *History*, v. p. 112.   [2] *Work and Wages*, p. 574.

I can conceive nothing more cruel, I had almost said more insolent, than to condemn a labourer to the lowest possible wages on which life may be sustained, by an Act of Parliament, interpreted and enforced by an ubiquitous body of magistrates, whose interest it was to screw the pittance down to the lowest conceivable margin, and to inform the stinted recipient that, when he had starved on that during the days of his strength, others must work to maintain him in sickness or old age. Now this was what the Statute of Apprenticeship, supplemented by the Poor Law, did in the days of Elizabeth. And if you go into the streets and alleys of our large towns, and, indeed, of many English villages, you will meet the fruit of the wickedness of Henry, and the policy of Elizabeth's counsellors in the degradation and helplessness of your countrymen. (*Ibid.* p. 425.)

At any rate, whatever our opinion about the Poor Laws may be, we cannot but see what vast and vital questions are bound up with the history of the "Abolition of Serfdom in England."

LECTURE V.

SLAVERY IN BRITISH COLONIES.

ALTHOUGH, as Blackstone says, "the law of England abhors, and will not endure the existence of slavery within this nation . . . and now it laid down, that a slave or negro, the instant he lands in England, becomes a freeman;"[1] yet at the time that Blackstone wrote, the slave-trade was practised extensively in British colonies. It may be well, therefore, to add a few words on the English slave-trade, and especially on the transportation of free British subjects into slavery.

When Mr. Bryan Edwards, in the beginning of the present century, wrote his *History of the West Indies*, he had to contemplate "the sad prospect of 45,000 reasonable beings (in the English islands only) in a state of barbarity and slavery."[2]

The Portuguese, under Prince Henry, in 1442, commenced the traffic in negroes through Gonsalez receiving, as part of the ransom for some Moorish prisoners, ten blacks. His countrymen, stimulated by his success, fitted out numerous ships for the same traffic, and in 1481 they built a fort on the Gold Coast, and the King took the title of Lord

[1] *Comment.* bk. i. c. 14. [2] Op. cit. ii. p. 39.

of Guinea. In 1517, Charles the Fifth granted a patent to certain persons for the exclusive supply of 4,000 negroes annually to Hispaniola, Cuba, Jamaica, and Porto Rico. The limitation as to number was due to the suggestion of the celebrated Las Casas, whose bitter regret for having in any way contributed to the enslavement of the negroes has been ably proved by Sir Arthur Helps.[1]

The first Englishman to engage in the slave-trade was the notorious buccaneer, Sir John Hawkins, who, in his voyages, discovered "that negroes were very good merchandize in Hispaniola, and that lots of negroes might easily be had on the coast of Guiney; he resolved to make trial thereof," and in 1562 sailed for Sierra Leone, where he soon got possession, "partly by the sword, and partly by other means," of 300 negroes, whom he sold in Hispaniola, and came back well satisfied with his success. Elizabeth was eager to share in so lucrative a trade, and appointed Hawkins to the command of a naval squadron, which sailed from Plymouth in 1564, on the same nefarious errand. Mr. Edwards justly calls him "a murderer and a robber."

In 1618, King James the First granted an exclusive charter to Sir Robert Rich and others for raising a joint stock for a trade to Guinea; and Charles the First erected by charter, in 1631, a second Company to enjoy the sole trade for thirty-one years. In 1662, a third Company was

[1] *Life of Las Casas*, Preface, p. xiii.

incorporated by Charles the Second, with his brother the Duke of York at the head of it, to supply our West Indian plantations with 3,000 negroes annually. In 1672, the fourth and last Company, called the "Royal African Company," was established, under the highest patronage, and exported goods to the value of £70,000 a year. After the Revolution of 1688, this Company came to an end, and the trade was thrown open. The British monopoly in the slave-trade passed through various phases of prosperity and failure; and, in 1771, 192 ships from Liverpool, London, Bristol, and Lancaster transported 47,146 negroes from Africa to the colonies. The total number of slaves transported by the British, French, Dutch, Danes, and Portuguese at the time when Mr. Edwards composed his work was 74,000 annually. On March 25, 1807, the Royal assent was given to the Act for the Abolition of the Slave-Trade, through the persevering efforts of Mr. Wilberforce. But it was not until 1833 that the Act for the Emancipation of all slaves in British territory was passed, with an indemnity of £20,000,000 to the slave proprietors.

There is, however, another phase of British slavery, which comes more distinctly within the scope of this work than that of negro slavery, viz., the traffic in white slaves. Mr. Froude gives proof of a sale of Spaniards at Dover in 1571:

The extraordinary spectacle was actually witnessed, of Spanish gentlemen being disposed of openly in Dover market at a hundred pounds apiece, and being kept in irons at the court-house till their friends could purchase their liberty.[1]

This was a manifestly exceptional case. Nevertheless, the legal "penal servitude" was for a long period literal slavery, especially in the case of those transported to America and the West Indies. The earliest *History of the Island of Barbadoes*, by Richard Ligon, gentleman, published in 1673, gives a graphic account of the island when that gentleman visited it in 1647, less than two years before the execution of Charles the First. He says:

The island is divided into three sorts of men, viz., masters, servants, and slaves. The slaves and their posterity, being subject to their masters for ever, are kept and preserved with greater care than the servants, who are theirs but for five years, according to the law of the island. So that for the time the servants have the worst lives, for they are put to very hard labour, ill lodging, and their diet very slight. . . . Upon the arrival of any ship that brings servants to the island, the planters go aboard; and having bought such of them as they like, send them with a guide to his plantation; and being come, commands them instantly to make their cabins, which they, not knowing how to do, are to be advised by other of their servants, that are their seniors; but if they be churlish, and will not show them, or if materials be wanting to make them cabins, then they are to lie on the ground all that night. . . . If they be not strong men, this ill lodging will put them into a sickness; if they complain, they

[1] *Hist.* vol. ix. p. 486. Pop. Edit.

are beaten by the overseer; if they resist, their time is doubled. I have seen an overseer beat a servant with a cane about the head, till the blood has followed, for a fault that is not worth the speaking of; and yet he must have patience, or worse will follow. Truly, I have seen such cruelty there done to servants, as I did not think one Christian could have done to another. (Op. cit. pp. 43, 44.)

Mr. Ligon tells a story which shows that this servitude was not merely an allotment to a master, but the "servants" actually became his property, so that he could sell them again.

There was a planter in the island that came to his neighbour, and said to him: "Neighbour, I hear you have lately bought good store of servants out of the last ship that came from England, and I hear withal, that you want provisions. I have great want of a woman-servant, and would be glad to make an exchange; if you will let me have some of your woman's flesh, you shall have some of my hog's flesh." So the price was set a groat a pound for the hog's flesh, and sixpence for the woman's flesh. The scales were set up, and the planter had a maid that was extream fat, lasie, and good for nothing; her name was *Honor*. The man brought a great fat sow, and put it in one scale, and *Honor* was put in the other; but when he saw how much the maid outweighed his sow, he broke off the bargain, and would not go on. Though such a case as this may seldom happen, yet 'tis an ordinary thing, there, to sell their servants to one another for the time they have to serve; and in exchange receive any commodities that are in the island. (*Ibid.* p. 59.)

These passages show only too clearly what was the fate that awaited not only felons, but those who were shipped out to the plantations as "servants." In the case of those who would now be called political prisoners, the term of five years' service was extended indefinitely, as will shortly be seen.

There is a curious passage in Ligon's book, which shows that some remnant of the old Catholic idea that Christians could not be made slaves of, still remained among these planters. A slave to whom Ligon had explained a compass was so impressed with his superior knowledge that he declared his intention of becoming a Christian; "for he thought to be a Christian, was to be endowed with all those knowledges he wanted."

I promised to do my best endeavour; and when I came home spoke to the master of the plantation, and told him that poor Sambo desired much to be a Christian. But his answer was, that the people of that island were governed by the laws of England, and by those laws we could not make a Christian a slave. I told him my request was far different from that, for I desired him to make a slave a Christian. His answer was, that it was true there was a great difference in that; but being once a Christian, he could no more account him a slave, and so lose the hold they had of them as slaves, by making them Christians; and by that means should open such a gap as all the planters in the island would curse him. So I was struck mute, and poor Sambo kept out of the Church, as ingenious, as honest, and as good a natured poor soul as ever wore black or eat green. (*Ibid.* p. 50.)

This scruple as to holding Christians in slavery does not seem to have disturbed the Puritans, who probably did not regard Catholics as Christians.

An example, which shows how little scruple these planters had in making slaves of free natives, has been given, in an embellished form, in the eleventh number of *The Spectator* by Sir Richard Steele. Ligon's original is as follows:

As for the Indians, we have but few, and those fetcht from the neighbouring islands, some from the main, which we make slaves. . . . We had an Indian woman, a slave in the house, who was of excellent shape and colour, for it was a pure bright bay. . . . The Indian dwelling near the sea-coast, upon the main[land], an English ship put into a bay, and sent some of her men ashoar, to try what victuals or water they could find, for in some distress they were. But the Indians perceiving them to go up so far into the country, as they were sure they could not make a safe retreat, intercepted them in their return, and fell upon them, chasing them into a wood, and being dispersed there, some were taken and some killed. But a young man amongst them, straggling from the rest, was met by this Indian maid, who upon the first sight fell in love with him, and hid him close from her countrymen (the Indians) in a cave, and there fed him, till they could safely go down to the shoar, where the ship lay at anchor, expecting the return of their friends. But at last, seeing them upon the shoar, sent the long-boat for them, and brought them away. But the youth, when he came ashoar in the Barbadoes, forgot the kindness of the poor maid, that had ventured her life for his safety, and sold her for a slave, who was as free born as he. And so poor Yarico, for her love, lost her liberty. (*Ibid.* pp. 54, 55.)

As early as 1618, one Owen Evans caused great consternation in Somersetshire by pretending a commission "to press maidens to be sent to the Bermudas and Virginia."[1]

Records are noted such as these: "Hope shortly to send 200 English to be exchanged for as many negroes."[2] Under Cromwell, the Council of State (1649) are "informed that 170 Irish have been taken at sea. Desire them to treat with those who trade to the English plantations to transport the common men thither, where their services may be made use of."[3] By order of Council of State, "liberty to be given to Henry Hazard and Robert Immans of the city of Bristol, merchants, to carry 200 Irishmen from any port in Ireland to the Caribee Islands, and to Robt. Lewellin, of London, merchant, to have 300 men."[4] "For a licence to Sir John Clotworthy to transport to America 500 natural Irishmen."[5] Licence to merchants of Boston to "pass to New England and Virginia, where they intend to carry 400 Irish children; directing a warrant to be granted, provided security is given to sail to Ireland, and within two months, to take in 400 Irish children, and transport them to those plantations."[6]

When Cromwell found that it was impossible to carry out his original design of extirpating the whole Catholic population of Ireland, he adopted

---

[1] Calendar State Papers, *Colonial* (1574—1660), p. 19.
[2] *Ibid.* p. 278 (A.D. 1638).   [3] *Ibid.* p. 328.
[4] *Ibid.* p. 387 (Aug. 20, 1652).   [5] *Ibid.* p. 401 (April 1, 1653).
[6] *Ibid.* 407 (Sept. 6, 1653).

the expedient of allowing the chieftains to expatriate themselves with a certain number of followers. According to Sir Wm. Petty, thirty-four thousand officers and men enlisted in the armies of France, Spain, Austria, and the republic of Venice.[1] Their wives and children were next to be disposed of; and the same author tells us that not less than six thousand boys and women were transported to the West Indies, where Lynch says they were sold for slaves. His words are:

They sent away to the most remote part of the Indies many droves of old men and youths, a vast multitude of virgins and matrons, that the former might pass their lives in hard slavery, and the latter maintain themselves even by their own prostitution. . . . Many priests (*mystæ*) are sent away to the islands of the Indies, that they might be sold by auction, and be set to the most degrading offices and employed in twisting tobacco.[2]

The number of exiles has never been ascertained. . . . After this drain the morality of the Irish people was protected by the following article of the Irish Republican Commissioners: "That Irish women, as being too numerous now, be sold to merchants, and transported to Virginia, New England, Jamaica, or other countries, where they may support themselves by their labour. (Porter, p. 292)."[3]

[1] *Political Anatomy of Ireland*, p. 313.
[2] *Cambrensis Eversus*. By Gratianus Lucius (Lynch). Published in 1662, and dedicated to Charles the Second. Reprinted by the Celtic Society. The above passages will be found in vol. iii. pp. 182, 198.
[3] Op. cit. vol. i. p. 24. Note by Editor, Rev. Matthew Kelly, who says in another note, p. 62, that he "heard from a person who was in the West Indies in 1800, that the Irish language was then commonly spoken in the island of Montserrat."

The Editor quotes a letter on the state of Ireland (1652—1656) by Father Quin, S.J.:

Whole cargoes of poor Catholics are shipped to Barbadoes and the islands of America, that thus those whom shame prevents from being murdered by the sword may fall under the doom of perpetual banishment. Sixty thousand, I think, have already been shipped; the wives and children of those who were banished in the beginning to Spain and Belgium are now sentenced to be transported to America.[1]

It is most difficult to get authentic information about these unfortunate exiles. Mr. Maurice Lenihan says:

Father O'Hartegan, who brought to Limerick the standards taken by Owen Roe, had been the agent of the Confederation at the Court of France. . . . We know nothing of Father Hartegan till the year 1650, when 25,000 Irishmen, sold as slaves in St. Kitts and the adjoining island, petitioned for a priest. Through the Admiral du Poenry, the petition was placed in Father Hartegan's hands. He was a Limerick Jesuit. He volunteered himself, and disappeared from our view. As he spoke Irish, English, and French, he was very fit for that mission, which was always supplied with Irish Jesuits from Limerick for more than a hundred years afterwards. It is thought that Father Hartegan assumed the name of De Stritch, to avoid giving umbrage to the English; for, in the year 1650, according to letters written five years after the petition, an Irish Father De Stritch was welcomed and blessed by the Irish of St. Kitts, heard the confessions of three thousand of them, then went disguised as a timber merchant to Montserrat, employed numbers of Irish as woodcutters,

[1] *Ibid.* p. 82.

revealed his true character to them, and spent the mornings administering the sacraments and the day in hewing wood, to throw dust in the eyes of the English.[1]

The same writer adds:

Before we leave the Irish slaves, we may say one word more about their missionaries. In 1699, Father Garganel, S.J., Superior in the island of Martinique, asked for one or two Irish Fathers for that and the neighbouring islands, which were full of Irish; for, continues he, every year shiploads of men, boys, and girls, partly crimped, partly carried off by main force for purposes of slave trade, are conveyed by the English from Ireland.[2]

A very rare little book, published at Innspruck in 1659, by F. M. Morison, O.Min., states:

Besides those whom they slew (1651), after a treaty had been entered upon and amnesty promised, they sent into perpetual exile 32,000 men and women from divers parts of the kingdom to different countries of the world.[3]

An. 1657, I myself saw this iniquitous law carried out into iniquitous execution in the city of Limerick in Ireland, by Henry Ingoldsby, Governor of the same city. A certain noble gentleman of Thomond, named Daniel Connery, was accused of harbouring a priest in his house and convicted on his own confession (although the priest had safe-conduct from the Governor himself), and declared guilty of death. And then, as he said, out

---

[1] *Limerick*. By Maurice Lenihan, Esq., p. 668. [2] *Ibid*. p. 669.
[3] *Threnodia Hiberno-Catholica*, p. 16. The copy of this work in the Grenville Library of the British Museum, has the following note in Thomas Grenville's own handwriting: "I have not been able to trace any other copy; probably few if any copies from Innspruck were circulated in this country." The book only contains 72 pages of large print, 18mo.

of mercy, the sentence was changed, commuted, and he was despoiled of all his goods, and bound in prison, and finally condemned to perpetual exile. This gentleman had a wife and twelve children. His wife was of a very noble family of Thomond, and she fell sick, and died in extreme want even of necessaries. Three of the children, very beautiful and virtuous virgins, were sent off to the East (*sic*) Indies, to an island which they call Barbadoes, where, if they are still alive, they pass their days in miserable slavery. The rest of the children, who from their tender years could not work, have either perished from hunger, or live unhappily under the cruel yoke of heretics.[1]

If a Catholic cannot pay the fine for non-attendance at the Protestant church, an. 1658, he will certainly be sold as a slave, sent away to the East Indies (*Indias Orientales*), where he passes the remainder of his life in miserable slavery.[2]

After the conquest of Jamaica in 1655, and the occupation of Barbadoes, the Governor of the latter island writes to Cromwell to assure him that the political prisoners shall not be released after the usual term has expired:

Such as hitherto have bin brought to this island from England, Scotland, and Ireland, have been landed on merchants accompts, who claimeing a propertie in the persons they bring as servants, for theire passage and disbursments on them, dispose of them heare, either for a tearme of yeares to serve, or for a summe of money, by which they free themselves from such servitude, either of which being performed, they have freedome to stay or departe hence, by the law and customes of the place. For the future, such as your highnes shall please

---

[1] *Ibid.* pp. 28, 29.   [2] *Ibid.* p. 34.

to command theire stay heare, I shall to the utmoste possibility of meanes to be used, labour to keepe them with us in pursuance of your highnes' commands.¹

Henry Cromwell, Major-General of the Forces in Ireland, writes to Thurloe, September 11, 1655:

I received yours of the 4th instant, and give you many thankes for your relation of Jamaica. . . . I have endeavoured to make what improvement I could in the short time allotted me toucheing the furnishinge you with a recruite of men, and a supply of younge Irish girles. . . . Concerninge the younge women, although we must use force in takeinge them up, yet it being so much for their owne goode, and likely to be of soe great advantage to the publique, it is not in the least doubted that you may have such number of them as you shall thinke fitt to make use uppon this account.²

Again, on September 18th, he writes:

I shall not need to repeate anythinge aboute the girles, not doubt- inge but to answerr your expectationes to the full in that; and I think it might bee of like advantage to your affaires their, and ours heer, if you should thinke fitt to send 1,500 or 2,000 younge boys of 12 or 14 yeares of age to the place aforementioned. We could well spare them, and they would be of use to you; and who knows, but that it may be a meanes to make them English-men, I meane rather Christianes.³

Lord Broghill to Secretary Thurloe, September 18th:

For women and maids, you must declare what you will give them on ship-bord, and what ther conditions

---

¹ Thurloe, *State Papers*, iv. 7. ² *Ibid.* p. 23. ³ *Ibid.* p. 40.

shall be, when ther. For my part, I beleeve you may get many more out of Ireland than heer, which I thought not impertinent to minde you of.[1]

Thurloe writes to Henry Cromwell, Sept. 25th:

I returne your lordship most humble thanks for the letter I received from you touching transporting of Irish girles to Jamaica.[2]

Again he writes:

I did hope to have given your lordship an account by this post of the bussines of causinge younge wenches and youths in Ireland to be sent into the West-Indies; but I could not make thinges ready. The comittee of the counsell have voted 1,000 girles, and as many youths be taken up for that purpose, &c.[3]

Thirty-three Royalist naval officers complain, on December 30, 1655,

That those who usurp the present power in England ... most barbarously have sold and sent away many of those our friends (free-born subjects to the crown of England) for slaves into some of the foreign plantations under the present power, &c.[4]

This transporting of free subjects into slavery did not cease at the Restoration, as appears from the letter of Father Garganel. In fact, it was applied equally to all persons convicted. Thus, in 1666,

The resolutions about the Scotch rebels is to hang all ministers and officers; of the common sort, one in ten is to be executed, or forced to confession, and the rest sent to plantations.[5]

[1] *Ibid.* p. 41.   [2] *Ibid.* p. 55.   [3] *Ibid.* p. 75   [4] *Ibid.* p. 360.
[5] Calendar State Papers, *Colonial* (1661—1668), p. 432.

Some observations on Barbadoes in 1667, note that there are

Not above 760 considerable proprietors, and 8,000 effective men, of which two-thirds are of no reputation and little courage, and a very great part Irish, derided by the negroes as white slaves. . . . Has inspected many plantations, and seen thirty or forty English, Scotch, and Irish at work in the parching sun, without shirt, shoe, or stocking; and negroes at their trades, in good condition; by which the whole may be endangered, for now there are many thousands of slaves that speak English, and if there are many leading men slaves in a plantation, they may be easily wrought upon to betray it, especially on the promise of freedom.[1]

When the infamous Judge Jeffreys held his "Bloody Assize" after the suppression of Monmouth's rebellion, out of those who escaped the gallows, "above eight hundred were given to different persons to be transported for ten years to the West Indies."[2] The historian says that "with respect to prisoners made in the field, it was argued [in the time of Elizabeth] that to them, as they might lawfully have been put to death on the spot, any fate short of death must be considered a favour: hence they were often transferred by gift or sale to others, who employed them as slaves, or by cruel treatment extorted from them or their relatives exorbitant ransoms. Afterwards, when colonies had been established in the West India Islands, these unhappy men were generally sold for a high price to the planters, to serve them

---

[1] *Ibid.* an. 1667.   [2] Lingard, vol. x. p. 181.

as slaves during life, or for a certain term of years."[1]

An authentic account by one of the victims has come down to us. Henry Pitman acted as surgeon to the forces of the Duke of Monmouth, and, though he had never been in arms, was taken prisoner after the defeat at Sedgemoor, in 1685, tried by Judge Jeffreys, and ordered to be transported to the Caribee Islands.

And in order thereunto, my brother and I, with nearly a hundred more, were given to Jeremiah Nepho, and by him sold to George Penne, a needy Papist, that wanted money to pay for our transportation. . . . He at length prevailed upon with our relations to give him £60, upon condition that we should be free when we came to Barbadoes; only owning some person, whom we should think fit to nominate, as a titular master. . . . And thus we may see the buying and selling of free men into slavery, was beginning again to be renewed among Christians.

When they got to Barbadoes, they found that a special Act of the Governor and Assembly of that island had been passed providing that no such arrangement as this should stand, but that every rebel sent out should serve his full time, and

Be obliged to serve and obey the owner or purchaser of him or them, in their plantations within this island, in all such labour or service as they shall be commanded to do by their owners, masters, or mistresses, or their overseers, for the full time and term of ten years from the day of their landing, and disposed of fully to be

[1] Lingard, vol. x. p. 183.

completed and ended; any bargain, law, usage, or custom in this island to the contrary, in any wise, notwithstanding.[1]

Pitman at first brought much gain to his master by his profession, but on his refusing to practise unless he got better food than the slaves,

> My angry master could not content himself with the bare execution of his cane upon my head, arms, and back, although he played so long thereon, like a furious fencer, until he had split it in pieces; but he also confined me close prisoner in the stocks (which stood in an open place), exposed to the scorching heat of the sun, where I remained about twelve hours, until my mistress, moved either with pity or shame, gave order for my release.[2]

Pitman's brother died of his hardships; but he himself contrived to escape, and, after many hairbreadth escapes, got back to England.

Henry and William Pitman both appear in the "Lists of convicted Rebels," as having been "sold and disposed of here in Barbadoes," with seventy others, by order of George Penne, Esq., 1685. The lists contain the names of 792 persons to be thus disposed of, but some of these died on the voyage.[3]

---

[1] *A Relation of the Great Sufferings and Strange Adventures of Henry Pitman, Chirurgeon to the late Duke of Monmouth*, 1689. Reprinted in Arber's *English Garner*, vol. vii. pp. 338—340.

[2] *Ibid.* p. 346.

[3] See *The Original Lists*, &c., 1600—1700. Edited by J. C. Hotten, pp. 315—344. The Editor says: "It must not be imagined that the following pages furnish by any means a complete list of the early settlers in America. . . . We learn incidentally that ships left England almost daily for America, but no records of them, or of their passengers remain." (*Introd.*)

There is no allusion in Bryan Edwards' *History of the West Indies* to this reduction of free British subjects to slavery; but it is too well attested to be doubted, and therefore we have thought it right to investigate it in connection with the subject of Slavery and Serfdom.

LECTURE VI.

THE ABOLITION OF SERFDOM IN EUROPE.

1.—France.

IT seemed more convenient, in the first place, to trace the abolition of serfdom in the British Isles, where it disappeared long before it was abolished in other European countries. But, in order to follow out the subject with regard to the rest of Europe, we must retrace our steps and go back to the ninth century, and recall the condition of the serfs under Charlemagne and his successors.[1]

We then saw how a serf, at any rate on the abbey lands, enjoyed much the same degree of comfort, and material and spiritual happiness, as a tenant farmer under a good landlord does at the present day. He could not be evicted from his holding, and he could appeal to custom for the maintenance of his privileges. But it must be confessed that much of his happiness depended upon the disposition of his lord. On the abbey lands and on the royal domains he was comparatively secure; but not so on the property of inferior and more capricious lords. The chartulary of the Abbey of St. Bertin traces the fortunes of that monastery

[1] See Lecture ii. pp. 73—81.

from the year 648, when it was founded, to 1176. For a large portion of this period the abbey was governed by the Counts of Flanders. Baldwin the Second, in 915, sent a knight named Winemar, who attacked Bishop Folco, the Abbot, on his return from Rheims, pierced him with his lance, and killed him. Winemar was excommunicated, but Baldwin obtained possession of the abbey, and is styled *comes et abbas monasterii Sithiu*.[1]

In 948, Arnulph, *abbas et comes*, being a very pious man, restored the abbey to the government of religious, and King Lothaire, in 962, secured its possessions to the Abbot. But, from time to time, the records disclose a lamentable succession of disorders in the abbey, in consequence of the claims of the officers of the Counts of Flanders to have free quarters therein, while collecting their lord's dues.[2] All sorts of abuses entered with this lay interference. To use the caustic expression of Abbot Simon, the *privilegium* was afterwards called the *pravilegium*, and the house of God became a *spelunca latronum*.[3] The serfs seem to have been crushed and demoralized under the frequent change of masters.

Even at the best serfdom was, after all, only mitigated slavery. There were four chains of slavery which still bound the serf. The right of pursuit, by which he was bound to his lord's property, and could be brought back and punished if he attempted to leave the territory. Secondly,

---

[1] *Cartularium Sithense*, pp. 135, 139.
[2] See op. cit. pp. 185, 190, 191.   [3] *Ibid.* pp. 171, 283.

he was taxable at the will of the lord, and might be set to do any work that was required of him. Thirdly, if he married without his lord's permission either a free woman or the serf of another lord, he forfeited his tenure, or at least a part of it, without any compensation. Lastly, when he died, unless he had relations living in the same house with him, his personal property as well as his tenure reverted to his lord. Custom, especially on the Crown and Church lands, made these chains so light as to be hardly felt; but it is easy to see how they might become, in the hands of a tyrannical lord, the cause of infinite misery to his serfs. This partly explains how it came to pass that the clergy, who made little haste to emancipate their own serfs, were diligent in inculcating on princes and nobles the merit of emancipation. The Kings of France took the lead in the emancipations, although there are few instances during the tenth and eleventh centuries.

From the twelfth century to the fifteenth, we meet with numerous royal charters of emancipation. The serfs of St. Denis were enfranchised in 1125, those of Orleans in 1180, of Auxerre in 1223, of St. Germain in 1250; those of Pierrefonds and Châtenay by Queen Blanche in the same thirteenth century, and all the serfs in the royal domains on the 3rd of July, 1315, of Dauphiné in 1367, and in part of Brittany in 1484. The serfs of the Duke of Burgundy were emancipated in the twelfth century. The serfs on the vast domains of the great Abbey of St. Germain des Prés were made free in the thirteenth century.[1] The motives of these emancipations are frequently expressed in the charters. When Louis the Seventh abolished serfdom in Orleans in 1180, he says he is "incited to this act by his royal piety and clemency, for the salvation of our soul, and those of our ancestors, and that of our son Philip." In 1311, Charles of Valois emancipated the serfs of his county, because "the human race, which is formed in the image of our Lord, ought generally to be free by natural right," and because he felt himself "moved with pity, for the remedy and salvation of our own soul, and in consideration of humanity and the common profit."[2] This last mentioned consideration doubtless, as in all human actions, had no small influence. Sometimes it is plainly stated, as by Hugh, Archbishop of Besançon, in a charter of emancipation, who gives several economical reasons, and adds: "Those who are bound by mortmain neglect their work, saying that they are working for others, and therefore they spoil their holdings, and do not care for more than their own sojourn on it, whereas, if they were certain that it would remain to their heirs, they would labour and reclaim it with heartiness."[3] In 1354, Guillaume Choiseul, in a charter to the inhabitants of Aigremont, and La Riviere, says that his serfs "left the houses to fall into ruins, and abandoned the country to withdraw

---

[1] Garsonnet, *Histoire des locations perpetuelles*, p. 488.
[2] Allard, *Esclaves, Serfs*, &c., p. 246.
[3] Perreciot, *L'Etat Civil des Personnes*, &c. vol. iii.; *Preuves*, n. 126, p. 251.

into the free towns, which has much desolated our heart."[1]

Another motive seems to have been the great lack of money that Kings and nobles experienced in the beginning of the fourteenth century. The decree of Louis the Tenth, in 1315, did not set the serfs free for nothing, but offered them freedom for a price, which it was well known they could afford to give. But these emancipations were not always accepted with eagerness. No sooner were some of the serfs set free, than they hastened to give themselves as serfs to the Church. The children of serfs and free women, who were free by the Frankish law, preferred the condition of their fathers to that of their mothers. The serfs of Pierrefonds, emancipated by Philip the Third, with the prohibition against their marrying serf wives under pain of returning to serfdom, lost no time in contravening the decree, and immediately applied to Parliament to ratify their return to their former state. The King was obliged to threaten to draft them into the army, and to levy a heavy war-tax upon them.[2]

Another cause of emancipation was the rise of village communes. The pastors of the Church saw the country constantly ravaged by the incessant wars of one prince or noble against another; which wars the royal authority was not powerful enough to repress. And in their Councils they prevailed upon the nobles to swear to keep the Peace of God, and not to molest clerics, monks,

[1] Allard, op. cit. p. 248. [2] *Ibid.* pp. 251—254.

travellers, labourers, and women; and to keep the Truce of God, that is, not to fight from the Wednesday evening to the Monday morning of each week, or during Advent, Christmas, Lent, and Rogation week. In order to keep these pugnacious gentlemen to their word, large associations, formed of the whole male population of the locality, marched, often under the leadership of the parish priest, to attack the castles of the nobles who violated the Peace or Truce. Louis the Fat found these village associations of great service to him in repressing the brigandage of turbulent nobles. But it is easy to see how rapidly a movement of this kind would swell far beyond the control of those who first set it in motion.[1] The community of interest, the meeting together for common action and mutual defence, taught them the power which their numbers gave them, and this power enabled them to dictate terms to their lords in places where serfdom was most oppressive, and to insist upon the customs of more favoured localities being introduced.[2]

[1] In 1358, when King John was a prisoner in England, after the Battle of Poictiers, the peasants in the neighbourhood of Paris broke out into open rebellion against the nobles. They stormed the castles, and slaughtered the nobles and their wives and children, with the most atrocious barbarity. The young Duchess of Orleans, and three hundred of the noblest ladies in France, were only rescued from the worst indignities by the Captal de Buck, a commandant of the Black Prince, who with sixty knights defeated with great slaughter some six thousand of these ruffians, who had invested the city of Meaux, where the ladies had taken refuge.

[2] Allard, op. cit. pp. 255–258. M. Allard quotes M. Semichon work, *La Paix et la Trêve de Dieu*.

O

The Crusades, again, powerfully contributed towards the emancipation of the serfs. The brotherhood in arms which they conferred upon all who took part in them, and the readiness with which many a needy noble would sell to his serfs their freedom, alike tended in the same direction. In many cases, the lords were leaving their families in their castles, without any other protection than the fidelity and good-will of their tenants and serfs; and we read of more than one noble, on the eve of his departure, calling together all his dependents, and bidding them publicly to proclaim any grievances under which they might be suffering, in order that he might do them justice and make restitution, if need be, before setting out on the far-off expedition.[1] Thus, in a variety of ways, did the Crusades help forward the work of emancipation.

To return to the subject of communities of serfs, especially in France, we find traces of them from a very early period. In the ninth century the *Polyptique* of Irmino informs us that farms (*mansi*) were often cultivated by two, and sometimes three families, who lived together, and were called *socii, consortes, domus fraternitatis*. Thus three families, nine persons in all, cultivated seventeen bonniers (about sixty acres) of land. Beaumanoir, in the thirteenth century, mentions similar societies. Masselin, in his *Journal of the States General of 1484*, speaks of a house in the village

---

[1] Sire de Joinville, *Hist. de S. Louis*, xxv.

of Chuc, in the district of Caen, which contained ten families, comprising seventy persons, living together and working in common.[1]

This kind of life was found advantageous even for free peasants; but the benefit in the case of serfs, or *mainmortables*, was immense. The family thus constituted never died: no heriot, relief, or succession fine for decease could be exacted; and, above all, the land did not revert to the lord. And thus was established the principle of customary right: "Serfs or *mainmortables* cannot leave property by will, and do not succeed to one another, unless so far as they live in common."[2] These associations were not necessarily formed of persons united by the ties of blood, yet they naturally were often thus united, and formed a patriarchal household, a tribe. The loaf of bread was the natural type of such a society, and thus its members were called *compani*, that is, those who eat their bread together. Thus, when they made up their minds to separate, the head of the company, according to the recognized custom, took a knife and divided a large loaf into several pieces, according to the divisions in the community.[3]

These associations elected a head, who, with the advice of the elder members of the community, acted as their representative in buying and selling cattle, borrowing money, giving or accepting a

---

[1] Allard, op. cit. pp. 342, 343.
[2] *Ibid.* p. 344. See Loisel, *Institutions Coutumières*, i. 74.
[3] *Ibid.* p. 346, from Troplong, *Du Contrat de Société*, Preface, p. xxxv.

lease, &c. It should be remarked that there is no trace of what are called communistic ideas in these primitive associations. Each one contributed his capital, his labour, and his skill, and the profits of the common labour formed a fund which belonged to the association. But, at the same time, each member preserved the proprietorship of the goods that he possessed before he entered the association. Moreover, each was bound individually to support his own personal expenses, such as giving his daughters their dowry. These daughters, though married outside the association, yet, provided they passed the first night of their married life under the common roof, preserved their rights in the association. For all others residence was a necessary condition of remaining a member of the company.[1] The advantages arising from this common labour and profit made many of these associations so prosperous that they did not care to have their condition altered; and thus, in Burgundy, many of them were found at the beginning of the eighteenth century, still nominally *mainmortables*, and better off than their enfranchised neighbours. In some communities of Auvergne, one part of the company employed themselves in cutlery, while the rest cultivated the land. The wages of the former were put into the common purse, while the association lived on the produce raised by the others.[2]

---

[1] Allard, op. cit. p. 348.
[2] *Ibid.* p. 355, note from Dareste, *Histoire des Classes Agricoles*, p. 235.

It would, however, be a serious mistake to suppose that these circumstances which mitigated serfdom, and rendered the condition of these serfs better in many respects than that of free peasants, is a desirable thing in itself. It could hardly be expected that such disinterestedness and forgetfulness of self as were necessary for the perfect working out of associations of this kind could ordinarily prevail. The strong and the industrious would soon weary of labouring for the weak and indolent; and these would be apt to get into the habit of depending on others. Hence divisions, discord, and ruin would ensue. It appears that these causes of disunion were increased by the introduction of strangers into the company by marriage. Besides, the crowding into one dwelling of several families injured both health and morals. The Abbe de Velard, in 1783, addressed a memorial to the Provincial Assembly of Berry, in which he said: "The habit of common life favoured that of premature marriages, which are one of the chief causes of the feebleness and laziness of the women, and contribute much to the degradation of the human race in Berry."[1] Still, in spite of these inconveniences, so strong was the attachment of the peasants in some parts of France to this common life, that some of these companies survived the Revolution; and M. Dupin, in 1840, visited a community in a corner of Nivernais which had kept up its continuous common life

---

[1] Allard, op. cit. p. 358.

to the well-being and happiness of its members.[1] It should further be noticed that in France the *villanus* was not a "serf," in the same sense as in England in the thirteenth century. His dues, whether in money or labour, were fixed; whereas in England they were at the will of the lord: in France, he could give testimony against his lord in a court of justice; in England, his evidence against his lord was not admissible. In

---

[1] M. de Lavelaye, in his work on *Property and its Primitive Forms*, has an interesting chapter on the Family Communities among the Southern Sclavonic Races in Croatia and Servia, in which he shows that the Servian laws have avoided alike the English extreme of merging all manorial property into immense estates, and the French extreme of so subdividing property that the occupier cannot get a living from it. "The result of English law has been to take landed property out of the hands of those who cultivate it, and to accumulate it in vast *latifundia*, for the benefit of a small number of families of princely opulence. The object of French law, on the contrary, is to secure the possession of the soil to the greatest number, by means of the equal division of inheritances. But this result is only attained by an excessive subdivision, which often cuts the field into strips that are almost too small for cultivation, and which is therefore opposed to any sound system of agriculture. The Servian laws, by maintaining the family community, make every man co-owner of the land which he cultivates, at the same time preserving to the holdings their suitable extent. By means of this association, the advantages of small properties are united with those of agriculture on a large scale. The cultivators may employ the farming implements and distribution of crops customary on large farms, while the produce is divided among the labourers, the same as in countries where the soil is subdivided among a multitude of small owners." (*Primitive Property*, p. 191, Eng. Tr.) Yet M. Lavelaye confesses that the *zadruga*, as this system is called, in spite of its many advantages, is falling into ruins. "In Croatia, the Diet in which the National party was predominant, recently (1874) voted a law forbidding the formation of new communities." (p. 194, note.)

France there was a vast variety in the degrees of serfdom, and there were numerous facilities for passing from the lower to the higher grades; and thus, while some of the remains of serfdom were to be found in that country even on the eve of the Great Revolution, yet in no other country in Europe had the peasantry succeeded in gaining and retaining possession of so much freehold land. This is remarked upon by De Tocqueville as one of the curious facts about the Revolution.[1] On the royal domains, Louis the Sixteenth abolished in 1779 the last remains of serfdom, the *mainmorte*. In 1772, the philippics of Voltaire called universal attention to the grievances of the serfs of the Canons of St. Claude. This was in Franche-Comté; and it was precisely there and in Burgundy that the communities of serfs had prevailed to the greatest extent, and reduced serfdom to the lightest possible yoke. In Lorraine,[2] when the remnant of serfdom was abolished there in 1771, it was commuted for two bushels of rye annually, as a composition for all services.[3] Other instances may be found, but the outburst of the Revolution swept away every vestige of serfdom from the soil of France.

---

[1] *France before the Revolution*, p. 30. (Eng. Edit.)
[2] Allard, op. cit. pp. 383—395. Perreciot, who wrote in 1786, states that one-third of the inhabitants of Franche-Comté were then *mainmortables*. See his work already quoted, ii. p. 119, note.
[3] Dareste, op. cit. p. 231.

2.—Germany.

Let us pass from France to Germany. Hallam tells us that "at the final separation of the French from the German side of the Charlemagne Empire by the Treaty of Verdun in 843, there was perhaps hardly any difference in the constitution of the two kingdoms."[1] The manorial system was firmly established throughout Germany. The laws of the Allemanni and of the Bavarians alike recognize the position of the *coloni* and the *servi*, as on the Frankish side of the Rhine. The feudal system was established in Germany at a somewhat later period than in France. It is very difficult to trace any vestige of the "Free Village Community" which under the name of "Mark" has played so important a part in modern political theories. As in France, slavery, at the time of the separation, was fast becoming merged into serfdom. The *hörigen* of the German manors were the *ascripti glebæ*, while the *leibeigener* of mediæval German law, although he repudiated the title of "slave," was as much the private property of his lord as the Roman *servus*. These two classes, however, became in time confounded, and the *leibeigenen* became attached to the soil. The enormous number of captives taken by Henry the Fowler, in his conquest of Hungary in the tenth century, must have plentifully supplied the country with slaves too rude for any but agricultural labour;

[1] *Middle Ages*, i. p. 202.

and these would naturally soon become attached to the land, and rise into serfs. Mr. Seebohm traces the process thus:

> On the estates of the Church in the early years of the seventh century the humanizing power of Christian feeling had silently raised the status of the slave. It had dignified labour, and given him a property in his labour, securing to him not only one day in seven for rest to his weary and heavy-laden limbs, but also *three days in the week* wherein his labour was *his own*. From slavery he had risen into serfdom. And this serfdom of the quondam slave had become, in the eyes of the still more weary and heavy-laden free labourers on their own land, so light a burden compared with their own —such was the lawless oppression of the age—that they willingly went to the Church and took upon them willingly the yoke of her serfdom, in order that they might find rest under her temporal as well as spiritual protection.[1]

Mr. Seebohm points out that the only early instances upon which G. L. Von Maurer relies for his theory of the original German mark system and free village community are taken from the Cartulary of the Abbey of Lorsch, from which he cites one hundred and seven surrenders of property to the monastery. But an examination of these surrenders shows them to have been mostly little villas with *liti, liberti, coliberti,* and *mancipia* upon them—by no means free village communities.

As in France, the same spirit of Christianity brought about the emancipation, first of the slaves

[1] *English Village Community*, p. 328.

and then of the serfs. In 967, the Abbey of St. Arnould at Metz emancipated the inhabitants of Morvill on condition of their paying a rent. In 1248, Henry Duke of Brabant liberated all the labourers on his domains, and freed them from the mainmorte.[1]

The existence of the free cities, which afforded asylum to serfs who had taken refuge in them, hastened on the emancipation. Bremen was the first city so privileged by Frederick the First in 1186. In 1220, Frederick the Second published general decrees at the Council of Frankfort, forbidding serfs or slaves to take refuge in any of the Imperial cities; but, in 1230, he granted the charters of asylum to the cities of Ratisbon and Vienna. In 1275 and 1290, Rudolph of Hapsburg granted to two cities of the northern league the privilege of enfranchising a refugee after only one year's sojourn. Still the progress of emancipation was much slower in Germany than in France. Where free peasants and serfs are mingled together, the two classes have a tendency to amalgamate. Either the serfs will rise to the level of the free peasants, or the free peasants, as was the case with the Roman *coloni*, will sink to the level of the serfs, according to the general tendency of the country. In France the tendency was towards freedom, and so the French *villein* was free; while in Germany, as in England, he was a serf. No doubt, the vast amount of property held by the great monasteries in Germany made

[1] Allard, *Esclaves*, &c. p. 299.

serfdom less oppressive; and the presence of so many Prince-Bishops at the Diet probably tended to mitigate the severity of the laws relating to the serfs. Yet the power of the German barons in their own little states was exceedingly great, and often arbitrarily abused. Robertson says that "the great body of the people was kept in a state but little removed from absolute servitude. In some places of Germany, people of the lowest class were so entirely in the power of their masters, as to be subjected to personal and domestic slavery."[1] He then goes on to describe what we know to have been the normal condition of serfs, and continues: "These exactions, though grievous, were borne with patience, because they were customary and ancient; but when the progress of elegance and luxury, as well as the changes introduced into the art of war, came to increase the expense of government, and made it necessary for princes to levy occasional or stated taxes on their subjects, such impositions, being new, appeared intolerable; and in Germany, these duties being laid chiefly upon beer, wine, and other necessaries of life, affected the common people in the most sensible manner. The addition of such a load to their former burdens drove them to despair."[2] In 1526, they flew to arms near Ulm in Suabia: "The peasants in the adjacent country flocked to their standard, . . . and the contagion, spreading from province to province, reached almost every part of Germany. Wherever they came, they plundered the monas-

[1] *Charles the Fifth*, bk. iv. p. 381.   [2] *Ibid.* p. 332.

teries, wasted the lands of their superiors, razed their castles, and massacred without mercy all persons of noble birth who were so unhappy as to fall into their hands."[1] A Catholic might be suspected of unjust prejudice if he were to say that this rising of the peasants was the natural result of Luther's tract on *Christian Liberty*, in which he had exhorted the Germans to throw off the yoke of the priests and monks; but it is not possible thus to evade the testimony of the Protestant Robertson, who says:

These commotions happened at first in provinces of Germany where Luther's opinions had made little progress; and being excited wholly by political causes, had no connection with the disputed points in religion. But the phrenzy, reaching at last those countries in which the Reformation was established, derived new strength from circumstances peculiar to them, and rose to a still greater pitch of extravagance. The Reformation, wherever it was received, increased that bold and innovating spirit to which it owed its birth. Men, who had the courage to overturn a system supported by everything which can command respect or reverence, were not to be overawed by any authority, how great or venerable soever. . . . No sooner, then, did the spirit of revolt break out in Thuringia, a province subject to the Elector of Saxony, the inhabitants of which were mostly converts to Lutheranism, than it assumed a new and more dangerous form. Thomas Münzer, one of Luther's disciples, had acquired a wonderful ascendant over the minds of the people. He propagated among them the wildest and most enthusiastic notions. . . . To aim at nothing more than abridging the power of the nobility,

---

[1] *Charles the Fifth*, bk. iv. p. 333.

was now considered as a trifling and partial reformation, not worth the contending for; it was proposed to level every distinction among mankind, and by abolishing property to reduce them to their natural state of equality, in which all should receive their subsistence from one common stock. Münzer assured them that the design was approved of by Heaven, and that the Almighty had in a dream ascertained him of its success. The peasants set about the execution of it, not only with the rage which animated those of their order in other parts of Germany, but with the order which enthusiasm inspires. They deposed the magistrates in all the cities of which they were masters, seized the lands of the nobles, and obliged such of them as they got into their hands to put on the dress commonly worn by peasants, &c.[1]

The princes and nobles assembled such of their followers as remained faithful, and by their superior generalship soon divided and defeated these unwieldy mobs of fanatics; and it is estimated that no less than one hundred thousand of the peasants perished in this outbreak. In his *Table Talk*, Luther did not hesitate to say: "I, Martin Luther, I have shed the blood of the rebellious peasants; for I commanded them to be killed. Their blood is indeed upon my head."[2] It was difficult for him to reply to the taunt of Erasmus: "You disclaim any connection with the insurgents, while they regard you as their parent, and as the author and expounder of their principles." He certainly exhorted the princes to put them down with terrible severity: "Strike, slay, front and rear; nothing is more devilish than sedition; it is a

[1] *Ibid.* pp. 335—337. [2] *Table Talk*, Eislaben Edit. p. 276.

mad dog that bites you if you do not destroy it. There must be no sleep, no patience, no mercy; they are the children of the devil."[1] Yet the demands of these poor deluded serfs, as set forth in their twelve articles, do not seem so unreasonable.

They demanded reduction of tithes, the abolition of serfdom, the restoration to all of fishing and hunting rights, and of the meadow-lands and commons which had once belonged to the people, the mitigation of forced labour, the right of cutting wood in the forests, the right of holding freehold land, and of holding mortgage on the land of others, and the abolition of the fines paid to the lord on the death of a peasant by his widow and orphan children. When Louis, Count Palatine of the Rhine, asked Melancthon his opinion of these articles, the Reformer replied, "That it was his settled conviction, that the Germans had been granted a great deal more liberty than was beneficial to people so rude and uncultured, and that, as Governments can do no wrong, they may confiscate the communal lands and forests, and no one has a right to complain; they may confiscate the wealth of the Church, and no resistance should be made."[2]

This unhappy insurrection threw back for at least a century the emancipation of the German serfs. The Bishops had disappeared from the Diets, and there was no one to plead their cause with the princess. "At the Diet of Güstrow, in 1607, the peasants were declared to be simple *coloni*, who

---

[1] Walch, xvi. 91.   See Alzog. iii. p. 58, American Edit.
[2] Alzog. l.c. p. 59.

were bound to give up possession of their lands, even of those that they might have held from time immemorial, at the desire of their landlords."[1] In 1621, an unlimited right of taxing them was assured to the lords, and if the serfs wished to run away, they were flogged. In 1660, the penalty of death was decreed against those who should leave the principality. In Pomerania, in 1616, the peasants were declared "serfs, and deprived of all civil rights."[2] In the eighteenth century, the serfs on the royal domains of Prussia were emancipated; but M. de Tocqueville informs us that—

In no part of Germany, at the close of the eighteenth century, was serfdom as yet completely abolished, and in the greater part of Germany the people were still literally *ascripti glebæ*, as in the middle ages. Almost all the soldiers who fought in the armies of Frederick the Second, and of Maria Theresa, were in reality serfs. In most of the German states, as late as 1788, a peasant could not quit his domain, and if he quitted it he might be pursued in all places wherever he could be found, and brought back by force. He could neither improve his condition, nor change his calling, nor marry without the good pleasure of his master. To the service of that master a large portion of his time was due. Labour rents (*corvées*) existed to their full extent, and absorbed in some of these countries three days in the week. The peasant rebuilt and repaired the mansion of the lord, carted his produce to market, drove his carriage, and went on his errands. Several years of the peasant's early life were spent in the domestic service of the

---

[1] Döllinger, *The Church and the Churches*, p. 92. (English Trans.) The whole chapter, on "The Church and Civil Freedom," is worth careful study.   [2] *Ibid.* p. 93.

manor-house. The serf . . . was obliged to till his field in a certain manner under the eye of the master, and he could neither dispose of it nor mortgage it at will. In some cases, he was compelled to sell its produce; in others he was restrained from selling it; his obligation to cultivate the ground was absolute.[1]

These "services" are legalized by the code of Frederick the Great, although that code declared that serfdom, properly so-called (*leibeigenshaft*), inasmuch as it established personal servitude, was abolished, but the hereditary subjection (*erbunter-thänigkeit*), which replaced it, and established these obligations, was certainly a kind of servitude. These provisions of the code were published by his successor at the time of the French Revolution.

Serfdom was abolished in Germany at the following dates:

In Baden, in 1783. In Hohenzollern, in 1804. In Schleswig and Holstein, in the same year. In Nassau, in 1808. In Prussia, on the royal domains, as early as 1717. In name by the code of Frederick; but in reality throughout Prussia, in 1809. In Bavaria, in 1808. In Westphalia and Lippe Detmold, in 1809. In Swedish Pomerania, from 1810. In Hesse Darmstadt, from 1811. In Würtemberg, from 1817. In Oldenberg, from 1814. In Mecklenburg, from 1820. In Saxony, from 1832. In Hohenzollern Sigmaringen, 1833. In Austria, Joseph the Second, like Frederick, had abolished the harsher kind of serfdom as early as 1782, but in its mitigated form it lasted until 1811.[2]

---

[1] *France before the Revolution*, bk. ii. c. i.

[2] De Tocqueville, op. cit. note vi. A German lady tells me her own experiences in Mecklenburg-Schwerin, when she was visiting

M. Tissot, in his entertaining work entitled *Unknown Hungary*, gives an interesting account of the condition of the peasants in that country, which he drew from the lips of an old peasant of considerable intelligence, from which it appears that although serfdom was legally abolished under Joseph the Second and Maria Theresa, yet many of its restrictions still remained.

Those who were discontented with their masters were allowed to leave them, and to establish themselves on the property of another proprietor, on the condition of giving six months' warning. The proprietor was also obliged to give up to the peasant a certain quantity of land, but he always managed to give him the very worst; in exchange, the peasant owed him so many days of labour on the roads. In the evening at sunset, when he returned home tired out with his day's work, and had already stretched himself on his bed, the *heidukes* (they gave this name to the private gendarmes of the proprietors) came, and knocking with their sticks at the door of the peasant's hut, warned him that if he were

there from 1867 to 1870. She says: "I found there to my astonishment a very distinct remnant of serfdom, probably that which is technically called *Erb-unter-thänigkeit*, although I do not remember hearing the expression. The fact was rather expressed by the tenants being *hörige*, the meaning of which would be 'belonging.' Neither the houses in which they lived, nor the small fields of which they had the use, were theirs; nor did they pay rent for them. No man is allowed to marry, or to leave the place without his master's permission. I do not know whether women are in the same position. There is no real poverty, because the master is bound to provide for all his tenants. He builds their school, pays the schoolmaster; the burial-ground is his. This is the general state in Mecklenburg." I have been told that in Hungary the tenant-farmers are even now obliged to arrange the marriages of their children exactly according to the dictation of their landlord.

P

not at work before daylight on the estate, he would be condemned to prison or the bastinado. Besides this, the peasant was forced to give so many days to carting; he had also to go into the forest to cut wood, and when his proprietor went out hunting, he had to beat the woods for game; he had also to pay a tax of a florin for each of his huts, and to furnish the kitchen of the château every year with two capons, two chickens, nineteen eggs, and five pounds of butter.

If the proprietor himself married, or gave one of his daughters in marriage, each peasant had to give forty-two kreutzers, or to furnish provisions at half-price. If the proprietor was thrown into prison, the peasants were obliged to subscribe to pay his ransom. Did the proprietor attend the Diet, the peasant paid a Diet-tax; that is, he had to furnish a certain sum for his master's expenses at the time. Did the peasant distil his brandy, he paid two florins for each cask of it; in fact, out of every kind of harvest he had to pay a nineteenth part to his lord, and a tenth part to the clergy, and the same tithe was due on his bees, sheep, goats, and pigs.

In exchange for this disguised form of serfdom, the law gave him permission to appeal to the King when he was condemned to death, or sentenced to receive a hundred blows with a stick, and also the privileges of becoming an artisan, a merchant, or a priest, and of being ennobled.

Such was the condition of the peasants in Hungary during the earlier part of this century. M. Tissot asked if he were better off since his complete emancipation by the revolution in 1848.

"No, he is no better off," answered the old Beri. "Before 1848, we had no land, because only those who were noble could become possessors of the soil; consequently we had nothing which they could take from us. But now, if we don't pay the taxes—and God knows they are augmented every year—they can seize our lands, and sell our furniture and our clothing, and turn us out into the road half-naked, and utterly without resources. Formerly, the proprietor gave us a field and a house, which could not be taken away from us, and so we had no cause for anxiety; we had, it is true, to give him two or three days' labour in the week, and our wives had to go to the château and spin, but, after all, that was not much. We did not suffer in bad years: in case of famine, the proprietor had always enough corn in his granaries to support us. But in the present day, you understand, the peasant is a free citizen, and he has no longer the right to have recourse to the liberality of his lord; he pays his tithe to the fiscal, good and bad years alike. Formerly the lord, as a rule, allowed his peasants to bring their oxen and sheep and horses to graze on his lands. The keep of our cattle cost us nothing, and we had oxen enough to cultivate our fields.

"But since 1848 the peasant has been obliged to sell such of his cattle as he was not able to feed, and in consequence the land is deteriorated. He borrows enough from a Jew to enable him to buy a pair of oxen. But, if there is not a good crop that year, he can't pay the bills he has signed, and his property is seized. These ruined peasants engage themselves to the great proprietors, and in this way compose a class of pariahs —poor fellows—much worse off than the former serfs. To sum up, the peasant has only changed masters. He is to-day in the power of the Jew, or of some rich speculator, who neither knows nor cares for him."

"Was justice managed better formerly?" I asked, continuing my inquiries.

"Better according to our ideas, for the interminable

cases were unknown. All was carried paternally before the lord, who settled the case on the spot; whilst now one must run at least ten times to the judge. Besides, punishment didn't cost anything more than a flogging, whilst to-day justice ruins you."[1]

In Denmark, serfdom had disappeared soon after its conversion to Christianity. You will notice that in the eastern counties of England, peopled to a great extent by the Danes, there were fewer slaves and fewer *villani*, and many more *sochmanni* and *liberi homines* than in any other part of England. The number of the cottars, or lower class of serfs, may be accounted for by supposing them to have been the remains of the Saxon population reduced to serfdom. In Denmark itself, serfdom reappeared in the twelfth century with the establishment of the feudal system. In the sixteenth century, the condition of the serfs was rendered far more grievous by the secularization of the monasteries, where the serfs had enjoyed comparative liberty. Dr. Döllinger quotes an English historian, Allen,[2] to the effect that the change in the sixteenth century for the Danish peasants was most disastrous. He says:

The inhabitants of the great ecclesiastical properties had to exchange the mild rule of the clergy for the heavy yoke of the nobles.

[1] *Unknown Hungary.* By Victor Tissot (English Translation), vol. ii. 2—6, 1881.
[2] Döllinger, *The Church and the Churches*, p. 85; Allen's *History of the Kingdom of Denmark*, which was voted a prize by the Copenhagen Society as the best work of its kind.

The forced labour was multiplied, and the peasants were treated as serfs. Agriculture fell below what it had been in the middle ages. The population diminished, the farms were abandoned. New privileges in favour of the nobility, cruel laws as to hunting—in 1537, by pulling out the eyes. Death for keeping a hound—completed the servitude and the degradation of the peasants, the burghers, and the clergy, so that the entire nation was trampled under the feet of eight or nine hundred gentlemen.[1]

In Sweden, Gustavus Vasa, after the subjugation and spoliation of the Church, "declared that the commonage lands of the villages and hamlets, and even also the rivers, weirs, and mining districts—finally, even all uncultivated lands, were the property of the Crown."[2]

Williams, in his *History of the Northern Governments*, writing of the eighteenth century, says:

The army of Denmark is composed of regular troops and militia. The greater part of the regular troops are foreigners, whom they pick up in different parts of Germany; and it cannot be otherwise, when one looks at the slavish condition of the peasants. The King believes that these serfs would make bad soldiers, and such is the idea that one has always had of them.

It was "not until 1804 that personal freedom was conferred on twenty thousand families, who had been in a state of servitude."[3]

Mr. Samuel Laing says:

About the year 1784, the spirit of the age began to make the feudal relations unprofitable as well as odious.

[1] Döllinger, op. cit. p. 85.   [2] P. 87.   [3] P. 86.

The serfs would enlist in the army, or desert to the free towns, Hamburg or Lübeck, or emigrate, and set themselves free, leaving none but the aged and infirm to labour without wages on the estate. Some nobles, among the first Count Bernstoff, emancipated their serfs, and paid day-wages for the labour they required on their estates. Some valued the serf's labour, and the land with his cottage, which he had for his subsistence, and converted the amount into a debt upon the little farm, which the serf had to pay interest for and redeem, but in the meantime was full proprietor of the land. . . . On the whole, the feudal vassals and serfs became proprietors of their several holdings, some remaining subject to a few servitudes, such as certain cartages of peat, wood, or corn, certain days' work in hay time or harvest, at certain rates, but all fixed, registered in the books of the local court, and placed beyond arbitrary exaction or oppression on the one hand, or evasion on the other.[1]

3.—Russia.

Hitherto we have been considering serfdom as a condition of things that existed in the middle ages, or at most in the last century, but our review would be incomplete if we neglected to look at serfdom as it existed less than thirty years ago in Russia. It was only in 1861 that the Tsar, Alexander the Second, emancipated the Russian serfs. In the volumes of Mr. Mackenzie Wallace we have a well-digested account of Russian serfdom past and present, gleaned chiefly from the works of M. Bêlaéf, and from his own personal investigations. Mr. Wallace begins by explaining how

---

[1] S. Laing, *Notes on Denmark and the Duchies*, 1852.

the Russian peasants became serfs, and tells us that—

In the earliest period of Russian history the rural population was composed of three distinct classes. At the bottom of the scale stood the slaves, who were very numerous. Their numbers were continually augmented by prisoners of war, by freemen who voluntarily sold themselves as slaves, by insolvent debtors, and by certain categories of criminals. Immediately above the slaves were the free agricultural labourers, who had no permanent domicile, but wandered about the country, and settled temporarily where they happened to find work and satisfactory remuneration. In the third place, distinct from these two classes, and in some respects higher in the social scale, were the peasants, properly so called.

These peasants were small farmers, . . . and were possessors of land in property or usufruct, and were members of a rural commune. The communes were free primitive corporations, which elected their office-bearers from among the heads of families, and sent delegates to act as judges or assessors in the Prince's Court. Some of the communes possessed land of their own, whilst others were settled on the estates of the landed proprietors, or on the extensive domains of the monasteries. In the latter case, the peasant paid a fixed yearly rent in money, produce, or labour, according to the terms of his contract with the proprietor or the monastery; but he did not thereby sacrifice in any way his personal liberty. As soon as he had fulfilled the engagements stipulated in the contract, and settled accounts with the owner of the land, he was free to change his domicile as he pleased.

If we turn now from these early times to the eighteenth century, we find that the position of the rural population has entirely changed in the interval. The distinction between slaves, agricultural labourers, and peasants has completely disappeared. All three categories have melted together into a common class, called serfs, who are regarded as the property of the landed proprietors of the State.[1]

An Imperial ukáz of Peter the Great seems to regret this state of things, for the Tsar says: "The proprietors sell their peasants and domestic servants, not even in families, but one by one, like cattle, as is done nowhere else in the whole world, from which practice there is not a little wailing."[2] Yet nothing was done to remedy the evil; and, in 1767 Catherine the Second, who professed the most liberal and philanthropic sentiments, by an ukáz, August 22nd, deprived the serfs of all legal protection, and commanded that if any serf shall dare to present a petition against his master, he shall be punished with the knout and transported for life to the mines of Nertchinsk.[3]

The binding of the peasants to the soil was the first stage in their loss of liberty.[4] This was in the interests of agriculture, and the free communes were as anxious to retain the cultivators of the land as the princes or landed proprietors. When the various independent principalities became concentrated in the Tsardom of Moscow, it was more

---

[1] *Russia.* By D. Mackenzie Wallace, vol. ii. pp. 234, 235.
[2] April 15th, 1721.   [3] Op. cit. p. 236.
[4] This was done by the Tsar Boris Godunóf, who at the beginning of the seventeenth century abolished the right which the peasants had hitherto enjoyed of changing their domicile on St. George's day.

easy to compel the residence of the peasants on the land. If the Tsar rewarded one of his boyars with an estate on which twenty families were living, it would make a vast difference in the value of the property if ten of these families migrated elsewhere, and the boyar would find himself unable to acquit himself of the services to his prince, to which he had bound himself on receiving the land. The communes had also obligations to the Tsar, which they could not fulfil if their members were allowed to depart at will. Hence came severe laws against those who attempted to change their domicile, and against proprietors who should harbour the runaways. As yet the peasant retained all the civil rights he had hitherto enjoyed. He could still appear before the courts of law as a free man, freely engage in trade or industry, enter into all manner of contracts, and rent land for cultivation. In the majority of cases he did not wish to travel far from home, and the restriction of domicile was probably not much felt. Yet, his connection with his lord being no longer voluntary, the weaker of the parties thus legally bound together naturally fell more and more under the power of the stronger. In other European countries the Government had interfered for the protection of the peasant, but the danger did not seem to have been perceived by the Russian Tsars, and the clergy do not appear to have stood forth there as they did in Western Europe to plead the cause of the poor and oppressed. In the absence of legislation as to the mutual obligation of lord and peasant, the proprietors made laws for the regulation of the peasants themselves, and enforced them by fines and corporal punishment. From this they went a step further, and began to sell their peasants without the land on which they were settled. Instead of forbidding this flagrant abuse, the Government winked at it, and even exacted dues on such sales, as on the sale of slaves. Finally, by imperial ukáz of the Tsar Alexis in 1675, and of Feodor the Third in 1682, the right to sell peasants without land was formally recognized. Peter the Great put the finishing stroke to the degradation of the Russian peasants, by ordering a census to be taken in which all the various classes of the rural population—slaves, domestic servants, agricultural labourers, peasants—should be inscribed in one category, and equally liable to the poll-tax, in lieu of the land-tax which had lain exclusively on the peasants.[1] The proprietors were made responsible for their serfs, and the "free wandering people" who did not wish to enter the army were ordered, under pain of being sent to the galleys, to inscribe themselves as members of a commune or as serfs to some proprietor. By making the proprietor pay the poll-tax for his serfs, as if they were slaves or cattle, the law seemed to sanction the idea that they were part of his goods and chattels. The free labourer no longer existed in Russia.

The discontent of the serfs under this change in their position led thousands to run away, and

[1] *Vide* op. cit. p. 245.

the Government authorized the proprietors to transport unruly serfs without trial to Siberia, or to send them to the mines. In 1762, Peter the Third abolished the obligatory service of the nobles, and the serfs expected that as the nobles were no longer bound to serve the Tsar, another ukáz would be issued emancipating them from service to their lords. They even imagined that such a decree had been issued, but that it had been suppressed by the nobles; and when Peter was assassinated in 1745, they imagined him to have been a martyr for their liberty.[1] Rumours were spread that he had escaped from his assassins, and a pretender appeared on the Don, who excited the serfs to revolt and massacred all the proprietors who fell into his hands. He was soon defeated and the insurrection was quelled. Peter's consort, Catherine the Second, found it her policy to cultivate the favour of the nobles, and during her reign the miseries of the serfs were at their worst. Serfs were bought and sold, and given as presents, sometimes in hundreds and thousands at a time, with or without the land, sometimes in families, sometimes individually.[2] The only legal restriction was that they could not be sold by public auction. Now and then cases of extraordinary cruelty came to the ears of the Tsar, and were punished, but these instances of interference were too exceptional to affect the proprietors as a class.

A certain lady called Saltykoff, according to the ukáz, had killed by inhuman tortures, in the course of ten or

[1] Op. cit. p. 247. [2] Ibid. p. 249.

eleven years, about a hundred of her serfs, chiefly of the female sex, and among them several young girls of eleven or twelve years of age.¹

A lady had murdered a serf boy by pricking him with a penknife, because he had neglected to take proper care of a tame rabbit committed to his charge.²

Catherine the Second secularized the monasteries, and instead of giving their lands to the nobles, as had been done in England and Germany, she transformed them into State demesnes. Catherine was succeeded by her son, Paul the First, one of whose first acts was to set at liberty Kosciusko and the Poles who were in prison, and for the first time distinct measures were taken by the Government for the protection of the serfs. He issued an ukáz that the serfs should not be forced to work for their masters more than three days in the week. From the accession of his son Alexander, in 1801, the Russian Government made many abortive attempts to improve the condition of the serfs. The Tsar Nicholas abolished the custom of giving land with peasants as grants to his courtiers; he placed some restriction on the power of proprietors, and some thousands of serfs were actually emancipated. Still, the legal powers of the proprietor were enormous. The laws laid down that—

The proprietor may impose on his serfs every kind of labour, may take from them money dues (*obrok*), and demand of them personal service, with this one restriction, that they should not thereby be ruined, and that

---

[1] *Ibid.* p. 251. [2] *Ibid.* p. 252.

the number of days fixed by law should be left to them for their own work. Besides this he had the right to transform peasants into domestic servants, and hire them out to other nobles. For all offences committed against himself or against any one under his jurisdiction, he could subject the guilty ones to corporal punishment not exceeding forty lashes with the birch, or fifteen blows with the stick; and if he considered any of his serfs incorrigible, he could present them to the authorities to be drafted into the army or transported to Siberia, as he might desire. In cases of insubordination, where the ordinary domestic means of discipline did not suffice, he could call in the police and the military to support his authority. In all cases the serfs were ordered to be docile and obedient, and unless a proprietor became notorious for inhuman cruelty, the authorities never thought of interfering.[1]

Mr. Wallace estimates [2]—

The entire population of Russia	60,909,309
Peasants of all classes	49,486,665

Of these latter there are—

Peasants on the State demesnes	23,138,191
Peasants on the lands of proprietors	23,022,390
Peasants on the Crown appanages	3,326,084

These numbers show that the Tsar owned more than half the serf population of the country. It would be unjust and untrue to imagine that the proprietors, as a class, were cruel and tyrannical. And when the proprietor habitually acted towards his serfs in an enlightened, rational, and humane

[1] Op. cit. pp. 261, 262   [2] Ibid. p. 254, note.

way, they had little cause to complain of their position. Mr. Wallace says:

> However paradoxical the statement may seem to those who are in the habit of regarding all forms of slavery from the sentimental point of view, it is unquestionable that the condition of serfs under such a proprietor as I have supposed was much more enviable than that of the majority of English agricultural labourers. Each family had a house of its own, with a cabbage garden, one or more horses, one or two cows, several sheep, poultry, agricultural implements, a share of the communal land, and everything else necessary for carrying on its small farming operations; and in return for this, it had to supply the proprietor with an amount of labour which was by no means oppressive. If, for instance, a serf had three adult sons, two of them might work for the proprietor, whilst he himself and the remaining son could attend exclusively to the family affairs. From those events which used to be called "the visitations of God," he had no fear of being permanently ruined. If his house was burnt, or his cattle died from the plague, or a series of "bad years" left him without seed for his fields, he could always count upon temporary assistance from his master. He was protected, too, against all oppression and exactions on the part of the officials; for the police, when there was any cause for its interference, applied to the proprietor, who was to a certain extent responsible for his serfs. Thus the serf might live a tranquil, contented life, and die at a ripe old age, without having been conscious that serfage was a burden.[1]

It was in March, 1856, soon after the conclusion of the Crimean War, that the Tsar, Alexander the

[1] Op. cit. pp. 258, 259.

Second, suggested to his nobles: "It is better to abolish serfage from above than to await the time when it will begin to abolish itself from below," and he requested them to consider how this could be put into execution. They did not take the hint, and he appointed a secret committee of the great officers of State to formulate the principles on which the emancipation could be effected.[1] The experiment was first tried on the Lithuanian nobles, who were Poles, and then a circular was sent to the Marshals of Noblesse in Russia proper, saying that the Lithuanian nobles "had recognized the necessity of liberating the peasants," and this "noble intention" had afforded peculiar satisfaction to His Majesty. So broad a hint from an autocratic Sovereign could not be mistaken, and the Press hailed the raising of the question with boundless enthusiasm. Mr. Wallace gives a graphic description of the excitement evoked:

The moralists declared that all the prevailing vices were the product of serfage, and that moral progress was impossible in an atmosphere of slavery; the lawyers asserted that the arbitrary authority of the proprietors over the peasants had no firm legal basis; the economists explained that free labour was an indispensable condition of industrial and commercial prosperity; the philosophical historians showed that the normal historical development of the country demanded the immediate abolition of this superannuated remnant of barbarism; and the writers of the sentimental, gushing type poured forth endless effusions about brotherly love to the weak and the oppressed.[2]

[1] Op. cit. p. 273. [2] Ibid. p. 277.

During 1858 committees of nobles were formed in almost every province to consider the question. But at length the Commission working under the immediate supervision of the Tsar received Imperial authority for a law which declared the serf personally free, marked off clearly the communal land from the rest of the proprietor's estate, transformed the labour dues into yearly money payments, and facilitated the redemption of them by the peasants, with the assistance of loans from the Government. With regard to the domestic serfs, it was enacted that they should continue to serve their masters during two years, and that thereafter they should be completely free, but should have no claim to a share of the land.[1]

As might well be supposed, there was great dissatisfaction on the part of the nobles, who were thus called upon to sacrifice, not only their right to the services of the peasants, but a very considerable slice of what they had regarded as their own land; but many of them shared the benevolent sentiments of the Tsar, and all saw that resistance was useless. The peasants were by no means so delighted with the change as might be expected. They imagined, in many instances, that the whole of the estate belonged to them. In the province of Moscow, one commune sent a deputation to the proprietor to inform him that, as he had always been a good master, the *Mir* would allow him to retain his

---

[1] Op. cit. p. 295. Mr. Wallace estimates that at the time of emancipation there were 20,158,231 peasant serfs, and 1,467,378 domestics.

house and garden during his lifetime. By degrees, and chiefly through the praiseworthy and conciliating efforts of the arbiters appointed to carry out the details of the emancipation, the serfs were not only liberated, but made also possessors of land, and put on the road to becoming communal proprietors; and the old communal institutions were preserved and developed. It is sad to reflect that the author of this beneficent act was destined to be barbarously murdered in his own capital.

Probably most of us would feel rather annoyed at the question being raised—Are the serfs any the better for their emancipation? Still, it is a question which those best acquainted with the subject are not so positive about, and it is well to hear what an authority like Mr. Wallace has to say on the matter. His opinion is that

> It is no easy matter to sum up the two sides of the account and draw an accurate balance, except in those exceptional cases in which the proprietor flagrantly abused his authority. The present money-dues and taxes are often more burdensome than the labour-dues in the time of serfage. If the serfs had a great many ill-defined obligations to fulfil, such as the carting of the master's grain to market, the preparing of his firewood, the supplying him with eggs, chickens, home-made linen, and the like, they had, on the other hand, a good many ill-defined privileges. They grazed their cattle during a part of the year on the manor-land; they received firewood and occasionally logs for repairing their huts; sometimes the proprietor lent them or gave them a cow or a horse when they had been visited by the cattle-plague or the horse-stealer; and in times of famine they

could look to their master for support. All this has now come to an end. Their burdens and their privileges have been swept away together, and been replaced by clearly-defined, unbending, un-elastic legal relations. They have now to pay the market price for every stick of firewood which they burn, for every log which they require for repairing their houses, and for every rood of land on which to graze their cattle. Nothing is now to be had gratis. The demand to pay is encountered at every step. If a cow dies or a horse is stolen, the owner can no longer go to the proprietor with the hope of receiving a present, or at least a loan without interest, but must, if he has no ready money, apply to the village usurer, who probably considers twenty or thirty per cent. a by no means exorbitant rate of interest. Sometimes it even happens that the peasant has to pay without getting any return whatever, as, for instance, when his cattle stray into the proprietor's fields, an accident that may easily occur in a country where walls and hedges are almost unknown. Formerly, on such an occasion, he escaped with a scolding or with a light castigation, which was soon forgotten, but now he has to pay as a fine a sum which is for him considerable. Thinking of all this, and of the other advantages and disadvantages of his new position, he has naturally much difficulty in coming to a general conclusion, and is perhaps quite sincere when, on being asked whether his new position is better than the old, he scratches the back of his head and replies, in a mystified, doubtful tone, "How shall I say to you? It is both better and worse!" —*Kak vam shadzát? I lútche i khúdzhe!*[1]

It is impossible to put back the hands of the clock of time; and it would be nothing less than

[1] Op. cit. pp. 352, 353.

criminal to attempt to bring back either slavery or even serfdom into any country from which it has been abolished. But it is a conviction that has impressed itself strongly upon my mind, since I have been following out these studies, that we ought to be very slow in passing condemnation upon those by whose influence slavery was abolished, because they did not, in the interests of the poor, think that it was advisable to hurry on the complete emancipation of the serfs. Christianity prepared the way for, and accomplished the deliverance of the slave; she prepared the way for, but a variety of other causes actually effected, the emancipation of the serf. One thing is certain: the abolition of serfdom in Europe has by no means solved those great social problems, upon the solution of which depends the happiness of the human race.

NOTE ON PAGE 176.

Prebendary Hingeston-Randolph, who is editing Bishop Grandisson's *Registers*, has kindly sent me the following specimen of his manumissions. Du Cange says : "*Nayvitas*, idem quod *nativitas*, Nativa servitus."

"*Manumissio*,—Universis Christi Fidelibus ad quos presentes Litere pervenerint Johannes, etc., salutem in Domino sempiternam.—Noverit Universitas vestra nos Willelmum Godefray, filium nativi nostri in Manerio nostro de Chuddeham, manumisisse, et ab omni servitute per Presentes liberum reddidisse. Ita quod nec nos, nec aliquis successor noster, aliquid servitutis seu nayvitatis in corpore predicti Willelmi clamare seu vendicare poterimus, seu poterit, in futurum. In cujus rei, etc. Datum in Manerio nostro de Chuddeleghe, X° Kalendas Januarii [23 Dec.]. Anno, etc. [1328]."

From the *Register of Bishop John de Grandisson*,
vol. ii. folio 102^b

INDEX.

Abbey, St. Albans, 92, 170.
  St. Ambrose, Milan, 80.
  Corbey, 80.
  Fleury, 74.
  St. Germain des Prés, 75, 77, 79.
  Kelso, 145.
  of Limoges, 104.
  St. Pierre de la Couture, 67.
  near Sherborne, 107.
Adamnan, St., redeems slaves, 127.
Aelfric, MS. Dialogue of, 104.
Aidan, St., redeems slaves, 128.
Aillt, a Welsh alien, 133.
Allard, M. Paul, on slavery, 2, 43; on free labour, 29; on Christian alumni, 41 n.; on serfdom, 43, 80; on emancipations, 207; on village communes, 208, 211.
Allodia, freehold, 69.
Allies, *Formation of Christendom*, 32.
Antrustions, trusty ones, 69.
Apuleius on slaves, 23.
Aredius, St., his will, 67.
Aristotle on slaves, 23.
Ascripti glebæ, 89, 93, 149, 150, 216, 223.

Barbadoes, Irish slaves in, 3, 128, 189—202.
Barbaric Invasions, 55.
Beaumanoir, on nobility and servitude, 77.
Bedeman, a Wycliffite, 172 n.
Beneficia of Charlemagne, 69, 71.
Beorwald, Abbot, holds a slave, 107.
Bertram, Bp., his will, 67.
Biot, M., on slavery in Eastern Empire, 54.

Black Death, The, 92, 156—158.
Bodmin Gospels, Manumissions recorded in, 110.
Bordarii, cottagers, 98, 104, 145, 192.
Bracton, Henry de, on villenage, 149, 152.
Brehon Laws, 114—120.
Brihtwald, Abp., redeems slaves, 107.
Bristol slave-dealers, 101, 112, 128, 193.

Caeth, a Welsh slave, 133.
Caius Cassius on slaves, 26.
Callistus, *see* Popes.
Caroticus enslaves Irish Christians, 126.
Caruca, a plough with four oxen abreast, 97.
Cato on slaves, 13, 16, 21, 24.
Charlemagne, 57; forbad serfs to be removed from land, 69; made this binding on his sons, 70.
Christianity abolished slavery, xv, 2, 29, 30, 41, 45.
  rehabilitated labour, 47, 49, 58, 61, 90, 107, 112, 128, 243.
Cibrario on slavery, 43, 82, 83.
Clement, St., of Rome, *see* Popes.
Clement, St., of Alexandria, on slaves, 37.
Coloni, 48—51, 54, 57, 76, 77, 135, 216.
Columella on *coloni*, 48, 110.
Communes in France, 208, 211.
Connery, Three Misses, sold as slaves, 3, 197.
Constantine, Laws of, on slavery, 17, 38, 46.

Q

Cotarii, cottiers, 95, 98, 145, 146, 182.
Constantius, Laws on slavery, 40, 50.
Co-tillage, 136, 137, 214.
Councils, Decrees on slavery of—
Agde, 65, 66.
Armagh, 128.
Auxerre, 64.
Berkhampstead, 64.
Celchyth, 68.
Chalons, 68.
Epône, 61.
London, 111.
Orleans, 35, 58, 61, 65.
Rheims, 59, 66.
Rouen, 64.
Toledo III., 59; IV., 59, 60, 66.
Welsh Canons, 129—133.
Cromwell sold Irish into slavery, 3, 128, 193, 197—199.
Cumerlach, a Scotch slave, 138.
Cumhal, an Irish female slave, 117, 119.
Cyril of Jerusalem, St., to slaves, 33.

Daer-tenant, daer-clanna, unfree, 122, 125.
Danes sold slaves, 111.
  revived serfdom in twelfth century, 228.
  more oppressive in sixteenth, 229.
Devonshire serfs, 102, 104, 175, 177.
Domesday Book, statistics of, 97, 103.

Ellis, Sir H. on Domesday, 101.
Elton, Mr. C., on serfdom, 152.
Emancipation of slaves, 37, 38, 45, 108, 110, 112, 128, 152, 176, 188, 206, 210, 218, 224, 227, 239, 242.
Ennodius, Deed of manumission, 39.
Epictetus, a slave, 24.
Epitaphs, Christian, never have the word "servus," 35.
Erw, a Welsh acre, 131.

Fergus, King of Ulster, Story of, 117, &c.
Feudal System, its origin, and effect in reducing slavery, 71.
France, Serfdom in, 75—80; abolition of, 204—215.
Franks, Slavery under, 56—63.

Gallicanus, St., liberated slaves, 45.
Garganel, F. on Irish slaves, 196.
Germany, Slavery in, 81.
  serfdom in, 216; abolition retarded by Luther, 222; accomplished, 224.
Germain des Prés, St., 75—79.
Grandisson, Bp., emancipates serfs, 175, 244 *n*.
Green, Mr., on abolition of slavery, 109.
Gregory the Great, St., *see* Popes.
Gregory of Tours, St., on Frankish slavery, 56; serfs removed from soil, 57; on cruelty to, 62, 63.
Gregory Nazianzen, St., on a slave Bishop, 32.
Guérard, M., how freemen became serfs, 72; on condition of serfs, 73; on the *Polypticon* of Irmino, 75.

Hallam on slaves of Church, 65, 73.
Hartegan, *alias* De Stritch, F., visits Irish slaves in St. Kitts, 195.

Ignatius of Antioch, St., on slaves, 37.
Ine, Dooms of, 64, 107.
Ireland, slavery in, 114, 128; ancient laws of, 114, 115; reformed by St. Patrick, 116.
Irish tribal system, 121, 122; plebeian tribes, 123; free tributes and servile, 125; converts enslaved by Welsh King, 126; Irish sold as slaves by Cromwell, 193, 200; liberated English slaves, 128.
Jacquerie, The excesses of, 209 *n*.

Justinian, Laws of, 29, 39, 41, 46, 47.

Lactantius on Slavery, xxxix.
Labour degraded, 4, 8, 28, 48.
Labour, dignity of, 27, 47.
Las Casas, advocate of slaves, vi, 83.
Lavelaye on Communities in Croatia, 214 *n*.
Leo XIII. *see* Popes.
Lucian on decay of Art, 9.

Macaulay on abolition of serfdom, 87.
Martial on slaves, 6, 13.
Mainmortables, 211, 212, 215.
Martin of Tours, St., guardian of slaves, 67.
Mansi ingenuales et serviles, 76, 77.
Montalembert, Facts related by, 67, 75.

Newman, Cardinal, on Roman Slavery, xvii.

O'Toole, St. Lawrence, liberates English slaves, 128.

Paedagogus, the, a slave, 13, 16.
Patrick, St., reforms Brehon Laws, 115, 116; excommunicates Caroticus for slave-hunting, 126.
Pelagia, St. liberates slaves, 46.
Peculium of slaves, 23, 39, 45, 50.
Penne, a Bristol slave dealer, 201.
Pitman, Henry, surgeon, sold as a slave, 201, 202.
Plautus on slaves, 7, 14—16, 24.
Pliny on slaves, 23.
Pope Clement I. on slaves, 37.
  Callixtus on slave-marriages, 37.
  Gregory I. liberates slaves, 52; defends slaves and *coloni*, 53.
  Adrian I. maintained slave-marriages as valid, xi. 62.
  Alexander III. declared that none is by nature a slave, xl.
  Innocent III. approved Trinitarian Order, xl.
  Honorius III. } approved Order
  Gregory IX. } of Mercy for redemption of slaves, xl.
  Pius II. condemned negro slavery, xlii. 83.
  Leo X. condemned slavery in Spain and Portugal, xlii.
  Paul III. condemned slavery in America, xliii. 83, 84.
  Urban VIII.   } repeated con-
  Benedict XIV. } demnation, xliii.
  Pius VII. condemned negro slavery, xliii.
  Gregory XVI. laboured for same end, xliii.
  Leo XIII. Letter on Slavery, xxvii.
Potamiaena, St., slave-Martyr, xvii, xxxvii, 31, 32.

Rectitudincon services due, 105.
Reeves on *English Law*, 142, 175, 177, 180.
Renan, M., on Church slaves, 65.
Roman slavery, 4. 26; a Roman entertainment, 11, 12; Roman *villa rustica*, 48; Roman ladies' cruelty, 18, 19.

Salvian on sack of Treves, 55.
Scotland, Serfdom in, 137—139.
Scyri, the, serfs not slaves, 51.
Seebohm, Mr. "English Village Community," 91, 93, 101, 105; on gradual improvement in condition of serfs, 153, 154.
Senchus Mòr, the Brehon Laws, 114, 115.
Seneca on slaves, 4, 25.
Serfdom, in Roman Empire, 50—54.
  in France, 56—80, 204—215.
  in Germany, 216—224.
  in Hungary, 225—228.
  in Denmark, 228.
  in Sweden, 229.
  in Italy and Spain, 84, 85.
  in England, 91—106, 146—177.
  in Russia, 230—242.
Serfs were originally *coloni*, 50,

51; how distinguished from slaves, 50, 53; confused with them under Franks, 56, 57; distinguished under Charlemagne, 69; of Abbeys, 65, 67, 73—80, 90, 107, 145, 170, 219, 228; life in the ninth century, 79, 80; their "Customs," 67, 80, 81; include *villani, cotarii, bordarii*, 104, 146—152; emancipation of, *see* Lectures IV. and VI.

Slavery, three epochs of, 2; its effect on working men, 4—8; on invention and art, 8, 9; on the masters, 13—19; on the slaves, 20—28; abolished by Christianity alone, 29, 90, 128, 129; means used in its abolition, 29—41, 58; modified into serfdom, 50, 51, 59.

Slavery in France, 56, 69, 70.
— in Germany, 81.
— in Italy and Spain, 82—84.
— in England, 106—113.
— in Wales, 129—133.
— in Ireland, 119—128.
— in Scotland, 138.
— in the Colonies, 185—202.

Slaves, Roman, condition of, 4, 5, 10, 11; let out on hire, 7; various kinds of, 10, 11; legal protection of, by Pagan Emperors, 17; by Christian Emperors, *ibid.*, 39, 40; their names, 20; classed with cattle, 21; marriage of, under paganism, 21; under Christianity, 36; children of, 22; 40,000 deserted to Alaric, 28; *see* Emancipation, Christianity, Slavery.

Smith, Sir Thomas, *Commonwealth of England*, 87—91.

Tacog, a Welsh *colonus*, 132, 133.
Tanistry in Ireland, 121.
— in Scotland, 138.
Theodosius, Code of, 46, 49.
Trev, a Welsh villein-township, 132.

Tyddyn, a Welsh homestead, 133.
Tye, twelve Welsh acres plough in common, 136.

Ulpian on slavery, 16, 20, 21.
Ulster Tenant-Right, origin of, 122.

Villani, in France free coloni, 28, 152, 214; in England serfs, villeins regardants, 89, 147; above Cotarii, 99; nativi, 93; bondi, 164; in Saxon, gebur and geneat, 104; their services, 94, 95; their holdings, 95, 98; proportion in different counties, 97; Devonshire, on Bp. Osbern's manors, 103; emancipation of, 110; by Bp. Grandisson, 175; means of emancipation, 140, 142; their condition steadily improved, 153; in the thirteenth century, 155; how affected by the Black Death, 157; by the "Statute of Labourers," 158; by Wycliffe's socialism, 160; their rebellion under Wat Tyler, 163; demands, 169; tenants "by copy of court-roll," 174; last legal mention of under Elizabeth, 177.

Wales, Slavery and Serfdom in, 129, 137.
White slaves, 193—202.
Wilfrid, St., emancipates slaves, 108, 109.
William the Conqueror, Laws of 112, 113, 140, 141.
William of Malmesbury on Danish slave trade, 11.
Welsh Laws,—Canons, 129, 130; Laws of Howel the Good, 130; system of co-tillage, 136, 137; land distribution, 133, 134; of food rents, 134.
Wulstan, suppressed Bristol slave-trade, 112.
Wycliffe, his socialism, 160, 161; his disciples, 165, 172, 173.

FROM

BURNS & OATES'

Catalogue

OF

PUBLICATIONS.

LONDON: BURNS AND OATES, Lᴅ.
28 ORCHARD ST., W., & 63 PATERNOSTER ROW, E.C.
NEW YORK: 12 EAST 17TH STREET.

1891.

NEW BOOKS JUST OUT.

Saint Ignatius Loyola and The Early Jesuits. By STEWART ROSE. With more than 100 Illustrations by H.W. and H.C. Brewer and L. Wain. The whole brought out under the immediate superintendence of the Rev. W. H. Eyre, S.J. Super Royal 8vo. Handsomely bound in Cloth, extra gilt. Price 15s. *net.* (Very suitable for a Prize or Gift.)

The Letters of the late Father George Porter, S.J., ARCHBISHOP OF BOMBAY. Demy 8vo. Cloth, 7s. 6d.

Acts of the English Martyrs, hitherto unpublished. By the Rev. JOHN H. POLLEN, S.J. With a Preface by the Rev. JOHN MORRIS, S.J., Quarterly Series (Vol. 75). Crown 8vo, cloth, in two styles, 7s. 6d.

The Christian Virgin in her Family and in the World. Her Virtues and her Mission at the Present Time. Handsomely bound in blue cloth, leather back, gilt top, 6s.

"The aim of the present book is to show how all those who, whether from choice or necessity, are led to live with their families or alone in the world may, by consecrating and sanctifying their state, lead a life, not only useful and meritorious, but amiable and pleasant to themselves and to society in general. The translation bears the imprimatur of the Cardinal Archbishop of Westminster."—*Tablet.*

The Blind Apostle and **A Heroine of Charity.** By the late KATHLEEN O'MEARA. With a Preface by the Cardinal Archbishop of Westminster. Vol. 3, "Bells of the Sanctuary" Series. Crown 8vo, cloth, gilt, 4s. 6d.

"Mgr. de Ségur's (the Blind Apostle) life is a story of our own time, and tells of the heroic courage in which, in spite of total blindness, he laboured for thirteen years, preaching, hearing confessions, and even contributing book after book to popular Catholic litcrature. Madame Legras (the Heroine of Charity) was the noble-hearted woman to whom St. Vincent de Paul entrusted the work of founding the order of the Sisters of Charity."—*Catholic Times.*

My Time, and what I've done with it. An Autobiography. By F. C. BURNAND. With Portrait of the Author. Crown 8vo, cloth, 5s.

"Interweaves with a partly fictitious plot Mr. Burnand's impressions of his boyhood and youth, especially of that period which he spent at 'Holyshade' (Eton), 'Tudor College' (Cowbridge), and 'St. Bede's' (Cuddleston). Each of these experiences yields to Mr. Burnand a little budget of portraits of the ruling powers. Dr. Keate, Canon Liddon, Bishop Wilberforce, and other celebrities, living and dead, are recognizable under their disguises. The author of 'Happy Thoughts' is an acute analyst of the sensations and unconscious reflections of boyhood as well as of manhood. For various reasons, then, this volume will be found entertaining."—*Times.*

Immediately.

The Autobiography of Archbishop Ullathorne. With Selections from his letters. By AUGUSTA THEODOSIA DRANE.

Ireland and St. Patrick. A Study of the Saint's Character, and of the results of his Apostolate. By the Rev. W. B. MORRIS, of the Oratory.

Succat; or, Sixty Years of the Life of St. Patrick. By the Very Rev. Mgr. ROBERT GRADWELL.

SELECTION
FROM
BURNS AND OATES' CATALOGUE OF PUBLICATIONS.

ALLIES, T. W. (K.C. S.G.)
Formation of Christendom. Vols. I., II., and III., (all out of print.) . . . .
Church and State as seen in the Formation of Christendom, 8vo, pp. 472, cloth . (out of print.)
The Throne of the Fisherman, built by the Carpenter's Son, the Root, the Bond, and the Crown of Christendom. Demy 8vo . . . . . : 0 10 6
The Holy See and the Wandering of the Nations. Demy 8vo. 0 10 6
Peter's Rock in Mohammed's Flood. Demy 8vo. . 0 10 6

"It would be quite superfluous at this hour of the day to recommend Mr. Allies' writings to English Catholics. Those of our readers who remember the article on his writings in the *Katholik*, know that he is esteemed in Germany as one of our foremost writers."—*Dublin Review*.

ALLIES, MARY.
Leaves from St. John Chrysostom, With introduction by T. W. Allies, K.C.S.G. Crown 8vo, cloth . 0 6 0

"Miss Allies 'Leaves' are delightful reading; the English is remarkably pure and graceful; page after page reads as if it were original. No commentator, Catholic or Protestant, has ever surpassed St. John Chrysostom in the knowledge of Holy Scripture, and his learning was of a kind which is of service now as it was at the time when the inhabitants of a great city hung on his words."—*Tablet*.

ALLNATT, C. F. B.
Cathedra Petri. Third and Enlarged Edition. Cloth   0 6 0

"Invaluable to the controversialist and the theologian, and most useful for educated men inquiring after truth or anxious to know the positive testimony of Christian antiquity in favour of Papal claims."—*Month*.

    Which is the True Church? Fifth Edition . . 0 1 4
    The Church and the Sects 0 1 0
    Ditto, Ditto. Second Series. . . . 0 1 6

ANNUS SANCTUS:
Hymns of the Church for the Ecclesiastical Year. Translated from the Sacred Offices by various Authors, with Modern, Original, and other Hymns, and an Appendix of Earlier Versions. Selected and Arranged by ORBY SHIPLEY, M.A.
    Popular edition, in two parts . . each   1 0 0
    In stiff boards 0 3 6
    Plain Cloth, lettered 0 5 0
    Edition de luxe 0 10 6

ANSWERS TO ATHEISTS: OR NOTES ON
Ingersoll. By the Rev. A. Lambert, (over 100,000 copies sold in America). Ninth edition. Paper. . . . £0 0 6
Cloth 0 1 0

B. N.
The Jesuits: their Foundation and History. 2 vols. crown 8vo, cloth, red edges . . . 0 15 0

"The book is just what it professes to be—*a popular history*, drawn from well-known sources," &c.—*Month*.

BAKER, VEN. FATHER AUGUSTIN.
Holy Wisdom; or, Directions for the Prayer of Contemplation, &c. Extracted from Treatises written by the Ven. Father F. Augustin Baker, O.S.B., and edited by Abbot Sweeney, D.D. Beautifully bound in half leather 0 6 0

"We earnestly recommend this most beautiful work to all our readers. We are sure that every community will use it as a constant manual. If any persons have friends in convents, we cannot conceive a better present they can make them, or a better claim they can have on their prayers, than by providing them with a copy."—*Weekly Register*.

BORROMEO, LIFE OF ST. CHARLES.
From the Italian of Peter Guissano. 2 vols. . . 0 15 0

"A standard work, which has stood the test of succeeding ages; it is certainly the finest work on St. Charles in an English dress."—*Tablet*.

BOWDEN, REV. H. S. (of the Oratory) Edited by.
Dante's Divina Commedia: Its scope and value. From the German of FRANCIS HETTINGER, D.D. With an engraving of Dante. Crown 8vo . . 0 10 6

"All that Venturi attempted to do has been now approached with far greater power and learning by Dr. Hettinger, who, as the author of the 'Apologie des Christenthums,' and as a great Catholic theologian, is eminently well qualified for the task he has undertaken."—*The Saturday Review*.

Natural Religion. Being Vol. I. of Dr. Hettinger's Evidences of Christianity. Edited, with an Introduction on Certainty, by the Rev. H. S. Bowden. Crown 8vo, cloth 0 7 6

(Other volumes in preparation.)

"As an able statement of the Catholic Doctrine of Certitude, and a defence, from the Romanist point of view, of the truth of Christianity, it was well worth while translating Dr. Franz Hettinger's 'Apologie des Christenthums,' of which the first part is now published."—*Scotsman*.

BRIDGETT, REV. T. E. (C.SS.R.).
Discipline of Drink 0 3 6

"The historical information with which the book abounds gives evidence of deep research and patient study, and imparts a permanent interest to the volume, which will elevate it to a position of authority and importance enjoyed by few of its compeers."—*The Arrow*.

Our Lady's Dowry; how England Won that Title. New and Enlarged Edition. 0 5 0

"This book is the ablest vindication of Catholic devotion to Our Lady, drawn from tradition, that we know of in the English language."—*Tablet*.

BRIDGETT, REV. T. E. (C.SS.R.)—*continued*.

Ritual of the New Testament. An essay on the principles and origin of Catholic Ritual in reference to the New Testament. Third edition . . . £0 5 0

The Life of the Blessed John Fisher. With a reproduction of the famous portrait of Blessed JOHN FISHER by HOLBEIN, and other Illustrations. 2nd Ed. 0 7 6

"The Life of Blessed John Fisher could hardly fail to be interesting and instructive. Sketched by Father Bridgett's practised pen, the portrait of this holy martyr is no less vividly displayed in the printed pages of the book than in the wonderful picture of Holbein, which forms the frontispiece."—*Tablet.*

The True Story of the Catholic Hierarchy deposed by Queen Elizabeth, with fuller Memoirs of its Last Two Survivors. By the Rev. T. E. BRIDGETT, C.SS.R., and the late Rev. T. F. KNOX, D.D., of the London Oratory. Crown 8vo, cloth, 0 7 6

"We gladly acknowledge the value of this work on a subject which has been obscured by prejudice and carelessness."—*Saturday Review.*

The Life and Writings of Sir Thomas More, Lord Chancellor of England and Martyr under Henry VIII. With Portrait of the Martyr taken from the Crayon Sketch made by Holbein in 1527 . . 0 7 6

"Father Bridgett has followed up his valuable Life of Bishop Fisher with a still more valuable Life of Thomas More. It is, as the title declares, a study not only of the life, but also of the writings of Sir Thomas. Father Bridgett has considered him from every point of view, and the result is, it seems to us, a more complete and finished portrait of the man, mentally and physically, than has been hitherto presented."—*Athenæum.*

BRIDGETT, REV. T. E. (C.SS.R.), Edited by.

Souls Departed. By CARDINAL ALLEN. First published in 1565, now edited in modern spelling by the Rev. T. E. Bridgett 0 6 0

BROWNE, REV. R. D.:

Plain Sermons. Sixty-eight Plain Sermons on the Fundamental Truths of the Catholic Church. Crown 8vo 0 6 0

"These are good sermons. . . . The great merit of which is that they might be read *verbatim* to any congregation, and they would be understood and appreciated by the uneducated almost as fully as by the cultured. They have been carefully put together; their language is simple and their matter is solid."—*Catholic News.*

BUCKLER, REV. H. REGINALD (O.P.)

The Perfection of Man by Charity: a Spiritual Treatise. Crown 8vo, cloth, . . . 0 5 0

"We have read this unpretending, but solid and edifying work, with much pleasure, and heartily commend it to our readers. . . . Its scope is sufficiently explained by the title."—*The Month.*

CASWALL, FATHER.

Catholic Latin Instructor in the Principal Church Offices and Devotions, for the Use of Choirs, Convents, and Mission Schools, and for Self-Teaching. 1 vol., complete £0 3 6

Or Part I., containing Benediction, Mass, Serving at Mass, and various Latin Prayers in ordinary use . 0 1 6

May Pageant : A Tale of Tintern. (A Poem) Second edition 0 2 0

Poems 0 5 0

Lyra Catholica, containing all the Breviary and Missal Hymns, with others from various sources. 32mo, cloth, red edges 0 2 6

CATHOLIC BELIEF: OR, A SHORT AND

Simple Exposition of Catholic Doctrine. By the Very Rev. Joseph Faà di Bruno, D.D. Tenth edition . . . . Price 6d.; post free, 0 0 8½

Cloth, lettered, ... 0 0 10

Also an edition on better paper and bound in cloth, with gilt lettering and steel frontispiece 0 2 0

CHALLONER, BISHOP.

Meditations for every day in the year. New edition. Revised and edited by the Right Rev. John Virtue, D.D., Bishop of Portsmouth. 8vo. 5th edition . 0 3 0

And in other bindings.

COLERIDGE, REV. H. J. (S.J.) *(See Quarterly Series.)*

DEVAS, C. S.

Studies of Family Life: a contribution to Social Science. Crown 8vo 0 5 0

"We recommend these pages and the remarkable evidence brought together in them to the careful attention of all who are interested in the well-being of our common humanity."—*Guardian.*

"Both thoughtful and stimulating."—*Saturday Review.*

DRANE, AUGUSTA THEODOSIA.

History of St. Catherine of Siena and her Companions. A new edition in two vols. 0 12 6

"It has been reserved for the author of the present work to give us a complete biography of St. Catherine. . . . Perhaps the greatest success of the writer is the way in which she has contrived to make the Saint herself live in the pages of the book."—*Tablet.*

EYRE, MOST REV. CHARLES, (Abp. of Glasgow).

The History of St. Cuthbert : or, An Account of his Life, Decease, and Miracles. Third edition. Illustrated with maps, charts, &c., and handsomely bound in cloth. Royal 8vo 0 14 0

"A handsome, well appointed volume, in every way worthy of its illustrious subject. . . . The chief impression of the whole is the picture of a great and good man drawn by a sympathetic hand."—*Spectator.*

FABER, REV. FREDERICK WILLIAM, (D.D.)

	£	s.	d.
All for Jesus	0	5	0
Bethlehem	0	7	0
Blessed Sacrament	0	7	6
Creator and Creature	0	6	0
Ethel's Book of the Angels	0	5	0
Foot of the Cross	0	6	0
Growth in Holiness	0	6	0
Hymns	0	6	0
Notes on Doctrinal and Spiritual Subjects, 2 vols. each	0	5	0
Poems (a new edition in preparation)			
Precious Blood	0	5	0
Sir Lancelot	0	5	0
Spiritual Conferences	0	6	0
Life and Letters of Frederick William Faber, D.D., Priest of the Oratory of St. Philip Neri. By John Edward Bowden of the same Congregation	0	6	0

FOLEY, REV. HENRY, (S.J.)

	£	s.	d.
Records of the English Province of the Society of Jesus. Vol. I., Series I. . . . net	1	6	0
Vol. II., Series II., III., IV. . . . net	1	6	0
Vol. III., Series V., VI., VII., VIII. . . net	1	10	0
Vol. IV. Series IX., X., XI. . . . net	1	6	0
Vol. V., Series XII. with nine Photographs of Martyrs . . . . net	1	10	0
Vol. VI., Diary and Pilgrim-Book of the English College, Rome. The Diary from 1579 to 1773, with Biographical and Historical Notes. The Pilgrim-Book of the Ancient English Hospice attached to the College from 1580 to 1656, with Historical Notes . . . . net	1	6	0
Vol. VII. Part the First: General Statistics of the Province; and Collectanea, giving Biographical Notices of its Members and of many Irish and Scotch Jesuits. With 20 Photographs . . . . net	1	6	0
Vol. VII. Part the Second: Collectanea, Completed; With Appendices. Catalogues of Assumed and Real Names; Annual Letters; Biographies and Miscellanea. . . . . net	1	6	0

"As a biographical dictionary of English Jesuits, it deserves a place in every well-selected library, and, as a collection of marvellous occurrences, persecutions, martyrdoms, and evidences of the results of faith, amongst the books of all who belong to the Catholic Church."—*Genealogist*.

FORMBY, REV. HENRY.

	£	s.	d.
Monotheism: in the main derived from the Hebrew nation and the Law of Moses. The Primitive Religion of the City of Rome. An historical Investigation. Demy 8vo.	0	5	0

FRANCIS DE SALES, ST.: THE WORKS OF.
Translated into the English Language by the Very Rev. Canon Mackey, O.S.B., under the direction of the Right Rev. Bishop Hedley, O.S.B.

Vol. I. Letters to Persons in the World. Cloth . £0 6 0

"The letters must be read in order to comprehend the charm and sweetness of their style."—*Tablet.*

Vol. II.—The Treatise on the Love of God. Father Carr's translation of 1630 has been taken as a basis, but it has been modernized and thoroughly revised and corrected. 0 9 0

"To those who are seeking perfection by the path of contemplation this volume will be an armoury of help."—*Saturday Review.*

Vol. III. The Catholic Controversy. . . . 0 6 0

"No one who has not read it can conceive how clear, how convincing, and how well adapted to our present needs are these controversial 'leaves.'"—*Tablet.*

Vol. IV. Letters to Persons in Religion, with introduction by Bishop Hedley on "St. Francis de Sales and the Religious State." 0 6 0

"The sincere piety and goodness, the grave wisdom, the knowledge of human nature, the tenderness for its weakness, and the desire for its perfection that pervade the letters, make them pregnant of instruction for all serious persons. The translation and editing have been admirably done."—*Scotsman.*

*** Other vols. in preparation.

GALLWEY, REV. PETER, (S.J.)
Precious Pearl of Hope in the Mercy of God, The. Translated from the Italian. With Preface by the Rev. Father Gallwey. Cloth 0 4 6

Lectures on Ritualism and on the Anglican Orders. 2 vols. (Or may be had separately.) 0 8 0

Salvage from the Wreck. A few Memories of the Dead, preserved in Funeral Discourses. With Portraits. Crown 8vo. 0 7 6

GIBSON, REV. H.
Catechism Made Easy. Being an Explanation of the Christian Doctrine. Fifth edition. 2 vols., cloth 0 7 6

"This work must be of priceless worth to any who are engaged in any form of catechetical instruction. It is the best book of the kind that we have seen in English."—*Irish Monthly.*

GILLOW, JOSEPH.
Literary and Biographical History, or, Bibliographical Dictionary of the English Catholics. From the Breach with Rome, in 1534, to the Present Time. Vols. I., II. and III. cloth, demy 8vo . . each. 0 15 0

*** Other vols. in preparation.

"The patient research of Mr. Gillow, his conscientious record of minute particulars, and especially his exhaustive bibliographical information in connection with each name, are beyond praise."—*British Quarterly Review.*

The Haydock Papers. Illustrated. Demy 8vo. . 0 7 6

"We commend this collection to the attention of every one that is interested in the records of the sufferings and struggles of our ancestors to hand down the faith to their children. It is in the perusal of such details that we bring home to ourselves the truly heroic sacrifices that our forefathers endured in those dark and dismal times."—*Tablet.*

GROWTH IN THE KNOWLEDGE OF OUR LORD.
Meditations for every Day in the Year, exclusive of those for Festivals, Days of Retreat, &c. Adapted from the original of Abbé de Brandt, by Sister Mary Fidelis. A new and Improved Edition, in 3 Vols. Sold only in sets. Price per set, ... £1 2 6

"The praise, though high, bestowed on these excellent meditations by the Bishop of Salford is well deserved. The language, like good spectacles, spreads treasures before our vision without attracting attention to itself."—*Dublin Review.*

HEDLEY, BISHOP.
Our Divine Saviour, and other Discourses. Crown 8vo. 0 6 0

"A distinct and noteworthy feature of these sermons is, we certainly think, their freshness—freshness of thought, treatment, and style; nowhere do we meet pulpit commonplace or hackneyed phrase—everywhere, on the contrary, it is the heart of the preacher pouring out to his flock his own deep convictions, enforcing them from the 'Treasures, old and new,' of a cultivated mind."—*Dublin Review.*

HUMPHREY, REV. W. (S.J.)
Suarez on the Religious State: A Digest of the Doctrine contained in his Treatise, "De Statû Religionis." 3 vols., pp. 1200. Cloth, roy. 8vo. . . 1 10 0

"This laborious and skilfully executed work is a distinct addition to English theological literature. Father Humphrey's style is quiet, methodical, precise, and as clear as the subject admits. Every one will be struck with the air of legal exposition which pervades the book. He takes a grip of his author, under which the text yields up every atom of its meaning and force."—*Dublin Review.*

The One Mediator; or, Sacrifice and Sacraments. Crown 8vo, cloth 0 5 0

"An exceedingly accurate theological exposition of doctrines which are the life of Christianity and which make up the soul of the Christian religion. . . . A profound work, but so far from being dark, obscure, and of metaphysical difficulty, the meaning of each paragraph shines with a crystalline clearness."—*Tablet.*

KING, FRANCIS.
The Church of my Baptism, and why I returned to it. Crown 8vo, cloth 0 2 6

"A book of the higher controversial criticism. Its literary style is good, its controversial manner excellent, and its writer's emphasis does not escape in italics and notes of exclamation, but is all reserved for lucid and cogent reasoning. Altogether a book of an excellent spirit, written with freshness and distinction."—*Weekly Register.*

LEDOUX, REV. S. M.
History of the Seven Holy Founders of the Order of the Servants of Mary. Crown 8vo, cloth . . 0 4 6

"Throws a full light upon the Seven Saints recently canonized, whom we see as they really were. All that was marvellous in their call, their works, and their death is given with the charm of a picturesque and speaking style."—*Messenger of the Sacred Heart.*

LEE, REV. F. G., D.D. (of All Saints, Lambeth.)
Edward the Sixth: Supreme Head. Second edition. Crown 8vo 0 6 0

"In vivid interest and in literary power, no less than in solid historical value, Dr. Lee's present work comes fully up to the standard of its predecessors; and to say that is to bestow high praise. The book evinces Dr. Lee's customary diligence of research in amassing facts, and his rare artistic power in welding them into a harmonious and effective whole."—*John Bull.*

LIGUORI, ST. ALPHONSUS.

New and Improved Translation of the Complete Works of St. Alphonsus, edited by the late Bishop Coffin :—
Vol. I. The Christian Virtues, and the Means for Obtaining them. Cloth elegant £0 4 0
Or separately :—
1. The Love of our Lord Jesus Christ . . . 0 1 4
2. Treatise on Prayer. *(In the ordinary editions a great part of this work is omitted)* . . . 0 1 4
3. A Christian's rule of Life 0 1 0
Vol. II. The Mysteries of the Faith—The Incarnation; containing Meditations and Devotions on the Birth and Infancy of Jesus Christ, &c., suited for Advent and Christmas. 0 3 6
    Cheap edition 0 2 0
Vol. III. The Mysteries of the Faith—The Blessed Sacrament 0 3 6
    Cheap edition 0 2 0
Vol. IV. Eternal Truths—Preparation for Death . 0 3 6
    Cheap edition 0 2 0
Vol. V. The Redemption Meditations on the Passion. 0 3 0
    Cheap edition 0 2 0
    Jesus hath loved us . . (separately). 0 0 9
Vol. VI. Glories of Mary. New edition . . . 0 3 6
    With Frontispiece, cloth 0 4 6

LIVIUS, REV. T. (M.A., C.SS.R.)

St. Peter, Bishop of Rome ; or, the Roman Episcopate of the Prince of the Apostles, proved from the Fathers, History and Chronology, and illustrated by arguments from other sources. Dedicated to his Eminence Cardinal Newman. Demy 8vo, cloth . 0 12 0

"A book which deserves careful attention. In respect of literary qualities, such as effective arrangement, and correct and lucid diction, this essay, by an English Catholic scholar, is not unworthy of Cardinal Newman, to whom it is dedicated."—*The Sun.*

Explanation of the Psalms and Canticles in the Divine Office. By ST. ALPHONSUS LIGUORI. Translated from the Italian by THOMAS LIVIUS, C.SS.R. With a Preface by his Eminence Cardinal MANNING. Crown 8vo, cloth 0 7 6

"To nuns and others who know little or no Latin, the book will be of immense importance."—*Dublin Review.*

"Father Livius has in our opinion even improved on the original, so far as the arrangement of the book goes. New priests will find it especially useful."—*Month.*

Mary in the Epistles; or, The Implicit Teaching of the Apostles concerning the Blessed Virgin, set forth in devout comments on their writings. Illustrated from Fathers and other Authors, and prefaced by introductory Chapters. Crown 8vo. Cloth 0 5 0

MANNING, CARDINAL.

	£	s.	d.
England and Christendom	0	10	6
Four Great Evils of the Day. 5th edition. Wrapper	0	2	6
Cloth	0	3	6
Fourfold Sovereignty of God. 3rd edition. Wrapper	0	2	6
Cloth	0	3	6
Glories of the Sacred Heart. 5th edition	0	6	0
Grounds of Faith. Cloth. 9th edition. Wrapper	0	1	0
Cloth	0	1	6
Independence of the Holy See. 2nd edition	0	5	0
Internal Mission of the Holy Ghost. 5th edition	0	8	6
Miscellanies. 3 vols. the set	0	18	0
National Education. Wrapper	0	2	0
Cloth	0	2	6
Petri Privilegium	0	10	6
Religio Viatoris. 3rd edition, cloth	0	2	0
Wrapper	0	1	0
Sermons on Ecclesiastical Subjects. Vols. I., II., and III. each	0	6	0
Sin and its Consequences. 7th edition	0	6	0
Temporal Mission of the Holy Ghost. 3rd edition	0	8	6
Temporal Power of the Pope. 3rd edition	0	5	0
True Story of the Vatican Council. 2nd edition	0	5	0
The Eternal Priesthood. 9th edition	0	2	6
The Office of the Church in the Higher Catholic Education. A Pastoral Letter	0	0	6
Workings of the Holy Spirit in the Church of England. Reprint of a letter addressed to Dr. Pusey in 1864. Wrapper	0	1	0
Cloth	0	1	6
Lost Sheep Found. A Sermon	0	0	6
On Education	0	0	3
Rights and Dignity of Labour	0	0	1

The Westminster Series

In handy pocket size.

The Blessed Sacrament, the Centre of Immutable Truth, Wrapper	0	0	6
Confidence in God. Wrapper	0	1	0
Or the two bound together. Cloth	0	2	0
Holy Gospel of Our Lord Jesus Christ according to St. John. Cloth	0	1	0
Holy Ghost the Sanctifier. Cloth	0	2	0
Love of Jesus to Penitents. Wrapper	0	1	0
Cloth	0	1	6
Office of the Holy Ghost under the Gospel. Cloth	0	1	0

MANNING, CARDINAL, Edited by.

Life of the Curé of Ars. Popular edition	0	2	6

MEDAILLE, REV. P.
Meditations on the Gospels for Every Day in the Year. Translated into English from the new Edition, enlarged by the Besançon Missionaries, under the direction of the Rev. W. H. Eyre, S.J. Cloth . £0 6 0
(This work has already been translated into Latin, Italian, Spanish, German, and Dutch.)

"We have carefully examined these Meditations, and are fain to confess that we admire them very much. They are short, succinct, pithy, always to the point, and wonderfully suggestive."—*Tablet.*

MIVART, PROF. ST. GEORGE (M.D., F.R.S.)
Nature and Thought. Second edition . . . 0 4 0

"The complete command of the subject, the wide grasp, the subtlety, the readiness of illustration, the grace of style, contrive to render this one of the most admirable books of its class."—*British Quarterly Review.*

A Philosophical Catechism. Fifth edition . 0 1 0

"It should become the *vade mecum* of Catholic students."—*Tablet.*

MONTGOMERY, HON. MRS.
Approved by the Most Rev. George Porter, Archbishop of Bombay.

The Divine Sequence: A Treatise on Creation and Redemption. Cloth 0 3 6
The Eternal Years. With an Introduction by the Most Rev. George Porter, Archbishop of Bombay. Cloth 0 3 6
The Divine Ideal. Cloth 0 3 6

"A work of original thought carefully developed and expressed in lucid and richly imaged style."—*Tablet.*

"The writing of a pious, thoughtful, earnest woman."—*Church Review.*

"Full of truth, and sound reason, and confidence."—*American Catholic Book News.*

MORRIS, REV. JOHN (S.J.)
Letter Books of Sir Amias Poulet, keeper of Mary Queen of Scots. Demy 8vo 0 10 6
Troubles of our Catholic Forefathers, related by themselves. Second Series. 8vo, cloth. . . 0 14 0
    Third Series 0 14 0
The Life of Father John Gerard, S.J. Third edition, rewritten and enlarged 0 14 0
The Life and Martyrdom of St. Thomas Becket. Second and enlarged edition. In one volume, large post 8vo, cloth, pp. xxxvi., 632, ... 0 12 6
or bound in two parts, cloth 0 13 0

MORRIS, REV. W. B. (of the Oratory.)
The Life of St. Patrick, Apostle of Ireland. Fourth edition. Crown 8vo, cloth 0 5 0

"The secret of Father Morris's success is, that he has got the proper key to the extraordinary, the mysterious life and character of St. Patrick. He has taken the Saint's own authentic writings as the foundation whereon to build."—*Irish Ecclesiastical Record.*

"Promises to become the standard biography of Ireland's Apostle. For clear statement of facts, and calm judicious discussion of controverted points, it surpasses any work we know of in the literature of the subject."—*American Catholic Quarterly.*

NEWMAN, CARDINAL.

Church of the Fathers £0 4 0
Prices of other works by Cardinal Newman on application.

PAGANI, VERY REV. JOHN BAPTIST,

The Science of the Saints in Practice. By John Baptist Pagani, Second General of the Institute of Charity. Complete in three volumes. Vol. 1, January to April. Vol. 2, May to August. Vol. 3, September to December . . . . each 0 5 0

"'The Science of the Saints' is a practical treatise on the principal Christian virtues, abundantly illustrated with interesting examples from Holy Scripture as well as from the Lives of the Saints. Written chiefly for devout souls, such as are trying to live an interior and supernatural life by following in the footsteps of our Lord and His saints, this work is eminently adapted for the use of ecclesiastics and of religious communities."—*Irish Ecclesiastical Record*,

PAYNE, JOHN ORLEBAR, (M.A.)

Records of the English Catholics of 1715. Demy 8vo. Half-bound, gilt top 0 15 0

"A book of the kind Mr. Payne has given us would have astonished Bishop Milner or Dr. Lingard. They would have treasured it, for both of them knew the value of minute fragments of historical information. The Editor has derived nearly the whole of the information which he has given, from unprinted sources, and we must congratulate him on having found a few incidents here and there which may bring the old times back before us in a most touching manner."—*Tablet*.

English Catholic Non-Jurors of 1715. Being a Summary of the Register of their Estates, with Genealogical and other Notes, and an Appendix of Unpublished Documents in the Public Record Office. In one Volume. Demy 8vo. . 1 1 0

"Most carefully and creditably brought out ... From first to last, full of social interest and biographical details, for which we may search in vain elsewhere."—*Antiquarian Magazine*.

Old English Catholic Missions. Demy 8vo, half-bound. 0 7 6

"A book to hunt about in for curious odds and ends."—*Saturday Review*.

"These registers tell us in their too brief records, teeming with interest for all their scantiness, many a tale of patient heroism."—*Tablet*.

POOR SISTERS OF NAZARETH, THE.

A descriptive Sketch of Convent Life. By Alice Meynell. Profusely Illustrated with Drawings especially made by George Lambert. Large 4to. Boards . . 0 2 6
A limited number of copies are also issued as an *Edition de Luxe*, containing proofs of the illustrations printed on one side only of the paper, and handsomely bound. 0 10 6

"Bound in a most artistic cover, illustrated with a naturalness that could only have been born of powerful sympathy; printed clearly, neatly, and on excellent paper, and written with the point, aptness, and ripeness of style which we have learnt to associate with Mrs. Meynell's literature."—*Tablet*.

QUARTERLY SERIES Edited by the Rev. H. J. Coleridge, S.J. 76 volumes published to date.
Selection.

The Life and Letters of St. Francis Xavier. By the Rev. H. J. Coleridge, S.J. 2 vols.	£0 10 6
The History of the Sacred Passion. By Father Luis de la Palma, of the Society of Jesus. Translated from the Spanish.	0 5 0
The Life of Dona Louisa de Carvajal. By Lady Georgiana Fullerton. Small edition	0 3 6
The Life and Letters of St. Teresa. 3 vols. By Rev. H. J. Coleridge, S.J. each	0 7 6
The Life of Mary Ward. By Mary Catherine Elizabeth Chalmers, of the Institute of the Blessed Virgin. Edited by the Rev. H. J. Coleridge, S.J. 2 vols.	0 15 0
The Return of the King. Discourses on the Latter Days. By the Rev. H. J. Coleridge, S.J.	0 7 6
Pious Affections towards God and the Saints. Meditations for every Day in the Year, and for the Principal Festivals. From the Latin of the Ven. Nicolas Lancicius, S.J.	0 7 6
The Life and Teaching of Jesus Christ in Meditations for Every Day in the Year. By Fr. Nicolas Avancino, S.J. Two vols.	0 10 6
The Baptism of the King: Considerations on the Sacred Passion. By the Rev. H. J. Coleridge, S.J.	0 7 6
The Mother of the King. Mary during the Life of Our Lord.	0 7 6
The Hours of the Passion. Taken from the *Life of Christ* by Ludolph the Saxon	0 7 6
The Mother of the Church. Mary during the first Apostolic Age	0 6 0
The Life of St. Bridget of Sweden. By the late F. J. M. A. Partridge	0 6 0
The Teachings and Counsels of St. Francis Xavier. From his Letters	0 5 0
Garcia Moreno, President of Ecuador. 1821—1875. From the French of the Rev. P. A. Berthe, C.SS.R. By Lady Herbert	0 7 6
The Life of St. Alonso Rodriguez. By Francis Goldie, of the Society of Jesus	0 7 6
Letters of St. Augustine. Selected and arranged by Mary H. Allies	0 6 6
A Martyr from the Quarter-Deck—Alexis Clerc, S.J. By Lady Herbert	0 5 0

VOLUMES ON THE LIFE OF OUR LORD.
The Holy Infancy.

The Preparation of the Incarnation	0 7 6
The Nine Months. The Life of our Lord in the Womb.	0 7 6
The Thirty Years. Our Lord's Infancy and Early Life.	0 7 6

The Public Life of Our Lord.

The Ministry of St. John Baptist	0 6 6

QUARTERLY SERIES—(selection) continued.

		£	s.	d.
The Preaching of the Beatitudes		0	6	6
The Sermon on the Mount. Continued. 2 Parts, each		0	6	6
The Training of the Apostles. Parts I., II., III., IV. each		0	6	6
The Preaching of the Cross. Part I.		0	6	6
The Preaching of the Cross. Parts II., III. each		0	6	0
Passiontide. Parts I. II. and III., each		0	6	6
Chapters on the Parables of Our Lord		0	7	6
Introductory Volumes.				
The Life of our Life. Harmony of the Life of Our Lord, with Introductory Chapters and Indices. Second edition. Two vols.		0	15	0
The Works and Words of our Saviour, gathered from the Four Gospels		0	7	6
The Story of the Gospels. Harmonised for Meditation		0	7	6

Full lists on application.

RAM, MRS. ABEL.

"Emmanuel." Being the Life of Our Lord Jesus Christ reproduced in the Mysteries of the Tabernacle. By Mrs. Abel Ram, author of "The most Beautiful among the Children of Men," &c. Crown 8vo, cloth . . . 0 5 0

"The foundation of the structure is laid with the greatest skill and the deepest knowledge of what constitutes true religion, and every chapter ends with an eloquent and soul-inspiring appeal for one or other of the virtues which the different scenes in the life of Our Saviour set prominently into view."—*Catholic Times.*

RICHARDS, REV. WALTER J. B. (D.D.)

Manual of Scripture History. Being an Analysis of the Historical Books of the Old Testament. By the Rev. W. J. B. Richards, D.D., Oblate of St. Charles; Inspector of Schools in the Diocese of Westminster. Cloth . . . 0 4 0

"Happy indeed will those children and young persons be who acquire in their early days the inestimably precious knowledge which these books impart."—*Tablet.*

RYDER, REV. H. I. D. (of the Oratory.)

Catholic Controversy: A Reply to Dr. Littledale's "Plain Reasons." Sixth edition . . . 0 2 6

"Father Ryder of the Birmingham Oratory, has now furnished in a small volume a masterly reply to this assailant from without. The lighter charms of a brilliant and graceful style are added to the solid merits of this handbook of contemporary controversy."—*Irish Monthly.*

SOULIER, REV. P.

Life of St. Philip Benizi, of the Order of the Servants of Mary. Crown 8vo . . . 0 8 0

"A clear and interesting account of the life and labours of this eminent Servant of Mary."—*American Catholic Quarterly.*
"Very scholar-like, devout and complete."—*Dublin Review.*

STANTON, REV. R. (of the Oratory.)
A Menology of England and Wales; or, Brief Memorials of the British and English Saints, arranged according to the Calendar. Together with the Martyrs of the 16th and 17th centuries. Compiled by order of the Cardinal Archbishop and the Bishops of the Province of Westminster. Demy 8vo, cloth ... £0 14 0

THOMPSON, EDWARD HEALY, (M.A.)
The Life of Jean-Jacques Olier, Founder of the Seminary of St. Sulpice. New and Enlarged Edition. Post 8vo, cloth, pp. xxxvi. 628 ... 0 15 0

"It provides us with just what we most need, a model to look up to and imitate; one whose circumstances and surroundings were sufficiently like our own to admit of an easy and direct application to our own personal duties and daily occupations."—*Dublin Review.*

The Life and Glories of St. Joseph, Husband of Mary, Foster-Father of Jesus, and Patron of the Universal Church. Grounded on the Dissertations of Canon Antonio Vitalis, Father José Moreno, and other writers. Crown 8vo, cloth, pp. xxvi., 488, ... 0 6 0

ULLATHORNE, ARCHBISHOP.
Endowments of Man, &c. Popular edition. ... 0 7 0
Groundwork of the Christian Virtues: do. ... 0 7 0
Christian Patience, do. do. ... 0 7 0
Ecclesiastical Discourses ... 0 6 0
Memoir of Bishop Willson. ... 0 2 6

VAUGHAN, ARCHBISHOP, (O.S.B.)
The Life and Labours of St. Thomas of Aquin. Abridged and edited by Dom Jerome Vaughan, O.S.B. Second Edition. (Vol. I., Benedictine Library.) Crown 8vo. Attractively bound ... 0 6 6

"Popularly written, in the best sense of the word, skilfully avoids all wearisome detail, whilst omitting nothing that is of importance in the incidents of the Saint's existence, or for a clear understanding of the nature and the purpose of those sublime theological works on which so many Pontiffs, and notably Leo XIII., have pronounced such remarkable and repeated commendations."—*Freeman's Journal.*

WARD, WILFRID.
The Clothes of Religion. A reply to popular Positivism. ... 0 3 6
"Very witty and interesting."—*Spectator.*
"Really models of what such essays should be."—*Church Quarterly Review.*

WATERWORTH, REV. J.
The Canons and Decrees of the Sacred and Œcumenical Council of Trent, celebrated under the Sovereign Pontiffs, Paul III., Julius III., and Pius IV., translated by the Rev. J. WATERWORTH. To which are prefixed Essays on the External and Internal History of the Council. A new edition. Demy 8vo, cloth ... 0 10 6

WISEMAN, CARDINAL.
Fabiola. A Tale of the Catacombs. .. 3s. 6d. and ... 0 4 0
Also a new and splendid edition printed on large quarto paper, embellished with thirty-one full-page illustrations, and a coloured portrait of St. Agnes. Handsomely bound. ... 1 1 0

www.ingramcontent.com/pod-product-compliance
Lightning Source LLC
Chambersburg PA
CBHW031906220426
43663CB00006B/785